Chris Johnson

Volume 1

The Best of Chris Johnson
Volume 1

Copyright © 2010
Chris Johnson
Kudzu Kid Press

*Columns reprinted by permission
of the Columbus Ledger-Enquirer*

Cover photographs by Sonja Johnson

ISBN: 978-0-615-35668-6

To contact the author:
kudzukid88@gmail.com

Read Chris Johnson's latest columns online at
www.ledger-enquirer.com/chris_johnson

Printed in the USA by
Morris Publishing®
3212 E. Hwy. 30 • Kearney, NE 68847
800-650-7888 • www.morrispublishing.com

Table of contents

To Saylor,
Never stop dreaming.

The boys of spring

This is Scoop Johnson, reporting live from Eufaula, Ala., site of the baseball game you've all been waiting for . . . yes, the mid-season showdown between the Techsonic Industries White Sox and the Eufaula Glass Company Blue Jays — led, of course, by my 7-year-old nephew, Cody.

Rarely have we seen so much tension at a coach-pitch game in the middle of the season. Wait a minute! The tension appears to have been relieved as the Blue Jays' coach begins his pregame inspirational speech. Let's listen in:

"OK, does anybody have to go to the bathroom?"

Maybe Bobby Cox should ask that question before the Braves take the field.

Now the action is really heating up. Cody slides into third base. Will slides into second. Austin slides into the dugout. Michael slides into Tyler. Dust is everywhere. Uniforms are torn and dirty. There is chaos on the field. Let's switch to our on-field microphone for the umpire's call:

"If you guys are through sliding around in the dirt, we'll start the game."

To the bottom of the first now, and the score is ... well, we don't know what the score is because this is coach-pitch and the score is not important; the important thing is that we learn the game and have fun. . . . Excuse me. . . . I have just been informed by Herbert's mom that the score is 2-0 White Sox.

As Cody comes to the plate, Little Billy leads the Sox' defensive s trategy, which relies not on positioning or slick fielding but on the incessant "Hey, batter batter! Hey, batter batter! Hey, batter batter!" The strategy works, as they never yell, "Swing!" thus confusing the Blue Jays' offensive attack. Sensing they're on to something, Little Billy and the White Sox never, ever stop yelling "Hey, batter batter!" They sound like a bunch of insane crickets.

To the third inning of a tight contest (6-5, Blue Jays, according to Herbert's mom) and Monica is trying to spark the offense with an attempt to draw a leadoff walk. Unfortunately for her coach and pitcher, there's no such thing as a walk in coach-pitch baseball. The count is now 11 balls and two strikes. Let's break for commercial.

Buy Chris Johnson's new book! On sale now!

OK, we're back, and the count is now 24 balls and two strikes. If little Monica weren't so cute with that blonde ponytail hanging out the back of her batting helmet, I think the coach might have beaned her with a fastball by now. But you've got to admire Monica's determination. While you're admiring that, let's break for a classic episode of "Sanford and Son."

To the fourth inning and our first major injury: Little Billy's jaw has locked up after yelling "Hey, batter batter!" for the 578th time. He may have to go on the injured reserve list. And, while we're on the subject, if I ever catch the guy who first came up with the idea of yelling "Hey, batter batter!" he's gonna go on the permanently injured list.

Don't mash that Tater

My newest second cousin, Charles Tate Moore, is just a few weeks old, but he's already making a name for himself in my family.

My cousin Chuck and his wife, SaBess, are calling their first-born by his middle name, but Tate is a little preppie for my taste. With a name like Tate, he's bound to wind up driving a Jeep Cherokee, wearing Tommy Hilfiger clothes, drinking Perrier and tucking in his shirt when it just ain't necessary. I'm not gonna stand by and see a member of my family, even a second cousin, start paying for water or wear anything you can't find at Wal-Mart under a yellow smiley face.

I think I solved a lot of problems for the little tyke when I leaned down to let him squeeze my finger and said, "Hey there, Tater." I thought nothing of it, but I noticed Chuck and SaBess glance at each other in a brief moment of terror thinking, "What have we done?!" In their heads, they heard the nicknames echoing in the locker-lined junior high school hallways of their memories:

"Mashed Tater! Baked Tater! Tater Tot! Sweet Tater! Tater Chip! Tater Souffle! Tater Salad! Mr. Tater Head! Po Tater! Irish Tater Famine!"

They pleaded with me to never call him Tater again, but he'll be Lil' Tater, Brother Tater, Sgt. Tater, Mayor Tater, Uncle Tater and

Grandpa Tater until he's the Late Great Tater. Once you open that can of worms, buddy, there ain't no going back.

With that name, junior high won't be easy. But junior high kids are gonna find some way to make fun of you anyway. In fact having that name may actually serve as a shield and protect him from entering high school with an even-worse moniker like "Bucktooth Tate" or "Big Ears Moore." Junior high kids have short attention spans and aren't likely to explore what's really funny about Tater beyond his first name.

A boy named Tate would have to be as tough as Johnny Cash's "A Boy Named Sue." In case you're one of those kids that grew up on geeky music like Beethoven and now listen to Yanni or Zamfir (MASTER of the pan flute), the climax of this country music legend's song is when the son tracks down the father who named him Sue. The father explains:

"Son, this world is rough and if a man's gonna make it, he's gotta be tough, and I knew I wouldn't be there to help ya along. So I give ya that name and I said good-bye. I knew you'd have to get tough or die, and it's that name that helped to make you strong."

Personally, I think a boy named Sue may have a better chance of making it through junior high alive than a boy named Tate. I thought Chuck would have been more understanding of this concept, because at age 11 he ordered the rest of the universe to quit calling him "Charles." That was just before junior high, and I guess he figured there were better reasons to get beat up.

Tater's definitely gonna stand out at family get-togethers. He's already got cousins Ansley, Kyle, MacKenzie, Zack and Caitlyn, all popular '90s names. Tate might fit in with that series, but Tater ain't got a chance. He might as well have been named Bubba, Jim Bob or Bo Diddley.

Chuck, an avid sports fan, soon will be teaching him how to throw a split-finger fastball or make a save from the sandtrap in hopes (like all dads) that his boy will become a sports legend. And if you're gonna be a sports star, what better name to have than Tater Moore. I could picture him coming up to bat in the bottom of the ninth with the bases loaded and the crowd chanting "Ta-ter! Ta-ter! Ta-ter!" And then the radio announcer would yell, "That ball's going, going, gone! Boy, he really mashed that tater! Braves win!"

And what a name for marketing. During the offseason, he could do ads like: "Hi. I'm Tater Moore and when I get through smacking homers in a game, I like to smack on Red Dot Mashed Taters at the dinner table."

Some of the greatest names are found in the sports world. As a sportswriter, I've written about a high school football linebacker named Crash Landin (a son of pilots with a sense of humor) and a college catcher named Stormy Weathers. And just look at the Baseball Hall of Fame. It wouldn't be the same without Babe Ruth, Catfish Hunter, Three-Finger Brown, Pee Wee Reese, Dizzy Dean, Cool Papa Bell and Rabbit Maranville. I think a Tater would fit right in at Cooperstown.

And he'll have me to thank for it. What if no thoughtful second cousin had come up with the names "Babe" Ruth and "Cool Papa" Bell? Do you think George Herman Ruth would have hit 714 homers, or James Thomas Bell would have been so fast that — as longtime Negro League teammate Satchel Paige said — he could turn out the lights and be in bed before the room got dark? Of course not. So, you owe me one, Tater. How 'bout a free ticket to the 2026 World Series?

Big bad bag boy

When the phone rings at my desk after 11 p.m., it's never good news.

The only people who know they can find me there at that hour are the newspaper's production department, various law enforcement agencies and my wife. I just hope it's not my wife.

"I need you to drop by the grocery store on your way home and pick up some milk, orange juice, toilet paper and various feminine hygiene products."

"Sorry," I say, "no can do."

I would print her response here, but in strict accordance with the Georgia Newspaper Decency Act of 1937, I'd better just print my side of the conversation.

"Yes, dear. Yes, dear. Yes, that would hurt. A cheese grater, huh?"

Needless to say, I follow orders because I know who the man of our house is, and I don't want her to get mad.

No offense to our local establishments, but I hate going to the grocery store. Maybe it's because I have flashbacks to my days as a Food Transferral and Arrangement Engineer (bag boy) making $3.25 an hour. I often scream out with night terrors, still seeing Mrs. Jones chasing me around C-Mart in Oglethorpe, Ga., with a squashed loaf of Wonder Bread in her hand. The only tip she'd give me was the tip of her walking cane to the back of my head. You know what they say: "Hell hath no fury like a woman whose bread got mashed."

Most of these tragic bread-mashing incidents occurred on Fridays. I also seem to recall Mary Jane in Checkout Lane 2 wearing tight blue jeans every Friday. But I'm sure that bagging groceries behind her and putting Wonder Bread in the same bag as a 10-pound tub of lard was pure coincidence.

Though the parking lot of the store was filled with angry victims of my ruthless scheme to mash the world's bread, it was safer than the inside of the store. Remember that Tyrannosaurus rex from "Jurassic Park?" Compared to my boss, that T-Rex would be considered cute and cuddly.

I'm fairly certain that he didn't like me. I deciphered that from subtle, tiny hints he would drop in our conversations, such as, "Hey, kid, did I remember to tell you today that I don't like you?"

"Yes, sir."

"I must have forgotten to scratch that off my to-do list. Now cut the chatter and get back to work!"

I'm not sure why he didn't like me. Maybe it's because Slim Jims began mysteriously disappearing from the checkout aisles after I was hired. Again, pure coincidence — just like it's pure coincidence that Slim Jims were suddenly overstocked after I quit.

Though I worked there for just a few months, I developed the skills that serve as the foundation for my career today — such as knowing where the boss is at all times and how to respond when caught sleeping on the job.

"Chris, are you snoring?" my boss asks a couple of times a day.

"Uh, no. I'm just thinking really hard. My brain always makes that sound when I think."

"Well, maybe you shouldn't think so hard. You're starting to drool on your desk."

Granted, I may not be much more of an asset to the newspaper than I was to C-Mart. But since we don't sell Slim Jims at the Ledger-Enquirer, I'm not too much of a liability, either.

Adventures in insomnia

Lately, I've been suffering from insomnia. And I mean "lately" as in since I was about three and couldn't sleep because I was worried about what was gonna happen to Brer Rabbit in the next bedtime story.

And you normal people miss so many wonderful things by going to bed early at night. To illustrate what you're missing, here's a moment-by-moment account of my night on Thursday.

12:31 a.m. — Get home from work. Close garage door. Check for Bogeyman in storage room.

12:32 — Thank God there is no Bogeyman in storage room.

12:33 — Make supper: 12 stale saltine crackers, a jar of olives and meat in bowl found in bottom of refrigerator (Could be taco meat. Or maybe chili). Scrape green, fuzzy stuff off discovered meat.

12:38 — Put olive on ceiling fan blade. Cut on ceiling fan. Run around living room in circle. Catch olive in mouth. Bow to imaginary audience.

12:39 — Realize ceiling fan blades really need dusting.

12:45 — Pick up guitar and sing "Margaritaville."

12:47 — Tell sleepy wife when she stumbles into the living room, "No, I don't hear anything that sounds like a hound dog run over by a garbage truck."

12:48 — See what's on TV.

12:50 — Flip through those 63 channels one more time just in case I missed something important. Stop on MTV. Pray for future of universe.

12:57 — Cut on computer and check e-mail. Learn how to be my own boss and earn $1,000 a day selling state-of-the-art toothpicks from the comfort of my own home. Check fantasy baseball statistics, see that I have firm grip on last place. Check stocks and mutual funds, make alternate plans for retirement.

1:01 — Put in subliminal tape to help me sleep.

1:11 — Tell myself, "I am a strong woman." Realize this is wrong subliminal tape.

1:28 — Flex muscles in front of bathroom mirror. Ask reflection, "You talkin' to me? You talkin' to me?"

1:55 — Deep thoughts: If Elvis really staged his death, why would he have done it by dying on the toilet?

2:18 — Notice frog hopping on patio. Wonder what would happen to a frog in a microwave.

2:30 — Finish cleaning microwave.

2:36 — Call telemarketer at home and tell her I've reconsidered. I would indeed like to know more about how I could save on all my long distance calls.

2:41 — Make note to self: Tell folks frog-in-microwave item was just a joke to avoid getting hate mail from angry amphibian lovers.

2:45 — Drive down street to home of teenie bopper with loud car stereo and one rap CD. Play Ernest Tubb song at 150 decibels.

2:56 — Enter Waffle House. Ask for nonsmoking section.

3:35 — Tell drunk man at Waffle House, "I'd really like to hear more about your alien abduction, but it's getting late."

3:42 — "Really, I must be going."

3:47 — "Look! It's E.T.!" Run like the wind.

4:15 — Crawl into bed. Warm cold feet on wife.

4:16 — Check in bathroom mirror to see if nose is broken.

4:17 — Strike Incredible Hulk pose again to see if muscles grew in last three hours.

Greasy dreams

I had a very naughty dream last night. I'll spare you most of the lurid details, but it went something like this.

I'm sitting alone in a dark restaurant. Suddenly, she appears before me, radiant in the candlelight. The temptation is unbearable. I look around nervously, but my wife is nowhere to be seen.

"Go for it. She'll never know," I tell myself. I reach out, pull the beauty across the table to my lips and bite the heck out of her.

Then I tell her, "You're the best double-chili-cheeseburger I've ever tasted."

Then I wake up as my wife slaps me.

"I can't believe you did that. You know you're not supposed to eat food like that — even in your dreams."

Ever since the doctor made the connection between my eating habits and death, my wife has monitored each morsel that goes into my mouth. It's not that she's so concerned about my health; she merely wants my 401K to mature a little before I die.

My doctor told me that if I don't cut down on my carbohydrates and protein, I'll die of diabetes. If I don't cut down on my fats and cholesterol, I'll die of a heart attack. Fortunately, I've had enough willpower to cut out all of that and won't die of either. Instead, it appears that I'll die of starvation.

I've been learning a lot about diet and nutrition from a hospital nutritionist whom I'm driving insane. She tries to be serious, explaining such important things as how one gram of fiber cancels out one gram of carbohydrates. Therefore, the more fiber in our diet, the better.

"So," I ask in all seriousness, "if I eat a whole container of Metamucil, does that mean I can eat an entire box of chocolates?"

"Mr. Johnson, I'm afraid I'm going to have to ask you to stand in the corner . . . again."

It's hard to change my diet. I've grown up on cheeseburgers, fried chicken, fried catfish, fried pork chops and just about any animal that would fit in a deep fryer, although I never got a chance to try my cousin Hank's recipe for deep-fried, beer-battered ferret.

At least my co-workers have rallied to help me make this difficult transition.

"Hey, Chris! We're gonna go out and get some pizza and cheeseburgers! Want some? Oh, I forgot! You'll die! Ha, ha, ha!"

That's all right. I'm getting skinny and discovering little-known facts about myself, such as my having only one chin. And folks at work are now calling me "Slim." That's much better than my old nickname, "Fat Tub of Goo."

But I'm so hungry for something greasy and loaded with fat and cholesterol that I'm looking forward to the day I walk into the doctor's office and he tells me I've got some entirely new disease like Chronic Ingrown Toenail Syndrome and have only six months to live. Then I'm going to eat myself to death in four months on pizza, chili cheeseburgers, fried chicken and catfish, barbecue and maybe a little beer-battered ferret.

Careful what you wish for

I wanted a new four-door car and a recliner. My wife wanted me to spend more time at home. A 16-year-old ran a red light, smashed into my car and broke my leg, hip and pelvis. All three wishes were granted. I've since traded in my Monkey's Paw for a rabbit's foot.

So, if you had been wondering if I had taken off for a few weeks to sail the Caribbean or something, well, that's just dumb. You oughta know that I can't afford to sail any farther south than Lake Eufaula on a Basstracker.

But I'm not bitter. Even though I've yet to get a dime from the kid's insurance company for medical bills and can't afford luxuries like food, I'm not bitter. Even though I can't pick up my 6-month-old son when he lifts his chubby little arms and cries for his daddy, I'm not bitter. Even though my left leg is worth about $15 in scrap metal and about as useful as an Atari 2600, I'm not bitter. I am so not bitter that if you had the nerve to accuse me of being bitter, I might just bite your head off.

See, you've got to find the positives in a situation like this. I made a list of all the great things about having your leg smashed to bits.

• I've had time to ponder the eternal question: How much leg hair can a man stand to have yanked out by surgical tape before he starts cussin'? By the way, it's 637 leg hairs.

• I haven't worn underwear since July 17. I now know the true meaning of freedom.

• I was able to flash nurses at the hospital without getting arrested ... for a change.

• I found inspiration to name my next child if it's a girl. Her name will be Morphina Darvocet Johnson.

• I have a cool footlong scar about which I can make up stories for my grandchildren someday. I am currently formulating tales of a shark attack, the 2008 World War against Greenland, and my battle with Xena, Warrior Princess.

• When my son has a dirty diaper, it's my wife's problem. My wife also spent weeks bringing hot meals to my recliner, helping me put on my shoes and socks and scratching hard-to-reach itches (sometimes on me, too).

• I now know nothing can stop my competitive streak. I challenged my Grandma to a walker race around the living room and won after nudging her into the coffee table on turn one. It's her own fault, for she knew in advance that walker racing is a dangerous sport, though it's not as interesting as those illegal sloth fighting rings.

• If I play my cards right, I may never have to mow the grass again.

• Even after my leg heals, I'm gonna have a really cool walk. And who knows? I might even be able to start a new dance craze, "The Drunk Chicken."

• Next time I get stuck in a boring conversation, I can end it with, "Did I tell you about the drainage that came out of my leg after surgery?"

• I'll forever appreciate having grown up in a town with just one red light instead of one every 12 feet.

• And my injury opened the door for that Dave Barry kid to run his column for a little while in this space. Maybe he'll get noticed and get his own weekly column or something.

Redneck millennium

The television airwaves have been jammed during the last couple of months with programs taking a look back at the great events and people of the last thousand years.

The important events are the same in every show — discovering America, World War II, the Wright brothers' first flight, the Reformation, man's landing on the moon, yadda, yadda, yadda.

Now, I know you're sick of anything related to the word "millennium," but the record must be set straight. Every one of these shows fails to mention how each of these events had a redneck connection. To illustrate this point, here are some of the supposedly significant events of the past thousand years. In parentheses, I've noted the redneck connection:

1000 — Chinese invent gunpowder. (First deer season opens.)

1150-67 — Universities of Paris and Oxford are founded. (English and French rednecks begin parking their RVs in the universities' parking lots, grilling burgers and drinking beer as they await the first college football game with the first tailgate parties.)

1337-1453 — Hundred Years War. (Rednecks are temporarily put in charge of counting how long wars last.)

1428 — Joan of Arc is burned at the stake by the English. (First English barbecue joint opens.)

1503 — Leonardo da Vinci paints the "Mona Lisa." (Bubba da Vinci paints the "Mona Lisa Nekkid.")

1543 — Copernicus says he thinks the Earth revolves around the sun. (His beer-drinking astronomy buddy, Big Larry-cus Howell, sees a UFO.)

1558 — Shakespeare begins writing "Hamlet." (Not to be outdone, Leroy Jones begins writing "Cannonball Run.")

1607 — First permanent English settlement established at Jamestown. (Twenty acres on west side of Jamestown sold to Wal-Mart.)

1614 — John Napier discovers logarithms. (Rednecks vow that if they ever run across a logarithm, they'll shoot it.)

1646 — Oliver Cromwell overthrows Charles I. (Charles I challenges Cromwell to steel-cage rematch with Jesse Ventura as a referee.)

1756 — Spain cedes Florida to Britain in exchange for Cuba. (British youths head to Panama City Beach — a.k.a. The Redneck Riviera — during spring break to drink beer and run around nekkid.)

1866 — Alfred Nobel invents dynamite. (European rednecks find a more efficient way to fish.)

1876 — Alexander Graham Bell patents telephone. (Little Jim Bob Dawkins calls 7-Eleven and asks if they've got Prince Albert in a can.)

1877 — Thomas Edison invents the phonograph. (First hit country song, "You're the Reason Our Children Are Ugly," is recorded.)

1915 — Einstein releases Theory of Relativity. (Rednecks try to figure out theory. Brains hurt. Drink beer. Feel better.)

1925 — First human features transmitted on television. (Plans made for "Dukes of Hazzard" pilot episode.)

1999 — NASA launches Mars Polar Lander. (Billy Joe Boondoggle invents a more powerful bottle rocket; NASA mysteriously loses contact with Mars Polar Lander.)

I might be a redneck

Hotter than a parrot in a microwave, it's Saturday's Silly Letters:

Dear Mr. Johnson,

Why do call yourself a redneck? I seen you at a restaurant the other day, and you ain't no more redneck than Pee Wee Herman. You drive that furrin four-door car, got your hair cut preppy and your belt buckle was barely visible from a hundred feet away. Bocephus rules! Yeehaw!

Big Larry Tunnamanoor
Possum Holler

Dear Mr. Big Tunnamanoor,

I am, too, a redneck. Am, too. Am, too, to infinity. OK, I see this is going to take some convincing, but I believe you'll come around to my way of thinking or be too drunk to care by the end of this column. Since I can tell you're not a fast thinker, I'll write slow as I present my case.

Exhibit A: Two ticket stubs. The first is from Merle Haggard's show at Buena Vista's Silver Moon back in 1994. And they didn't serve any Perrier at that honky tonk, buddy — at least not at my table. The second is from 1995. Yes, Hank Williams Jr. and Lynyrd Skynyrd in the same show. I haven't seen so many Confederate flags since the first Battle of Bull Run.

Exhibit B: A dead squirrel. Granted, I haven't killed a deer or any of my cousins (not for lack of effort, mind you), but I did take the life of a mammal with a firearm. I was 12 and dang near cried as I put that .22 between the little feller's eyes after he fell from a tree and cowered next to a stump. But, by golly, I've shot an animal to death. And I've shot a few road signs to death, too — and hundreds of tin cans and bottles.

Exhibit C: Two scars on my forehead. Ever crushed a beer can on your forehead? Ha! That's for beginners. Try crushing a whiskey bottle on your forehead. If you don't have the guts to do that, go to Booger Bottom Country Club and ask Jim Bob Walker if you can cut in while he's dancing with Louann Poovey — and he'll do it for you. The other scar came courtesy of a tire tool. You can't be a real redneck without at least one story involving the improper implementation of a tire tool.

Exhibit RV: A videotape. On it, "The Dukes of Hazzard" reunion special. Granted, I was trying to tape a "Friends" episode, but I haven't erased it yet. I also once asked a paint and body shop if they could paint my car like the "General Lee" and weld the doors shut so I would have to hop in through the window like Bo Duke. They said they didn't think that was legal with a Nissan Sentra in the state of Georgia.

Exhibit IOU: My first vacation? Panama City. Senior trip? Panama City. Honeymoon? Panama City.

My only witness: Betsy the cow. "Moo. Moo. Moo." For the record, your honor, the witness has clearly identified me as the redneck who tipped her over on the night of June 20, 1988. I rest my case.

Judge: I heard that.

Here comes Bubba Claus

(Note: There are thousands of plagiarized versions of this column on the Web, but here's the original. Why anybody'd wanna steal it, I have NO idea. I didn't even like it myself!)

An open letter to the citizens of the Bi-City area from Santa Claus:

Dear ya'll:

I regret to inform you that, effective immediately, I will no longer be able to serve your area on Christmas Eve. Due to recent changes in my union contract renegotiated by North American Fairies and Elves Local 209, I now serve only certain areas of northern Wisconsin and west Michigan. I also get longer breaks for milk and cookies.

However, I'm certain that your children will be in good hands with my replacement, my third cousin from the South Pole, Bubba Claus. He shares my goal of delivering toys to all the good boys and girls, but there are a few differences between us, such as:

• There is no danger of a Grinch stealing your presents from Bubba Claus, who has a gun rack in his sleigh and a bumper sticker that reads: "These toys insured by Smith and Wesson."

• Instead of milk and cookies, Bubba Claus prefers that children leave an RC and pork skins on the fireplace. And Bubba doesn't smoke a pipe. He does dip a little snuff, though, so please have a spit can handy.

• Bubba Claus' sleigh is pulled by floppy-eared, flyin' coon dogs instead of reindeer. I loaned him my reindeer one time, and Rudolph's head now rests over Bubba's fireplace.

• You won't hear "On Comet, on Cupid, on Donner and Blitzen ..." when Bubba Claus arrives. Instead, you'll hear, "On Earnhardt, on Wallace, on Martin and Labonte. On Rudd, on Jarrett, on Elliott and Petty."

• "Ho, ho, ho!" has been replaced by "Yeehaw!" And you also are likely to hear Bubba's elves respond, "I heard that!"

• As required by Southern highway laws, Bubba Claus' sleigh does have a decal depicting "Calvin and Hobbes" comic strip character Calvin relieving himself ... but not on a Ford or Chevy logo. His decal shows Calvin going wee wee on the Tooth Fairy.

• The usual Christmas movie classics such as "Miracle on 34th Street" and "Ernest Saves Christmas" will not be shown in your area. Instead, you'll see some lesser-known movies about Bubba Claus made in the late 1970s. Many feature Burt Reynolds as Bubba Claus, Jackie Gleason as a Grinch who says "You scumbum!" a lot and dozens of state patrol cars crashing into each other.

• Bubba Claus doesn't wear a belt. I'd turn the other way when he bends over to put presents under the tree.

• Lovely Christmas songs have been sung about me, including Elvis' "Here Comes Santa Claus" and Madonna's remake of "Santa Baby." Until this year, songs about Bubba Claus have been played only on AM radio stations in Mississippi. They include such classics as Mark Chesnutt's "Bubba Claus Shot the Jukebox," David Allan Coe's "Willie, Waylon, Bubba Claus and Me," and Hank Williams Jr.'s "If You Don't Like Bubba Claus, You Can Kiss My Icicle."

Don't trust those cows

Last week I had business back home, which meant a long, lonely drive down two-lane roads through the countryside.

The sun was shining, and I decided to roll down the window and breathe some of that fresh country air shortly after I left Buena Vista on Highway 41. I rolled it up two seconds later ... in a hurry.

I had forgotten what we country folks mean by the term "fresh country air." There's no such thing. It's an inside joke we country folks play on city slickers. We enjoy seeing the looks on the faces of city folks when they come to the country and take a big whiff of "fresh country air," better known to us as cow poopee.

It was the first time this year I'd seen cows. Living in the big city of Columbus, you don't see many cows, front porches with swings or drivers who use turn signals. I miss all of them.

But I still think cows are up to something. Every time I passed a herd, they all looked up at me very suspiciously. I'm sure as soon as my car was out of sight, one of the cows would say, "All right, roll the nuclear missile back out from behind the haystack and let's get back to work."

Intelligence-wise, cows are the most underrated animals on the planet. Sure, you think that all they do is lie around all day, eat and pass gas — kinda like your typical married man. But when you look into a cow's eyes, you can tell it is deep in thought — totally unlike your typical married man.

When I look at cows, I always think they're talking about me. Or maybe I'm just paranoid because I carry a leather wallet.

"Hey, Betsy. Moo. See that redneck over there? Moo. I think he tipped me over once while I was sleeping. Moo."

Yes, I admit it. I used to go cow-tipping. We small-town folks didn't have racquetball and we were too poor to play golf at the country club, so for recreation we piled into a pickup, crawled through a barbed-wire fence and tipped over sleeping cows ... and prayed we weren't in a bull pen.

These small-town Saturday nights have led to the formation of such crazy groups as FACT (Friends Against Cow-Tipping). They even have an Internet site with a link to a cow-tipping alternative for animal lovers — online electronic cow-tipping. They even moo when you push them with your mouse.

Some of you city folks also may think cow-tipping is cruel, but they get their turn. Each year a bunch of bulls chases humans who loiter in the streets of some podunk town in Spain to a stadium where a guy in a funny hat and tights (called a matador) dances around as bulls chase him and Spanish folks in the stadium shout "Ole!" which in English means, "Hey you idiot in the funny hat, look out! There's a bull behind you!"

Now, that is cruel. Cow-tipping is harmless fun. The only cruel thing about cow-tipping is what happens to your clean sneakers. And you thought your mom got mad when you tracked mud across the living room carpet.

Captain Jim and the birds

I was backing the car down the paved cliff known as our driveway when my wife yelled, "Stop!"

Figuring I was about to run over Mrs. Crabtree again, I slammed on the brakes. Instead, my wife pointed to a tree in our back yard and asked, "Is that a bald eagle?"

It was. The king of birds. The symbol of American pride. As I gazed at the majestic feathered creature, I wondered how Ben Franklin could have ever sought to have the turkey declared our national bird. Of course, we are talking about a guy who flew kites in thunderstorms.

I ran to the side of the house to get a better view as my neighbor, Mark, was pulling into his driveway. "Look, Mark! A bald eagle!" I pointed at the pine tree and — of course — the bird was gone. Mark just looked at me kinda funny and went back to cleaning off his "Home for sale" sign.

I felt like the guy from the cartoon with the frog who danced and sang, "Hello, my baby. Hello, my honey. Hello, my ragtime gal." But every time the guy tried to prove it to someone, the frog would merely sit there and go "ribbet, ribbet."

Nevertheless, seeing the eagle made my day. But buying bird food for the back yard is going to be a lot more expensive now. How much are hamsters these days anyway? Oh, never mind; Mark has a cat. "Here, kitty, kitty!"

When I delivered the exciting eagle news at work, nobody seemed interested. After sending the computer message — "I saw a bald eagle in my yard today" — all I got was smart-aleck responses, started by my boss, Larry:

"Propecia might help."

Now I know how Captain Jim felt. Captain Jim's the guy who carried my wife and me around the San Juan Islands between Washington and British Columbia last March in a search for killer whales. Unfortunately, we saw nothing but seals and a bunch of rare birds that made Captain Jim — an avid bird watcher — dang near wet his pants.

"Look! It's the orange-necked yellow-bellied hookbilled oystercatcher!"

We'd look at him as if he'd just said, "Actually, my name's not Captain Jim. It's Elvis. Ya'll ever been to Graceland?"

"That's a rare bird," he would explain upon seeing the blank looks on our faces. "If you tell your bird-watching friends, they'll be excited for you."

Yeah, well, my bird-watching friends didn't pay $200 to bop around these islands looking for invisible orcas. Come to think of it, the bird-watching friends I have watch them only while toting a shotgun in a baited field and gnawing on a Slim Jim. They couldn't tell a orange-necked yellow-bellied hookbilled oystercatcher from an emu.

If only Captain Jim could see me now. I've come a long way from a rookie bird watcher who couldn't spot a chicken unless it came with mashed potatoes and a biscuit. Now I'm watching eagles. Well, I gotta go. It's time to feed the birds.

"Here, kitty, kitty!"

Interstate pit stop

"What'll it be, hun?"

This is the sound of music to me at 2 a.m. on some forgotten exit along the interstate. Not only will this sweet lady keep my cup filled with hot coffee and bring me a plateful of eggs, grits, sausage and toast, but she calls me "hun." Even my wife won't call me "hun" unless it's accompanied by "Atilla."

It's one of my favorite guilty pleasures, stopping at these 24-hour breakfast joints far away from home. You know the place by some name — Waffle House, Huddle House, Omelet House, Coffee Kettle, etc. As Shakespeare said, "A Waffle House by any other name would smell just as much like cigarettes and grease."

I like sitting here alone, a total stranger that no one will remember one minute after I walk out of here — though they do steal glances at me as I jot down notes in my reporter's notebook. What kind of freak stops in a Waffle House to write at 2 a.m.? "If that's sober," the man staring at me from three booths away is thinking, "I'll stay drunk, thank you."

The crowd in here is the same as it is every 2 a.m., though this is my first time in this particular Waffle Huddle Omelet Coffee House. A few stools down sits an old man with his coffee and Camels. When one goes out, he lights another. I figure he's been sitting there awhile, probably since the Beatles split.

Behind me is a table of teen-age boys discussing graphically — though unrealistically — their exploits with the ladies before Saturday evening turned into the wee hours of Sunday morning. Nothing wrong with a little macho fantasy talk, I guess. Been there, done that. Besides, when they're ready for reality and have $50 to spare, there's always that lady over there by the pay phone.

In the corner booth sits a couple laughing and pumping quarters into the jukebox, which, thank goodness, has a slew of Merle Haggard songs. I don't think these two folks knew each other too well before tonight, but I get the feeling they'll know each other all too well by morning.

And, of course, there are the two ladies waiting tables. Linda's in her 40s, Sally Ann's in her 50s. Linda is happy to see me. Everybody else in here is simply riding out the night and probably spent most of their money before coming here. I'm a sober stranger who might actually leave a decent tip. And I always do — a least a quarter per "hun."

And there's the intense cook, who seems to be cooking for 500 customers instead of the dozen that are here. He can't stop to breathe while Linda and Sally shout out, "Number three, scattered and smothered, over easy, scorch it with extra cheese!" Where he found time to get those four dozen tattoos, I have no idea.

"Here you go, darlin'," Linda says as she delivers my meal. "Darlin" — that's worth two quarters. Linda looks at me funny as I sample the grits and say, "My compliments to the chef." The "chef" glares at me briefly, wishing it weren't too late to spit in my cheese grits.

I drop two bucks on the table as I leave — two "darlins" and four "huns" — and then stick two quarters in the jukebox and request the same song ("Achy Breaky Heart") three straight times. They're gonna remember me for more than a minute after I leave, by golly.

Chicken supreme

Sometimes the best stories are true ...

Growing up in rural Macon County, Ga., I've seen my share of chickens. But none can hold a candle to Peep, Georgia's champion clucker.

Peep showed up one Sunday morning on my Uncle Fred's doorstep. Uncle Fred lives in the middle of urban Warner Robins, the heart of booming Middle Georgia. No one knows how this little chick made its way to the city, but I suspect he hijacked a Tyson truck or had compromising photos of Colonel Sanders.

"Oh, Daddy, he's so cute!" my then 7-year-old cousin Lisa squealed. "Can I keep it?"

"No way! Absolutely not! No! Don't give me the sad, puppy dog eyes! Stop! Arghhhh! . . . OK, you can keep it."

Lisa could turn up those big, brown eyes and ask Uncle Fred, "Daddy, can I please have a nuclear weapon to play with?" and there would be a missile in the back yard in 10 minutes.

Peep grew up a true city chicken. He slept in the house and ignored the sunrise. Instead, he crowed when the alarm went off. During the day, he stayed in the back yard, but he expected to be let back in the house at dusk. If no one remembered, he would hop the fence and run to the side storm door and peck loudly on the aluminum. If there were still no response, he'd fly up to the living room window, flap his wings, crow and peck on the window.

Uncle Fred hated the chicken — with good reason. Never having seen a hen, Peep was under the impression that Uncle Fred's shoes were hens. Every now and then, often while Uncle Fred was snoozing in front of a ballgame, Peep would get the urge and charge into the living room with his wings spread wide, and Uncle Fred would awake to find this crazed rooster in the throes of passion with his feet.

One night, when Uncle Fred was home alone, he refused to let Peep in the house. When Lisa and my Aunt Clarice got home, they found Peep had pecked that door until he fell unconscious on the stoop. They laid the chicken down in the living room, fussing at Uncle Fred as they went to get water to revive him. When the ladies left the room, Peep sprang to life and mocked Uncle Fred, who threw a shoe at him. You don't throw shoes at a chicken that thinks shoes are hens.

Lisa convinced Uncle Fred to take her and Peep to the annual pet show at the Museum of Arts and Sciences in Macon in 1987. But under no circumstances, he said, could she enter the chicken.

"No! Not the eyes again!"

Peep, to everyone's chagrin, won the miscellaneous category. An hour later, Uncle Fred left running from the building with the chicken in front, Lisa in one arm and a 4-foot-high "Best of Show" trophy in the other. A mob of rich, poodle-owning ladies was trying to kill this man who had beaten their fancy-schmancy dogs with a chicken that wasn't even talented by poultry standards.

Lisa was heartbroken when Peep flew to that ol' coop in the sky at the ripe old age of 10. Uncle Fred couldn't have picked a worse night to bring home KFC.

But Peep's spirit lives on. The giant trophy from a dozen years ago still rests in the living room, mocking the tiny awards and plaques Uncle Fred has won in the insurance business. And he still hates that chicken.

Sleeping on the job

American companies recently have made much progress in the

way they treat their employees and have been rewarded with more loyal, efficient workers.

While foreigners bleed and sweat to make our sneakers in strange lands such as Vietnam, Laos and Southern California, we American workers enjoy such perks as 401(k) plans, ergonomic chairs, and access to the Xerox machine to make copies of personal documents and our butts when the boss goes home. (Of course, I've never photocopied my butt because this is unsanitary for those of us who use the Xerox machine for regular daily tasks at work, such as making copies of our faces.)

With unemployment near an all-time low in America, now is a great time to request even more perks from companies desperate to attract and keep good workers, merely adequate workers and those whose criminal records are three pages or less.

One trend sweeping the nation now is nap breaks. With people working an average of seven hours more per week than they did 10 years ago, companies have found that a short nap boosts tired workers' productivity.

We tried this experiment here at the Ledger using me as a test subject. I slept all day, and productivity soared and errors were cut by 20 percent. Based on that, I've proposed that by allowing me to stay home and sleep all week, we could wipe out errors altogether.

A study by the Sleep Research Center at Loughborough University in Britain (and this is true) has found that for each hour less than eight that you sleep each night, you can temporarily lose one IQ point. Fifteen points could easily be lost in a week, the study says, making a person with an average IQ of 100 "borderline retarded." This means a lack of sleep could render Dennis Rodman a complete vegetable. If you find "Ace Ventura" funny, you may want to go home and take a nap immediately.

Numerous other studies conducted by the National Sleep Foundation here in the colonies have yielded similar results. This leads to the obvious question: "What the heck is the National Sleep Foundation and how can I apply for a job there?" I could picture myself in a position there:

WASHINGTON (AP) — National Sleep Foundation director of research Chris Johnson announced the results of a five-year, $40 million study on insomnia Friday and reports that watching Ted

Koppel or Barney the purple dinosaur really helps. Or try a hot bubble bath.

But I may not be qualified because lately I've been having trouble sleeping at work, especially when people bang on the bathroom stall and ask, "You all right in there? You've been in there for three hours."

"Yeah, my wife tried to cook again last night. How's productivity going?"

"We've been unusually productive and efficient for the past three hours. Too bad you missed it."

A picture worth saving

My wife ordered me to clean my room last night.

"My room" is the spare bedroom where I keep my computer, books, old trophies, various sports memorabilia and "tacky" art such as the $2 print of dogs playing roulette.

I like my room just the way it is. I can find all my old papers amid the 10 gallons of trash covering my 1-gallon trash can. And there's a unique sense of order, mostly maintained by an array of spider webs.

I decided to shift the trash around a little to appease my wife and even made vacuum cleaner noises when she walked past the door.

Among the many items I discovered while climbing over the trash pile were really bad stories I wrote in college, photos of people I don't know but probably am related to and various woodland creatures.

Most of this junk found its way into a trash bag after all. Then I came across an item worth saving — my fifth-grade class photo.

I've seen only a handful of these boys and girls in the past decade. Most seem to have fallen off the face of the earth. Very few stayed home.

Of course, there's me, the class clown, sitting up front with my bowl haircut styled by Mom. I was also the kickball king, spelling bee champ and elementary school Valentino. I married every girl in the class at least twice in playground ceremonies. Gee, I hope those weren't official; I can't afford the alimony.

There's Paul on the left. The whole schoolyard circled us one day as we fought over a ponytailed cutie named Paula. Because we were friends, we never landed a punch. Dennis, the class tyrant, was so disappointed no blood was spilled that he told on us for fighting in the first place. Ten years later, Paul was a groomsman in my wedding. I don't know where Dennis is, but I bet the mafia or FBI does.

There are the teacher's pets — Darrell and Angela. I've seen Darrell once since high school. We played golf when he flew home on a break from his doctorate studies in Native American literature in New Mexico back in 1996. Angela is a well-paid geologist with a dog that goes to a pet psychiatrist. I hope I never get that rich and successful.

There's Stephen, the outcast no one played with, on the right. He went on to become a football star in high school. A couple of weeks before graduation, he and some buddies were goofing off in a hot rod when he lost control and crashed. He was paralyzed from the neck down. Last year, he decided he'd had enough of this world and rolled his wheelchair off a fishing dock at his college.

Even without the photo, I'll never forget Robin. With bright blue eyes, long blonde hair and a Texas accent, she's still the cutest 10-year-old girl I've ever seen. She was my first crush and my first heartbreak as she moved back to Texas before sixth grade began. I wonder where she's at. I wonder where they're all at.

I should clean my room more often.

History lesson

The following column is a public service for students who will be taking history classes this year:

Most of what your history teachers tell you in class is true — such as, if Billy shoots one more spitball, he will indeed get detention. However, there are a few discrepancies between what's in the history books and the actual truth. Lucky for you, I'm here to set the record straight. For instance ...

• Ben Franklin did not discover electricity by flying a kite in a thunderstorm. Come on, what genius would fly a kite in a thunderstorm? Franklin actually discovered electricity when he stuck his finger in an outlet in his living room and got shocked. But what clued him in for sure was when he got his Georgia Power bill at the end of the month.

• Your teacher may try to tell you that just before being hanged by the British, Revolutionary War hero Nathan Hale said, "I regret I have but one life to lose for my country." What he actually said was, "Please, please don't hang me. I'm scared of heights. How about 50 bucks and an apology? Or, here, take my wife and hang her. I regret I have but one wife to lose for my country."

• Paul Revere is credited with warning the colonists of the impending invasion by riding his horse and yelling, "The British are coming!" This is partly true. Paul Revere was paranoid and rode through town yelling something every night. Sometimes he'd yell "The aliens are coming!" or "Y2K will be your doom!" He was bound to be right sooner or later, kind of like those tabloids that predict the world will end every year.

• You may be told that Abraham Lincoln read books by candle-light in his log cabin. Again, partly true. He was just reading the Cliffs Notes.

• The Louisiana Purchase was not a purchase at all. Thomas Jefferson won it in a poker game with Napoleon.

• You may hear that Thomas Edison patented the phonograph in 1877. Wrong. What would be the point of that? There were no records. He wouldn't have anything worthwhile to play on a phonograph until 1974 when Jimmy Buffett released his "A1A" album. Nobody would have invented the phonograph to listen to a bunch of hooey by Beethoven and Mozart.

• In 1903, the Wright brothers did indeed make their inaugural flight in Kitty Hawk, N.C. But the flight lasted only a few seconds as Orville landed and told Wilbur, "It was flying OK, but I had a sudden craving for salted peanuts. Besides, I wasn't sure if my seat could be used as a flotation device."

• That same year, Henry Ford organized Ford Motor Co. True. But what you won't be told is production was immediately shut down when the first car to roll off the line accidentally turned out to be a Corvette instead of a Model A. Attempts to restart the plant were then delayed by a United Auto Workers strike.

• And, of course, there's that edited version of man's first walk on the moon. Neil Armstrong did in fact say, "That's one small step for man ..." But before he could get to the next part, he actually said, "Yuck! I think I've steeped in dog poopee. I thought we were the first people here." To which Buzz Aldrin replied, "We are, but German shepherds landed here in 1956. Those are some smart dogs."

Buffalo burgers

I recently read that the federal government is buying millions of pounds of bison meat (that's buffalo to you uncultured folks) to use for making hamburgers in our nation's school cafeterias.

I knew buffalo were still roaming America because I've eaten their wings at several area restaurants. (It's no wonder those big ol' animals can't fly.) But I had no idea that schools were using real meat these days.

Maybe it was because I went to school in an area so poor (we all got free lunches) that we were served those meatless mushy soy-bean-fungus burgers. If they had used real meat when I was in high school, I wouldn't have ditched school lunch every other day to eat at a cheap back-alley burger joint in downtown Montezuma.

Even though I returned before the next class began, my principal warned me there would be repercussions for leaving the school grounds to go to Troy's Snack Shack (even though I had a permission slip). What were they going to do? Give me an F in lunch? Or — heaven forbid — put it on my permanent record?

(Editor's note: For more information, please refer to Chris Johnson's Permanent Record, now available online at www.fbi.gov. It's right after the part about his writing "Bocephus rules!" in his 10th-grade English book.)

I'd have probably had perfect attendance at lunch if I could have got a big ol' buffalo burger. But school lunch just didn't cut it.

I remember my first school lunch back in the first grade. I thought it was a pick-and-choose cafeteria deal like Piccadilly's or Morrison's. I was saying things like, "I'll have the mashed taters, please. No cole slaw, please. Is the fried chicken included in the Super Dilly?" But they just slapped whatever they felt like on my plate. Plop! Cole slaw.

I loved eating, but school lunches were too small in those pre-buffalo days. Who in the world eats one slice of pizza? I wanted the whole pizza and breadsticks. And they put gravy on everything. Gravy on mashed taters is great, but not on vanilla ice cream. And milk? Yuck! Who eats pizza and washes it down with milk? Everybody knows you serve beer with pizza.

Another school lunch problem is the seating arrangements. I never knew where to sit. They should have posted signs above each table such as Jocks, Nerds, Cool Kids, Geeks, Young Republicans or Metallica Fans. I could have walked to the correct table every time if I'd have seen a big, flashing sign that said: Boys With Ugly Cars And No Date For Friday Night.

I must confess, though, that I loved school lunch my freshman year. Our cafeteria burned down, and we had to eat in the school gym — even as the P.E. classes went on below us. It was fun to boo and laugh at the students and bet pickles on who'd win the basketball games. But it was dang near impossible to concentrate on eating a taco when Jenny Jerome was playing volleyball.

The story of Odysseus Bob

This is for you college students out there who may have to read Homer's "The Odyssey" for the first time this year. I'm here to help. Having taken English 201 three times in college, I'm an expert.

I have written an easy-to-understand version of "The Odyssey." Better than Cliffs Notes, it's Chris Notes:

There once was this fellow, Odysseus Bob, who was a real hot shot in his hometown, but he got lost for 20 years on Lake Eufaula after taking off for the weekend with his buddies.

It turns out that he spent years shacking up with this girl Calypso Lou while his boy, Telemachus Joe, was taking care of Odysseus Bob's doublewide, mowing the grass and all. Telemachus Joe couldn't wait for his pa to come home because these drunk rednecks kept hanging out at the doublewide, hitting on his mama, Penelope Sue, and watching wrasslin' and "Jerry Springer" on Odysseus Bob's satellite dish. But Penelope Sue kept hoping her common-law husband would come back someday.

A lot of bad stuff happened to Odysseus Bob around Lake Eufaula. Like there was this one time a one-eyed hillbilly trapped Odysseus Bob and his buddies. Well, when the hillbilly — Larry Polyphemus — asked his name, Odysseus Bob replied, "I ain't nobody."

Then one night Odysseus Bob jabbed Larry Polyphemus in his one good eye with a broken beer bottle and blinded him. Larry Polyphemus ran and told his brothers, "Ain't Nobody done blinded me." They just laughed and laughed and went back to watching their bug zapper.

Then this guy, Aeolus Jim, gave Odysseus Bob a bag of wind and told him not to open it just yet. But his buddies thought Odysseus Bob was hiding some treasure in there like an RC and some pork skins. They opened it and the wind blew them into the back yard of a witch named Circe Mae who turned his buddies into hogs. Odysseus Bob then threatened to beat up Circe Mae if she didn't turn them back into men — which she did, except for Bubba, whom they barbecued.

Then they went by this old shack where the Sirens lived — Jolene, Irene and Irmalene Siren. They sang pretty songs men just couldn't resist. His buddies put in earplugs, while Odysseus Bob tied himself up so that he could hear the Sirens, but could not stop the boat and yield to temptation when they sang Loretta Lynn's "Don't Come Home a Drinkin' With Lovin' on Your Mind."

After some big dude named Hey Zeus slapped Odysseus Bob's Basstracker with a stick of dynamite, killing all his buddies, he washed up on a sand bar called Ogygia where he borrowed a fancy new Jet Ski and went home disguised as an old man by wearing knee-high black dress socks and polka-dot shorts pulled up to his armpits.

Penelope Sue then said that whoever cranks Odysseus Bob's old pickup can marry her, knowing that nobody but he could crank it. He hopped in, tapped the gas pedal a few times, banged on the dashboard and jiggled the key until it cranked. They knew Odysseus Bob had finally come home. He then grabbed a tire tool out of the back and opened up a can of you-know-what on the rednecks.

Then Odysseus Bob kissed Penelope Sue right smack on the mouth and they lived happily ever after.

Exposing Tinky Winky

Jerry Falwell has an interesting way of picking his battles. He could go up against strip clubs, obscene music and President Clinton. Instead, he's declared war on the popular public TV children's show "Teletubbies."

Falwell claims that Teletubby Tinky Winky is gay and therefore "damaging to the moral lives of children."

He is convinced that Tinky Winky is gay because Tinky Winky carries a purse. Well, he claims it's a purse. The Itsy Bitsy Entertainment Co. maintains that it's actually "a magic bag." Does Itsy Bitsy's argument fly? I doubt it.

Picture this: Ted and Bill step onto an elevator at the office. Ted is carrying a briefcase, Bill a paisley purse.

Ted: Ha! Ha! You're carrying a purse. What are you, gay or something?

Bill: This is NOT a purse. It's my magic bag.

Ted: Oh, well, that's different. Say, how 'bout coming over to my house after work to watch the game, drink beer, cuss, play songs with our armpits and other fun macho guy stuff.

Bill: Sorry, can't tonight. There's a Judy Garland tribute at the Fox.

Personally, I don't really care if Tinky Winky is gay or straight. I'm very secure in my sexuality, though I did see "The Wizard of Oz" when it was re-released and I danced and sang along to the Village People's "YMCA" on the way to work today. And just yesterday I mustered up the courage to get a Diet Coke from that machine with Dale Earnhardt on the front.

It's not that I don't like Dale, for my brother-in-law would run over me with his pickup truck if I didn't. It's just that the machine dispenses its product between Dale's legs and I wasn't real interested in reaching between Dale's legs to get anything, even a Diet Coke.

I feel bad for Tinky Winky and believe he would be well-served to choose another name, maybe Bubba Winky or Tinky Joe. Gays have enough stereotypes to live down — assuming Tinky Winky does prefer other Tinky Winkys — without having to overcome a name like Tinky Winky.

Would you be scared to fight "Iron" Mike Tyson if his name were Mike "Tinky Winky" Tyson? I'd fight Mike "Tinky Winky" Tyson even without earmuffs.

Can you imagine this promo for TBS' "Movies For Guys Who Like Movies?"

Macho announcer voice: Tonight on "Movies For Guys Who Like Movies," Clint Eastwood is Tinky Winky!

But unlike Mr. Falwell, I don't have a problem with kids watching Teletubbies, be they gay, straight or undecided. Although, if I walked into my living room and saw a 3-year-old watching a purple creature with a "magic bag" and a TV in its stomach, I probably would freak out.

Me: Yikes! What's that strange creature?!

Wife: It's a Teletubby, Tinky Winky.

Me: No, that thing in front of the TV!

Wife: It's a child, Chris.

Me: Well, get it out of here! You know those things give me the heebie jeebies!

Men in the shower

There are numerous reasons I'm glad I'm not a woman: My hairy legs would not look good in stockings. I would no longer be able to burp really loud in public. And, Lord knows, I would never be able to get my bra on and off without help.

Last weekend, I was reminded of another reason I'm glad I'm a man — when I drove my wife to Americus so that she could attend the baby shower for my cousin's wife, Robyn, thrown by my cousin's cousins at the home of the mother-to-be's mother-in-law's sister. Or something like that.

Women go to more showers than men take showers. They are forced to cram their feet into uncomfortable shoes, eat miniature sandwiches and "oooh" and "aaah" over cute rug rat clothes that will be covered with vomit in three months.

I actually enjoy baby showers ... because I'm not there. I'm at a friend's house watching football and scratching myself where I want, when I want.

I wonder what it would be like if men threw baby showers while the women sat at home and watched "Oprah" on the big-screen television.

"I'm so glad y'all could come to my baby shower. And many thanks to Mickey's Bar for use of the conference room — the urinals have never been so shiny. Now let me open this first gift. This newspaper wrapping is so pretty. What's that, Bubba? You want to save the bow? Here, you weenie. Wow! A baseball bat."

"Oooooooo."

"Now, let's see. From Junior. Something to decorate the baby's room — a Pamela Anderson calendar."

"Aaaaahhh. Oooooh. Aaaaahh!"

"But what if the baby's a girl, Junior?"

"Well, you can exchange it, can't you?"

"Yeah, I guess. You got the receipt for this?"

"No, I meant the baby."

"I don't know. Now, from Big Larry. Oh, how cute, the head of a 12-point buck, already mounted."

"Awwwww."

"Shot him just last week. Thought you could hang it over the crib."

"That's sweet of you, Big Larry. I'm sure the moment I hang it over the crib will require an instant diaper change. Now, from Hank — something to keep the baby quiet: heat-duct tape."

"Aaaahhh."

"From Jim Bob — leopard-print bikini Pampers."

"Ooooooh."

"Well, Chris, you know how kids are always getting undressed in day care. The girls will love him in these. It works for me."

"Well, I don't know if the little girls in day care have as much class as your crowd, but you're the fashion expert, Jim Bob, and may I say you're looking lovely today in that Hank Jr. T-shirt. Would you mind pulling it down over your belly button?"

"And, finally, from Sammy — bibs, footies, diapers, shirts, shoes, baby powder, a baby monitor, a blanket and a Barney doll."

"Huh?"

"What am I supposed to do with all this useless junk, Sammy?

Can't you come up with something thoughtful like Big Larry here? You're not invited to any more of my showers. And don't even think about grabbing a free beer and Vienna sausages on the way out."

Lester's loose in Heaven

Over the years, various editors have allowed me to write about dang near anything in my column, so long as I stayed away from one dangerous topic: religion.

"Whatever you do, if you've got any sense at all, don't write about religion. Do you understand? Want us to talk real slow?" they'd ask.

"No problemo," I'd reply.

Today's column is about religion. It can be confusing stuff, but I've got a pretty good grip on it because I spent a year in the Royal Ambassadors in my church back home. I'm still not sure what we RAs were supposed to do, but in Oglethorpe we played a lot of Ping-Pong.

And my dad was a preacher for a while until he went to try out for a pulpit opening and totaled his Corvair on a cow in the road. He took this as a sign from God that he had not received the calling after all. The cow took it as a sign from God not to play in the road.

But for the really tough religious questions, I go to my buddy, Herman Snodgrass. Herman started studying the Bible extensively after he got a spanking following an RA class when our teacher told us God was omnipotent, and Herman asked, "Is that why Jesus is his only son?"

Herman later found the Lord after a frat party our freshman year of college. He said he saw the Lord playing volleyball in the back-yard of the frat house. I found out later "The Lord" playing vol-leyball was not Jesus Christ, but Jesus Hernandez, a student from Mexico. Good thing Herman didn't see Jesus funneling beer later that night.

Since meeting Jesus, Herman has been living right. He quit drink-ing and goes to church every Sunday except Super Bowl Sunday. "Some things are still sacred," he says. Herman wants to be a preacher, but no church has invited him just yet. So, on Mondays he preaches to the squirrels down at the park. And he offers me spiritual guidance on poker night.

When I had my recent accident and other woes, I went to Herman with a question that has perplexed generations: "Why do bad things happen to good people, Herman?" — only people don't usually follow that question with "Herman."

"That's Lester," Herman said. "Sometimes when God's not looking, Lester starts pushing the buttons up there."

"What about those Mormon sects in Utah that still practice polygamy?" I asked him. "Is that right?"

"Shoot naw!" he said. "Have you ever heard a preacher say, 'And do you take this woman and this woman and this woman to be your lawfully wedded wives?'"

"What's God gonna do to Benny Hinn when He gets His hands on him for duping all these folks?"

"I don't know, but I wish he'd make him the Falcons' head trainer."

"Do all dogs really go to heaven?" I asked.

"Yep, unless they got fleas, that is. Fleas go to hell. Gnats, too."

"Are there streets of gold in heaven?"

"Yeah, but you'd better not get caught running any red lights — unless you like fleas and gnats."

Back in the dating game

I went out on a date last Friday. This may not be a big deal to you. In fact, you've probably stopped reading this already and moved on to today's "Jumble," which is a real shame because there's more to my story, though I'm sure the "Jumble" is equally fascinating.

Unlike most of my previous dates, this one was with a married woman. Wipe that disgusted look off your face! Don't jump to conclusions, I'm talking about my wife.

It took my wife only seven years of nagging to get me to take her out on a date, and it wasn't so bad. Shoot, I might even take her out on a second date in three or four years.

The best thing about dating my wife is that I don't have to make a good impression, not that I could even if I wanted to. She's fully aware of the repulsive creature a man becomes after marriage.

I don't have to examine myself in the mirror for a half hour before going out, making sure every strand of hair is in its proper place (not that there are as many strands to worry about these days anyway). I don't have to blow on my hand and see what my breath smells like (thank goodness), nor do I have to douse myself with cologne to mask that "man smell" — a combination of sweat, motor oil, fishing bait and beer that seems to stick with you your whole life.

In fact, I haven't owned a bottle of cologne in years. You're doing pretty good if I remember to put on deodorant now. And instead of having some stranger on a date asking, "What's that scent you're wearing? Eau de possum?" I can get straight to the point with my wife and tell her to sniff me before we leave the house.

"Do I stink?" I ask.

"Not bad. At least, not from a distance. How close are the tables at this restaurant?"

Another good thing about my return to dating was the movie experience. We went to the 4 p.m. show to get in cheap. And unlike when I began dating, every movie did not star Molly Ringwald and Anthony Michael Hall. Now, they all star Sarah Michelle Gellar and Sandra Bullock. Unfortunately, Hollywood still hasn't made a great movie since "Ferris Bueller's Day Off."

Best of all, though, I didn't have to take her to one of those fancy-shmancy tie-wearing restaurants where they cook your 'maters, serve your green beans raw and dim the lights so you can't see what you're eating anyway. I used to take girls to such restaurants to make them think I was classy and had money. But my wife knows I'm about as classy as Jethro Bodine, and she keeps the checkbook and knows exactly how poor we are.

The conversation was so much easier, too, because we didn't actually have to talk to each other. We talked to each other once back in 1991 and realized neither of us is very interesting. In fact, I think the only time we spoke was when she asked, "Did you remember to bring the coupon?"

The teens on their dates around us shrieked in horror, but that's romantic dinner conversation to us. And you should have seen the twinkle in her eyes when I said yes.

Attack of the ninja kayaker

When I vacation at my favorite spot on Earth — St. Simons Island — I seek relaxation, not adventure. I like to hang out at the pier, where an assortment of creatures come together at sunset: dolphins, sharks, seagulls, fishermen, Canadian transplants with their dogs (all named Fifi), those cool smoking and swearing teenagers, and the ghosts of pirates, Indians and slaves. And, of course, me.

But on my most recent visit, my wife refused to let me spend every day watching the sun rise and set, snoozing to the tide's ebb and flow in the meantime. She insisted we participate in some sort of physical activity. Yikes! As we strolled by a quaint outdoors shop in the village, a sign caught her eye: "Kayak Tours."

"No, no, no. Can't we just ride the trolley around the island or take a dinner cruise?" I begged.

My wife has had the nerve to include me in a variety of adventures over the past year, a time span that has seen us try snorkeling, snow skiing and, now, kayaking, for the first time. She apparently wants us to be bad at many different activities. She wants us to be well-rounded adventurers, in the same sense colleges use the term "well-rounded" as an excuse to produce graduates who know hardly anything about a whole lot of stuff.

I can't say for sure why this kayaking quest bothered me. After all, I relish any chance to canoe down the Flint River. Maybe it's because while canoeing offers an up-close look at gators, ducks and deer, sea kayaking provides a close-up view of sharks, giant squid and two-headed sea monsters. Or maybe it was because the expedition she picked out was labeled "a three-hour tour." I was raised by a television, and somewhere in the back of my mind I was hearing those words set to TV theme song music: A three-hour tour, a three-hour tour. If the weather started getting rough and our tiny ship was tossed, I was prepared to jump ship, Mary Ann or no Mary Ann.

Fortunately, our guides — Cindy and Hank — were expert kayakers and unbelievably patient. Cindy is a young biology major who bears a striking resemblance to Gwyneth Paltrow, and Hank's look can best be described as Jimmy Buffett meets Maynard G. Krebbs, and his resume will always look a lot like mine under the education header: "Some college."

Right off the bat, they performed two amazing manuevers: (1) convincing me to ride in a tandem kayak with my wife and (2) easing my wife's terror as we started our journey in the spooky marsh instead of the sea as we had expected. I figured asking my wife and me to cooperate on guiding a tandem kayak was a certain recipe for divorce. As we pushed the kayak into the marsh's tiny, winding tidal creek, I told my wife, "I'm getting the good car."

She wasn't paying attention. She was on snake watch. She's terrified of the reptiles and rarely will set foot outdoors in "snakey" areas such as Glynn County or North America. I, too, was somewhat uneasy as we slid off the bank into the murky water and heard another voice from the dark dungeon of my subconscious. It was that fuzzy monster sheriff from Six Flags' Monster Plantation: "Don't go into the marsh! You humans never listen!"

My job was to supply all the power and do all the steering for the kayak; my wife's job was to use her paddle backward on the wrong the side of the boat and to sling water in my eyes. But I dared not tell her she was using the wrong side of the paddle because I figured the less paddling she did, the better our chances of survival. Besides, she is a dangerous woman. If you don't believe me, ask Karen, another member of our kayak tour group.

When our boat got stuck in the current at a difficult bend and we made 47 unsuccessful attempts to make a turn, Cindy came up with a solution to free us. She told Karen to ram us with her kayak to get us going in the right direction again. Karen accidentally sent us into the sawgrass once again where my wife found herself in an extremely "snakey" area and began to panic, paddling left, right, front and back and making no progress. In the midst of her terror, she finally used the right side of her paddle ... using it to smack Karen in the face. The bad part is that I saw it coming. I was thinking, "Surely she knows Karen is right beside her. Surely she won't hit her with that wild paddle. ... Oh well."

Poor Karen, who would be apologized to throughout the day, straightened her glasses and paddled away dazed and confused as to why she had been assaulted by my ninja kayaker wife. Cindy took over and rammed us correctly. Cindy bore no fear, for she had survived two earlier assaults by my wife before entered the water — once with a paddle and another time in a very awkward spot with the pointed front end of the kayak. I'd never heard a person scream, "Wooooaaaa! Excuuuse meeeee!" quite that way before.

We eventually made it into the sound and would later paddle into the surf, surprisingly, without dying. We were spared further embarrassment until my wife walked away from the tour still wearing the outdoor shop's lifejacket. Cindy ran down the thief before we got away, and I took Cindy aside and defended my wife's absent-mindedness as any good husband would.

"I'm sorry, Cindy. She's a cleptomaniac. It's kind of embarrassing."

Bathtime burglar

As much as I've come to enjoy living in Columbus, I can't get used to the fact that you have to lock your doors around here.

Growing up in tiny Oglethorpe, Ga., we never bothered to lock our doors. We felt safe. Even when we did bother to lock the front door, we were courteous enough to leave a note for friends and relatives such as, "The key is under the flower pot." Good thing many criminals are illiterate.

But once you venture away from the friendly confines of the Oglethorpe city limits — an area some call "The Modern World" — danger lurks. Thieves lurk. Stuff's just lurkin' all over the place. You better lurk out.

The only time I ever heard of anyone almost getting robbed back home was when my Uncle Johnny spotted a man climbing into his bedroom window. He quickly devised a scheme to scare him away.

"Sue! Hand me my shotgun!"

My aunt responded, "Johnny, you know we ain't got no gun!"

My first brush with thievery came when I was in college at Georgia Southwestern in Americus. I had a new car, and — just as I had always done with my piece-of-junk 1978 Celica — I kept the keys under the seat.

On the first day I drove it to school, I returned from classes only to find an empty parking space where I was sure I had parked my car. After a desperate hour of searching, I found the car at the other end of campus with a note from my sneaky ex-girlfriend attached to the steering wheel: "Love your new car. Drives great."

My closest brush with theft came in 1992 in Valdosta, Ga., where we were wise enough to keep the doors to our apartment locked.

I had a rare day off and was taking a hot bath with Mr. Bubble (that's a soap, not a man) when I heard the venetian blinds of the living room rustling. I got out of the tub and, sure enough, there was a burglar unhooking my VCR and television — which made up pretty much all of our wordly possessions — from the wall.

"Hey!" I yelled. And at that very moment, he and I both came to a realization: I was nekkid. He gave me a deer-caught-in-the-head-lights look that the word "fear" just can't explain.

He dashed out onto the patio, and I followed. Although, like a dog chasing a car, I didn't know what I was going to do with him if I caught him. Fortunately for both of us, he got away. Unfortunately, the fear turned to laughter for several housewives taking their after-noon walks around the lake.

I guess the thought of tangling with a wet, naked man will make just about any guy run like a gazelle chased by a lion. I've got a bum left knee, yet I can guarantee you that no wet, naked man will ever lay a hand on me.

I'll make an exception, though, for Mr. Bubble.

The night stars fell

A couple of weeks ago, I took in the Leonid meteor shower at Pine Mountain. After getting off work, I gassed up my wife's car, bought a Slim Jim and a Diet Coke and was at the overlook across from the Callaway Store by 1 a.m.

Expecting a crowd, I was pleasantly surprised to find just three cars and a secluded spot from which I could watch the biggest Leonids show since 1966. I couldn't use that "not being born yet" excuse this time. And being haunted by this feeling I won't be around 33 years from now for the next big show, I wanted to make the most of the night.

I lay on the hood of the car and stared at the sky. As the moon called it a night in the west and my eyes tuned out the southern glow from Columbus, I caught an occasional falling star overhead.

Though I nearly froze to death, it was nirvana for a loner like me. It reminded me of those nights back home when I was a kid and followed the railroad tracks to "my thinking spot" under the trestles on the moonlit banks of the Flint River. Oglethorpe had no Riverwalk, nor a library bigger than my bedroom, but there are still few things that can beat that milelong trek on the tracks past the kudzu patches and grunting gators with their eyes aglow in the sloughs outside my hometown.

As I did on those walks, I went to Pine Mountain seeking inspiration. Maybe I'd return with the seeds of the next great American novel — or at least next week's column. Maybe I'd find the meaning of life. But mainly I came for the show.

A carload of teen-agers pulled up beside me after a half-hour or so. They were drinking, smoking and cussing, but seemed to be good kids beneath their MTV shells. A dozen years ago, I'd have shared a bottle of Boone's Farm with them, though I was never much for smoking or cussing. They left me to my thoughts, probably because any guy who sits atop a mountain by himself in the middle of the night might be a serial killer. I couldn't help but eavesdrop as they discussed everything from galaxies to the proper use of swear words. By the time they got to religion, I understood why there is a minimum drinking age.

Unimpressed by the occasional meteor streaking across the sky, the teens and others soon left the mountain to me and the stars. I saw about a hundred falling stars in two and a half hours — not spectacular but more than enough to impress me. I appreciate moderation. That's why I like our little ol' Pine Mountain — high enough for a splendid view, but small enough to remain one of Georgia's many secret treasures.

I thought about how insignificant I was against the heavenly backdrop of billions of planets in billions of solar systems in billions of galaxies. I wondered what was there before the "Big Bang." How could there have been such a thing as nothing? Is there another planet like Earth? Most certainly, somewhere. But are humans the top species, or do rats rule and perform lab experiments on humans?

About 3:30, a huge meteor streaked all the way from the northeast sky to Alabama. I made a wish. Years ago, I might have wished for a date with Becky Breeze or just yesterday for a million bucks. But I wished only for my son to be born healthy next year, nothing more.

You've got to make the most of a night like this.

Even men can cry

There are a few moments in my life that I could not forget even if I tried to — the first time I saw my Dad cry at my Granddaddy's funeral, first real kiss from a girl at tennis camp and the first time I saw my wife in college and she smiled.

But no moment will ever surpass 9:56 p.m., Feb. 22, when the doctor put my son, Saylor Trey, on my wife's stomach and I saw my eyes. I refused to cry because I'm a man. But I wanted to.

My wife ignored the eyes and pointed out that he had her nose. "Don't worry," I told her. "They can do wonders with plastic surgery these days."

He was 9 pounds, 10 ounces and 22 inches long with a head full of black hair like I did when I was born 30 years ago. Because he was so unexpectedly big, the birth was traumatic for both him and my wife — just how much so we would not learn until later.

I didn't know how I'd react to having a boy. I had hoped — until the second ultrasound revealed his sex — that we would have a girl. Nothing in the world is cuter than a little girl, and I wanted a daddy's little girl for whom I would run off potential boyfriends with a shotgun.

But it did not take long to adjust. While my wife rested on his first day, I promised him that I would teach him how to read, how to throw a spiral and how to whistle at pretty girls.

Then, at 3 a.m. the next morning, a doctor woke us to report that Saylor had a seizure, that tests were being run and that he was being taken to the high-risk nursery. The cause was a mystery. I forgot to be macho and cried for hours with my wife as we faced an uncertain future.

About 6 a.m., we visited Saylor in the high-risk nursery. I had to push my wife down the hall in a wheelchair, for it would be days before she could walk again on her own. As with the first moment I saw him, nothing could prepare me for seeing him in that nursery, hooked up to an IV, an oxygen tube and monitors, while encased in an incubator.

Most babies in there are two and three pounds, so he looked like a giant. As one of the nurses said, "You shouldn't have named him Saylor; you should have named him Cruise Ship."

Slowly, but surely, he came around and we learned the seizure was merely a result of head trauma during the birth and was temporary. A nurse snapped a Polaroid of him so that we could put it by our bed as we came home from the hospital without him. It was not how we had pictured coming home, but we were able to bring him home only a few days later. The wait for some of the other parents with children in that nursery would be much longer. We wished them the best.

The stress of wondering whether he would make it has been replaced by the normal stress of sleepless nights and messy diapers. And when the doctor told us that he was fully recovered, we took a balloon from a bouquet sent to us at the hospital and released it in the backyard, along with our fears and worries.

Though it barely floated inside the house, it rose so high into the clear, blue sky that folks flying Delta knew, "It's a boy!" I didn't know where the balloon was headed as it disappeared into the heavens, but that wasn't important. All that mattered was that it could fly. And God only knows where we go from here.

The perfect friend

If there's one thing I miss about being a kid or teenager — and there were about 427 things at last count — it's my old friends.

We still consider ourselves friends, of course, but we're all so scattered now. Mike and Thad are living the concrete life in Atlanta. Paul's holding down the fort back home. And Keith, who was my best friend in addition to being my first cousin, is trying to keep the "peace" in Bosnia. So, you can see why it's kinda hard to get everybody together to cruise round and round my hometown Dairy

Queen these days. And, anyway, at least three of us have been advised by our doctors to stay away from Blizzards and triple cheeseburgers.

When I get home from work, I can't get anybody up for a touch football game anymore. Nobody's got a handful of quarters for the Donkey Kong machine down at the Suwannee Swifty. And not only is there no one to give me a boost to peek in the girls' locker room at school, but now we'd get arrested instead of merely suspended.

But I've learned to cope by observing children, and I've found the solution to my problem: bedwetting. No, wait. That's not it. Oh yeah, the imaginary friend.

This is not my first imaginary friend. There was Buford back when I was seven and spent a lot of time in the corner of my second-grade classroom standing on one foot in a trash can for heckling during readings of Dr. Seuss. He was my imaginary friend until I was 15 and dropped him for Denise Huxtable.

I haven't seen Buford since then, but did get a letter from him saying he was being chased by O.J. Simpson for being "the real killer." He's now working in D.C. as the Washington Post's anonymous source.

My new imaginary friend is named Homer. I met Homer in the hospital last July. He was moved into my room the same night they gave me a morphine pump.

There are some great things about having Homer as my best friend: He never asks for money (maybe because we're so close he knows I have none). Like me, the only shows he watches on TV are "Biography," "The Andy Griffith Show" and "SportsCenter." And I don't have to buy a ticket for Homer when I go to sporting events.

Then again, having an imaginary friend has its drawbacks. High-fives are a little dangerous. Sometimes Homer will act crazy between me and a pretty girl at the mall and my wife thinks I'm looking at the girl. He also gets me in trouble with my wife at the gutbuster buffet when he slips things like fried chicken and cheesecake on my plate while I'm not looking. And I almost got slapped at the Springer when I asked him if my breath stunk during a play and the lady next to me thought I was talking to her.

But there's one way Homer's just like the rest of my old friends: When he found out I got a truck, he offered me pizza and beer if I'd help him move his imaginary furniture into his imaginary apartment, where he has stolen imaginary cable.

Of course, I agreed. What are friends for?

Early lessons in love

I don't remember what age I was when I started to get interested in girls. Maybe 10 or 11. I can't wait until I get old enough to understand them. I did have some early crushes, the first of which was on my kindergarten teacher, Miss Hunt. Then there was Jessica Lange from "King Kong," who wouldn't respond to my love letters, but fell for a giant dead monkey.

Fortunately, my experience of being rejected by Jessica Lange helped me deal with a brief period of rejection later on — a period I like to refer to as "the '80s." But, hey, when you've been turned down in favor of a monkey, you don't go into high school with a lot of expectations.

That all leads up to why I'm worried about my son, Saylor. It all started when he was about 6 months old and threw down the remote control when he was accidentally flipping channels and spotted Britney Spears. And he's been a babe hound ever since.

Now, six months later, he's got his eye on a 1-year-old at his daycare. For about the past month, when I've dropped Saylor off, he and his little girlfriend run up to each other with their arms extended and little hands waving.

If they were adults, it would be very romantic. However, adults who are in love usually don't show affection by running up to each other and drooling on each other — unless it's around last call at the singles bar or maybe spring break in Panama City.

I'm worried that Saylor might get burned out on love before he even reaches kindergarten. You never know what could happen when you fall in love so early. Just when you think things are going swell, little Gracie's liable to get swept away by a giant monkey.

The relationship has already had some rocky moments. Its roots can be traced to the day Saylor ran crying to a daycare worker with a fresh set of toothmarks in his left arm. Of course, in his right hand was a lock of auburn hair. These years are all about learning, and I think in grasping Gracie's hair, he also grasped the concept of cause and effect.

I reported this incident to a buddy who has never been married but is currently planning a wedding for the second time. "I'm proud to see that he has already learned early about girls and the pain they inflict," he replied in an e-mail.

That might be a bit harsh, for rarely have I been bitten by women, not since my senior trip to Panama City, anyway. This biting thing likely will pass. Hopefully, the hair-pulling thing will, too. If not, he'll have to court Sinead O'Connor when he's old enough to date. And even if Sinead decides to grow her hair out, she probably won't still have teeth by the time he's old enough to date.

Lately, Saylor and Gracie have kinda cooled down a little bit. Maybe it's over. Who knows? There's a lot of other hair out there to pull and more little boys to bite. But someday, years from now, Saylor will hear a song on the radio that brings forth a rush of nostalgia as he reflects on his daycare love. I bet it'll be Def Leppard's "Love Bites."

Leapin' lizards

My wife called me the other night to let me know there would be something waiting for me on the stove when I got home from work around midnight. I thought that was a good thing. I was wrong.

Usually when my wife calls, it's to tell me about my son's latest accomplishment. These all happen while I'm at work. He's either pointing at things and naming them or doing something a bit more complex, such as programming the VCR to tape a Britney Spears video.

Other times, it's bad news about the baby: He's wide awake because the teeny-boppers keep cruising by the house with their rap music, he's teething, or she realizes why those disposable diapers were just $5.99 a pack.

"When you get home, there'll be a Tupperware dish on the stove . . ." she began.

"Cool!" I interrupted. "What's in it? Chili? Chicken and dumplins? Mashed 'taters?"

"No, a lizard."

"Is it deep-fried or baked?" I asked.

"No, you dufus! It's still alive."

"Still alive? That's worse than sushi. You know if I don't eat raw fish, I sure as heck ain't eating raw reptiles."

"It's not for your supper!"

"Well, what's for supper?" I asked.

"When's the last time I had supper waiting for you when you got home?"

"September 22, 1994. But there's always hope."

"I trapped it, and I want you to get rid of it as soon as you get home. He keeps looking at me."

"How do you know it's a he?"

"Well, I don't know for sure. It's only about 4 inches long."

"For a little reptile, that definitely sounds like a he."

"The LIZARD is 4 inches long."

"Oh. Why don't you get rid of it?"

"No way. You know I haven't touched anything like that since we saw 'Jurassic Park'. That's your job."

"Oh yeah, and what if I don't?" I asked defiantly.

"Remember John Wayne?"

"Yeah, loved his movies."

"Not that one. John Wayne Bobbit."

"OK, OK, I'll do it. To quote Lorena Bobbit, you can kiss that lizard good-bye."

I admit it: I'm scared of lizards. I'm not really sure what a lizard could do to me — barring some kind of nuclear accident that turns it into the T-rex from "Jurassic Park" — but it looks too much like a dinosaur to mess with.

I crept up on the lizard in the Tupperware dish and he stared at me as I slid a piece of paper underneath and turned the dish over with the paper serving as a ceiling. I felt the lizard jump up and down, trying to knock the paper off and cause me to have a heart attack as a 4-inch reptile unleashed its fury on my poor, little 190-pound body.

I flung him into the cold night and he landed somewhere in the vicinity of Pine Mountain. I pounded my chest and screamed, "I am the lizard king!"

I was feeling pretty macho until my wife woke up and found that same Tupperware dish — unwashed — back in the cabinet.

For at least a week, I've been demoted from the lizard king. I'm now the dishwasher king.

Cole slaw conspiracy

A couple of weeks ago, we were dining at one of those all-you-can-eat, gutbuster buffet-and-steak places when a table went flying beside me. I hadn't witnessed such a sight since I saw Merle Haggard at the Silver Moon seven years ago. Only this table wasn't thrown by a drunk or even somebody high on the free cheesecake. It was thrown by an angry waitress.

The police were called, and a manager apologized to the family for their children's brush with death, but that was it. Any manager worth their pay would have at least paid for their meal.

That was one of my more pleasant recent dining experiences. In one day, I had to walk away from two restaurants before I finally found one staffed by humans with common sense. And, yes, such animals still exist. But if you're a rare human with common sense, beware: At any moment, you may be shot in the backside with a tranquilizer dart and wake up with a beeping transmitter dangling from your ear.

We began the night at one of our town's many bar-and-grill restaurants. I settled on the Fisherman's Platter. Of course, it came with cole slaw and fries. I'd rather go down a water slide made of cheese graters than eat cole slaw.

"What can I get besides cole slaw?" I asked the waiter.

"You can't substitute for cole slaw."

"I don't like cole slaw," I explained.

"You can substitute the french fries."

"I like french fries. How 'bout some mashed taters in place of the cole slaw? Pretty please."

"You can't substitute for cole slaw."

"You mean to tell me that we can send men to the moon, but we haven't figured out a way to NOT put cole slaw on a Fisherman's Platter? I'm sure I read in a recent article where scientists at MIT found a way to put mashed taters right where cole slaw was supposed to go on a Fisherman's Platter, and nothing blew up."

"You can't substitute for cole slaw."

As we walked out, I felt sorry for the poor waiter. Some night, he's gonna find himself on a date with a beautiful girl, and he'll gaze into her eyes, but with his limited vocabulary all he'll be able to say is, "Darling, you can't substitute for cole slaw."

"Oh yes, Jimmy! I love cole slaw! Take me, I'm yours!"

We settled for the drive-through of a chicken place, where the girl taking our order began deciding that we wanted combos instead of meals and got both of us pretty confused. After I repeated part of the order, she blared, "That's what I said, sir!" Stunned, I sat there in silence. Surely, she couldn't have said what I thought she'd said. She broke the silence. "That's what I said, sir!!" with two exclamation points this time.

I suggested an original place to put her chicken leg and drove away.

Denied fish by cole slaw and denied chicken by cole-slaw-for-brains, we settled on barbecue and warned the staff of our previous two tries at eating. They bent over backward for us out of pure fear.

Forget cole slaw; there's no substitute for customer service.

Bigger not always better

I can see several buildings 40 stories high to my left. There's a major river to the right and a whole 'nother country on the other side. There are thousands upon thousands of folks working here in downtown Detroit and millions of people living in the vicinity. Yet I might as well be lost in the swamp back home.

As I walk the streets, I see parking lots charging a couple of bucks an hour. There are restaurants under the impression that I'm gonna pay five bucks for a hot dog. And people look straight ahead as they walk. Nobody dares make eye contact.

Back at the hotel, I search through the tourist guides for something to do. There are casinos, but I don't gamble except for the occasional office pool. Joe Louis Arena is across the street, but the dang Kings knocked the Red Wings out of the NHL playoffs. The

Tigers are out of town. There are a lot of advertisements for dancing nekkid women, but that kind of entertainment comes at a high cost — mine being that my wife reads this column and owns a couple of iron skillets.

Detroit has its interesting nooks and crannies, such as Greektown and the tunnel under the river and into Canada just a couple hundred yards from here. But to me it's just another city. It's just an Atlanta without the Braves.

It's not totally unlike Columbus, because just an hour ago (and I swear this is true) a waitress at the bar and grill across the street told me I couldn't substitute the cole slaw on my steak dinner. This cole slaw thing is getting out of hand, I'm telling you.

Columbus leaders talk a lot about growth. Why? By the time you get the size Columbus is today, every benefit gained from growth is countered by a drawback. The tax base increases, but so do the things you have to fund with tax money. Businesses get more customers, but more businesses spring up, and the competition never stops. I don't want Columbus to grow anymore. Why don't we take all the energy we use trying to turn Columbus into another Atlanta and simply boost the quality of life? When do we draw the line and say enough is enough? How about now?

As I look down at the streets of Detroit, I know there's more to see, and I plan to see much of it. It's so big, though, I don't know where to start. And with a 15-month-old at the house, mainly I plan to sleep EIGHT STRAIGHT HOURS every night. And, in the event my bosses are reading this, I might even do a little work, too.

But I can't help but be a little homesick — not just for my family in Columbus, but for my tiny hometown of Oglethorpe, where "downtown" was the post office and Suwanee Swifty, where the lights outside my window came from other galaxies instead of skyscrapers and where the closest thing to mass transit was getting the Thornton kids in the back of their pickup.

Maybe Columbus can find a happy medium between Oglethorpe and Detroit. We'd better, because the day I have to pay five dollars for a hot dog on Broadway after paying two bucks for a bad parking space is the day I pack up my pickup truck and move to the first town where folks wave at me for no particular reason. Then I'll know I'm home again.

Better than Wimbledon

You'd have to try pretty hard to be any geekier than I was 16 years ago.

I was all set to become a computer programmer as I mastered the ins and outs of my high-tech Commodore 64, which had 64 — yes, a whopping 64 — kilobytes of memory. I had quit baseball because I was convinced I had simply forgotten how to play. Turns out I was dang near blind and had to get glasses — as if I needed an accessory to go with my mom-styled bowl haircut.

But I wasn't a geek at heart. I was Casanova at heart. At least, I was in my dreams — though even in those dreams I somehow kept winding up late for algebra class in my underwear. Then, and only then, did the girls at school notice me. Then I'd wake up and be invisible to them once again.

So, at 14, I had pretty much decided that I would never, ever get a French kiss from a girl. Unless you count that one unexpected encounter with a female giraffe at the zoo.

And with baseball out of the picture, I had to choose another sport. Either that, or stay at home and subject myself to such horrors as mowing the grass and washing Dad's truck. I chose tennis. Why? Two words: tennis skirts. Of course, the high school coach told me I'd have to wear regular white shorts. Oh, well.

I went to a crash course in tennis, a summer camp at Florida State University. In June 1985, FSU's Cash Hall played host for a week to high school participants in baseball, football and basketball camps. All the camps mingled some around the courtyard pool, but players of each of the sports had to retreat to their unisex dorm floors at night — except the tennis players. Our camp was so small that the guys and girls shared a floor. And my life would never be the same.

We were all geeks, with the exception of one wild 15-year-old girl from Thomasville, Ga. As sweet goddess Fate would have it, we were paired in the mixed doubles tournament.

I don't remember exactly how it happened. It was about midnight, and we were sitting on the floor at the end of the dormitory hall. I'd been avoiding the inevitable all day long. I knew I'd have to kiss her at some point, and I knew I'd screw it up. It would be just like the giraffe experience, only she'd wind up throwing peanuts at me. Finally, she gave me a subtle come-on:

"Are you gonna kiss me or not? I'm getting sleepy!"

I knew it was now or never, or then or never since this is past tense. I lunged in, mouth open and tongue flying around like a retriever hanging his head out a car window. I was in panic mode. What if my tongue started going the wrong way? What if she caught me peeking? What if she thought, "Man, this is like kissing a retriever."

By the time the kiss ended, about 2 a.m. in the same spot at the end of the hall as our counselor, a 21-year-old player on the college tennis team, stepped over us as if we were a ripple in the carpet, my mind was at ease. Of course, my tongue was tired.

We finished second in the mixed doubles tournament, by the way. We each got awards. But as far as I was concerned, it wasn't for second place; it was for first base.

Free Taliban vacation

(Note: This column was written pre-9/11. I thought the Taliban deserved blowing up long before that.)

The following is an official announcement from the Taliban Tourism Association:

Tired of lounging around the beach? Can't afford to be entertained by a giant Mouse? Lost your freakin' mind? If so, we've got the vacation for you! Come to Afghanistan and feel all right, but not too all right or we'll have to stone you to death.

The first 100 people to respond to this once-in-a-lifetime offer will receive an all-expenses-paid vacation in Afghanistan, land of the, uh, rocks and stuff. We're not just the Gateway to Uzbekistan anymore!

We'll fly you nonstop from Bubba bin Laden's Airport, just outside of Possum Holler, Ga., to beautiful downtown Kabul, where you'll begin your weeklong stay in paradise at the Kabul Hilton, overlooking, uh, a bunch of rocks and stuff.

You'll find all our rooms at the Kabul Hilton equipped with all the latest amenities — except, of course, for televisions, VCRs, radios, books, magazines, newspapers or Nintendos. No more of those annoying "Free HBO" signs at every hotel; the Taliban Facade Board wouldn't stand for it anyway.

Be sure to bring the wife and daughters — we'll lock them in a dark room for you while you men and your sons have fun. And if they dare set foot on the streets or try to learn anything while you and the boys are out, we'll stone them for you.

On your second day, you and the boys will head to Margo Desert where you'll see, uh, sand and stuff. And the night will conclude with a wet T-shirt contest. There will be no women in the T-shirts, of course. But there will be T-shirts, and they will be wet.

On day three, you'll get free passes to Six Flags Over Afghanistan, which is just like Six Flags Over Georgia except for not having any rides or music or entertainment whatsoever. But you will get to walk around on hot pavement and sweat all day long, just like in Georgia. And, if Bugs Bunny pops up anywhere, you get to stone him to death.

On day four, it's family day and graduation at Ghazni University, renowned for its geology program, which is the study of rocks and stuff. But beware: The Taliban Religious Police will be patrolling the aisles watching for anyone clapping, laughing, cheering, smiling, breathing or, Allah forbid, sleeping. Anyone caught by the police will have to spend four weeks in Taliban summer school, breaking rocks and stuff.

On day five, treat yourself to a concert by ZZ Top. True, we usually even squash crickets and birds when they sing, but ZZ Top looks kinda Taliban-ish with their beards. Some of the lyrics have been changed however, such as, "She's got legs, but we can't see 'em."

Then, visit any one of our equally fun-loving border countries — Iran, Pakistan, China, Tajikistan, Uzbekistan or Turkmenistan. It's the land of the "stans."

And, finally, you'll visit the cliffside in the Bamiyan Valley where we shelled those annoying giant Buddhas dating back to the third and fifth centuries. Now, well, they're a bunch of rocks and stuff. We showed those Buddhists that our God can beat up their God. He can beat up yours, too.

Bishops, queens and drugs

In case you missed it, delegates at the U.S. Chess Federations have agreed to begin drug testing at tournaments. The reason: because the Federation Internationale des Esches (FIDE, though I don't know if it's bona-FIDE) is trying to make chess an Olympic sport, and the International Olympic Committee requires routine drug testing in every Olympic sport.

This raises some obvious questions:

One, is there more than one chess federation in the United States? I started to look into this and get you an answer but got distracted by a banner ad telling me how I can buy cool lunch boxes from the '70s and, let's face it, "Charlie's Angels" trumps chess.

And, two, why would we want chess in the Olympics?

Before I go on, let me confess that I used to play chess a lot, and I'd play it more at home now if my wife didn't call the knight a "horsey" and the rook a "lighthouse."

But an Olympic sport? That's the craziest thing I've heard since solo synchronized swimming became an Olympic event — as if team synchronized swimming weren't silly enough.

When I think of the Olympics, I think of those traditional events the ancient Greeks started — those tried-and-true tests of physical prowess such as the marathon, wrestling and ballroom dancing. If some Greek tried solo synchronize swimming, everybody would have said something like, "Hey, Perzeusemona, you been playing around in Socrates' medicine cabinet again?"

And if they tried to play chess, all the other Olympians would have said something like, "Hey, Desdaramis, what you doin' with that horsey and lighthouse? Why don't you put that down, and we'll have a toga party!"

I haven't had a steady chess partner in about six years, not since my friend Andrew and I would play while listening to Pink Floyd and drinking beer. Any sport that can be played effectively to the tune of "Comfortably Numb" and the buzz of a Bud Light doesn't belong in the Olympics.

And the ancient Greek Olympians used to compete in the nude. You never know when they might start that back up again. How many chess players (me, for instance) have you seen that you wished you could see naked? I'm assuming, of course, that Jennifer Lopez does not play chess.

Then again, maybe I'm just prejudiced because I'm merely an average chess player. I'll never be a grandmaster, which means I'm probably using my brain's medial temporal lobe when I play. See, scientists found in tests that amateur players experienced tiny "focal gamma bursts" in their medial temporal lobes for a few seconds after making chess moves. Grandmasters, on the other hand, experienced focal gamma bursts in their frontal and parietal cortices.

And this is why I'm against drug-testing potential chess Olympians, for if I experience any bursts in my head, be they gamma or dynamite, I'm gonna need some drugs or at least a Bud Light. And in severe cases, maybe even some Pink Floyd.

America will sing again

It's so easy to lose perspective in this life.

I spent Monday getting my wisdom teeth cut out and then spent about five hours that night at the emergency room after an unexplained fainting spell. I didn't care, because I was more worried about my stepmother, who was in surgery that day as doctors worked to rid her body of cancer.

I reckon I was fine. My stepmother's prognosis was positive. Then something happened to put our individual struggles in perspective. Thousands died at the hands of cowards and launched us into a war that will be unlike any other.

This won't be like World War II. There will be no D-Day, no Iwo Jima, no Hiroshima, no Bataan Death March. It will be a war on a much smaller scale, but much more complicated. It's a war against evil, which knows no boundaries. The battle will be won by freedom-loving Americans, but the war against evil is as old as time itself.

What happened Tuesday is forever etched in my mind. I can put the Civil War, Pearl Harbor, the Kennedy assassination and Kent State in historical perspective. But I can't truly know how it felt. My grandfather, who used to ride me around in his wheelchair after losing both of his legs in World War II, knew how it felt. My parents knew how it felt when Macon County High students were told their president was killed. It hurt. And this hurts. We hurt for America and its shattered families.

I played hooky from school the day the Challenger exploded and watched it happen live on television. To this day, I still feel guilty about it. I saw Reagan shot, John Lennon killed. I rejoiced with millions as one little girl singing nursery rhymes was saved after falling down a well. Those images will stay with me forever.

Many images from Tuesday will stay with me forever, too. Planes crashing into skyscrapers. People leaping to their deaths. Palestinian children dancing in the streets. But there's one image that gives me hope and keeps it all in perspective.

The U.S. Congress, just a week ago bitterly partisan, was united that night. Lawmakers bowed their heads for a moment of silence and then sang "God Bless America." It was hardly unexpected, but moving nonetheless.

But that's not the image I'll recall best. When the Congress finished singing, my 18-month-old son, Saylor, clapped and giggled. He had no idea why Mama and Daddy had been glued to the television while he stacked blocks and jumped off sofa cushions. He only knew that folks were singing, and he likes singing.

The next generation won't know the pain, anger and sorrow America felt Tuesday. They'll read about it, and teachers will help them put it into historical perspective. But they'll never truly know. And they'll have their own Tuesdays to deal with, as well as their share of triumphs.

Saylor will have many more days to laugh and clap, as will generations to come. Time does — and must — march on. And so will America.

Giant hamster thingies

Like many previous rainy or cold Monday nights, I spent a good two hours of this past one (prior to Monday Night Football, of course) at Hollywood Connection, where my son, Saylor, and I go to ride the "choo choo," Ferris wheel and carousel.

But this last trip marked Saylor's first time in the gargantuan indoor playground. I don't know the official name of these evil places, but I know they were originally built during the Cold War out of fear that radioactive hamsters would grow to be about 3 feet tall. That's why I call it the Giant Hamster Thingy. Or maybe they are former Martian child traps.

Giant Hamster Thingy rules state that you must take off your shoes before playing. I didn't understand why before I had a child, but now I do: Someday we're going to lose Saylor in that Giant Hamster Thingy, and we'll at least have the $20 shoes to take home.

My wife and I spent most of the night dodging rugrats in the Giant Hamster Thingy, looking up toward tubes, slides and nets and every now and then saying something like, "There he is. There he goes." Meanwhile, all we heard from above were what sounded like gremlins in socks: "Hee hees" and the pitter-pat of tiny feet.

When I was a kid, there were no Giant Hamster Thingies or even Little Hamster Thingies. There were a few playgrounds at random McDonald's along the interstate with maybe a slide, and they were all outdoors, so if it was 25 degrees you froze your little buns off.

Of course, when my dad was a kid, their idea of fun was working in the fields and freezing their buns off --- or sweating their buns off, depending on the season. So, I guess I can't complain about how tough I had it, but kids today have got it made.

Maybe they should build Super Giant Hamster Thingies for adults like me who were deprived in their childhood of such wonders. I'd climb up in the quiet tube with the hammock and remote control. Like Saylor, I might not come down voluntarily, either.

When your kid climbs up into one of these, it's like dropping your coin in the slots of a casino: You might get it back, you might not. You might get two. And Hollywood Connection has the policy that any kids left in the Giant Hamster Thingy become property of the establishment. And buying your kid back from the Hollywood Connection costs 40 points — or you win your kid back playing Skee Ball.

Employee: For 40 points, you can get the paddle-ball set or the 22-month-old with the head full of hair.

Me: Does the paddleball set sleep through the night?

Employee: No, but it's potty-trained. Well?

Me (to wife): You know, honey, those paddleball sets are more fun than they look.

I had to beg some 10-year-old to retrieve my son from the Giant Hamster Thingy, done by dragging him down the slide. I checked him close to make sure he was mine, for he was in there so long that he grew a couple of inches. I hope he'll come down potty-trained next time.

Wrong or white

This is going to come as a shock to my friends, family and co-workers, but I have a confession to make: I'm a fashion moron.

I know that's hard for you to believe. I know you're looking up at that good-looking guy at the top of this column and thinking, "Who'd have thought that a boy from Oglethorpe, Ga., who drives a pickup, worships Jimmy Buffett and thinks the remote control is mankind's greatest invention would not be hip to the latest fashion trends?

However, I don't know tweed from Tweety Bird or a catwalk from catnip. I haven't worn a suit since June 1999 and have worn the same pair of sneakers since October (2000, that is). And my favorite designer is Gustervo Onsale, who usually only posts his last name on giant yellow signs over large bins of his clothing near the front of stores.

But there's one trend that truly disturbs me: You're not supposed to wear white — especially shoes, pants and hats — between Labor Day and Easter. It bothers me because (a) there's no good reason for the rule, just like ties, and (b) I just found out about it last week, though it's apparently been around since the late 19th century.

I was dumbfounded and quite vocal about the ridiculousness of this white rule and was met with resistance from three groups in the newsroom — (1) those who believe the rule is absolutely necessary for the human race to survive, (2) those who think it's a little silly but don't have the guts to make their own fashion statements, and (3) those who wish I'd shut up so they can get some work done.

How was I supposed to know about this rule? Was it among the Ten Commandments that Moses broke when he got down the mountain? Were the public service announcements broadcast only on Lifetime and C-SPAN? Did Mr. Roarke on "Fantasy Island" know about it? And, is there really any good time to wear white shoes?

Maybe it's a woman thing. Guys never sit around and say things like, "You know, Bubba, camouflage ain't the new black." If guys (and I mean beer-drinking, truck-driving, football-watching kind of guys) had more input, ties would be obsolete, runway models would have curves, short skirts would always be in and Britney Spears would always be on the least, uh, I mean best-dressed list.

Of course, I've never been much for rules anyway, which is another shocker for folks around here. But I at least like to know the reason for a rule before I break it. All I get from folks around here is "because that's the way it is and the way it's always been."

No, I want some concrete rules. Give me, "You can't wear white shoes in winter or your toes will fall off." Or, "If you wear that white hat, they'll put you in a higher tax bracket."

How can we point fingers at the Taliban for making women wear those silly burqas when we have folks trying to find something purple to wear because it's January?

You all can go about your white rules, and I'll keep my vintage sneakers. Just promise me that if I ever die in the winter, the Hawaiian shirt thing I've got planned for my funeral is still on.

Sorry about this

I had every intention of writing a column when I sat down here in my study tonight, but I just can't come up with a column idea. Problem is, I can't think with the steady stream of teenie-boppers with their boom-boom car radios parading by my house.

I just can't write with all this noise around me. I'd go into work and write it, but there's noise there, too: telephones ringing, televisions blaring breaking news like the 1,200th showing of "Coal Miner's Daughter," computers beeping, drink machines spitting out cans of cola and those ants stomping their little feet when they march past the crumbs on my desk.

If only Raid worked on boom-booming Jeep Cherokees like it

does on those ants at work, I could produce a column. Or if I could crush that dang Cherokee with my fist like I do the ants, that would work, too. But it takes so much more work to beat a Cherokee to death. And I don't have the energy. So, no column tonight.

I've given it the old college try, something I learned at an old college. I've gone so far as to put on headphones and listen to some Internet radio. I've tried to relax to the tunes of Andy Narell and Boney James on the smooth jazz stations and the light sounds of Jimmy Buffett on the Net's Radio Margaritaville, but you just can't write thought-provoking words of wisdom while listening to Buffett tunes like "My Head Hurts, My Feet Stink, and I Don't Love Jesus." Besides, I'm going to see him (Buffett, not Jesus) play live Thursday in Tallahassee, so Cyber Bubba just doesn't measure up tonight.

Noise in general — or in specific — bothers me. But totally unnecessary noise — leaf blowers (Why does everyone here hate leaves?), annoying tunes from cell phones, rap music, C-SPAN, car engines that sounds like jet planes, and canines with short-dog complexes who bark at everything that moves — bother me even more. Actually, I'd probably buy a leaf blower if it were powerful enough to blow loud teenie-bopper vehicles off the road. But they don't, so no column writing will happen tonight.

I guess I could have written a column earlier today when the teenie-boppers were still in school, but there was only a narrow opening for a nap between my son's playtime at a certain noisy pizza place with a giant mouse — and naptime always trumps column-writing time. When you've got kids (particularly 2-year-olds) naptime trumps everything. ("Yes, honey, I know the house is on fire, but I'm sleepy. It'll be a while before the blaze makes its way to the bedroom.")

I'm thinking about drilling a hole in Pine Mountain and moving my study about three miles into a cave. But I'm scared I might forget to shave, and you don't want to be coming out a cave with a beard these days.

If it were quiet, perhaps I'd write a column about that idea I came up with to solve the violence in the Middle East, Northern Ireland and Colombia. But it's so noisy around here, I can't remember what it was. There went our one chance for world peace.

Oh well, maybe next week.

Winter whites

With the Winter Olympics being held in the United States for the first time since 1980, I'm supposed to be feeling some great sense of pride and excitement. Sorry, I just don't care a whole lot.

That's no slap at the athletes, for I'm sure this crop of Winter Olympians is one of the best ever. I'm just not in a Winter Olympics state of mind.

The only athlete I really care about at the Games is downhill skier Picabo Street (though she bowed out of the Games with a disappointing 16th-place finish Tuesday). Despite being very serious about her sport and being the greatest American female skier in history, she's a fun-loving girl and has her head on straight. Besides, four years ago she broke her leg in almost the exact same spot as I did nearly two years ago, so I've got to root for her. And how can you root against somebody named Picabo?

But other than Picabo, the Games can't hold my interest. If I were there perhaps it would be different, for I wouldn't have to watch the four TV interviews for every minute of action. Then again, if I were there, I'd probably be sitting in a Jacuzzi while drinking hot chocolate and just reading about the Games in the paper the next day.

Maybe I'm not interested because the games are in Utah. I've never been to Utah, but I've heard it's quite beautiful. I've also heard it's not the kind of place you'd want to go for Mardi Gras or spring break. Any state where the majority of folks would rather hear the Mormon Tabernacle Choir than Bocephus just ain't my kind of place. And I'm still upset about the New Orleans Jazz moving to Utah and keeping the name Jazz. There's nothing Jazz about Utah.

Or maybe it's because it looks pretty darn cold there. They should hold the Winter Olympics somewhere a little warmer for folks like me who hate cold weather. Why doesn't Miami bid for the Winter Games? They've got ice hockey down there. Granted, luge and downhill skiing wouldn't be quite as exciting in a county where the highest point is 35 feet above sea level, but you could get a nice tan on the way down because it would take an hour and a half to complete the course. Of course, in Miami, the bobleds would have

62

to leave their blinkers on for two miles.

Perhaps the Winter Olympics is just too large a gathering of white folks to interest me. Being one of them, I don't really have anything against white folks, but you should never get too many in one spot — something I've learned from various family get-togethers. Large gatherings of white folks also have been known to spawn such scary things as curling, polka, "The Lawrence Welk Show" and Utah.

What this Winter Olympics is missing most of all, however, is Tonya Harding. If you're gonna have an Olympics with this many white folks, you can at least add a dash of color with some white trash.

I guess I'm just a big Tonya Harding fan. Any girl can skate and twirl around in a skimpy outfit, but a girl who can skate and twirl around in a skimpy outfit and hurl a hubcap with the best of 'em, well, that's just a girl after my heart.

The old home place

I did something this past weekend I haven't done in at least 11 years: I went traipsing around my family's land, a few dozen acres somewhere in the triangle between Ellaville, Andersonville and Oglethorpe.

On one side of me was my Dad, who is leaning toward an early retirement next year, and on the other was my son, Saylor, who will force me into an early retirement if these terrible twos keep up.

My Dad was there to point out a spot in the middle of acres of old hardwoods where he plans to build a cabin next year. I was there to get back in touch with my roots and soak up the silence. Saylor was there to hit trees, rocks and relatives with sticks.

I did a lot of growing up on that land. My Grandma lived many years in a small tin house along the dusty dirt road that splits the land in half. We spent many summers and many days after school out there. Actually, the tin house was just a pit stop for us before we embarked on one of our thousand or so adventures in the woods.

Even before I was 10 years old, those dozens of acres just weren't enough. We'd gas up with a little cold water from the hose near the well house and then head north or south, or wherever the breeze happened to guide us. Usually it guided us — us usually consisting of my cousin Keith and me — through briars, around bauxite mines, up trees, over beaver dams and into trouble before the sun set. By the end of the day, the sunsets provided a comforting purple haze as we hunted for our switches.

Much has changed.

Great-Uncle George is no longer around to holler, "Who's out there aggravating them chickens?!" The old grassy make-out spot to which I used to sneak off with pretty girls in my ugly '78 Toyota Celica is buried by the straw of adolescent pines reaching high above. And Grandma's tin house has long since burned down, but she's doing just fine at 92 in a Warner Robins retirement home. She doesn't get around as fast as she used to, but neither Keith nor I have yet mustered enough guts to say "no" if she ordered us to get a switch this very day. And we both still deserve it from time to time, though not as much as when we used to fire shotguns into the air so that the pellets would rain down on her tin roof.

Even though the cabin is a project for the future, it's more about the past. I think my Dad always wanted me to be into hunting and fishing, but I never got a big thrill out of blowing holes in animals. I'd gladly eat deer meat over a campfire, but the blast of a gun was just one more noise I didn't need. Not then, not now. It probably skips a generation. I'll probably have to wear earplugs out there 14 years from now while Saylor blows holes in cute, furry creatures. Hopefully by then hunters will be using silent ray guns.

Or maybe my Dad can take Saylor hunting, since it's probably all just a way to relive his childhood. All I want, however, is a nice, quiet thinking spot. But if any shotgun pellets rain down on the roof, somebody, probably my son or Dad, is gonna pay.

The roots of my raisin'

Like a lot of 21-year-olds, I've spent a lot of time trying to find myself. Unlike a lot of 21-year-olds, I'm 31.

My latest quest to find myself didn't begin as such. It began merely as a trip to the hospital where I was born. The only reason I was headed there was so my mother could show off her grandson to colleagues there. It was supposed to be a simple trip for lunch with Mom.

We indeed had a simple lunch, but what transpired beforehand was far more complicated. And like much of my searching over the years, I'm not exactly sure what I came away with. Perhaps another piece of the puzzle. Perhaps another hole in it.

Somewhere on Georgia 49 from Americus to Macon County, my 33-pound travelling companion dozed off. That happens sometimes after a big lunch at Monroe's Hot Dogs, even for 183-pound travelers like myself. Anyway, there's an unwritten but well-known rule among parents of 2-year-olds: On the rare chance that they actually go to sleep, take advantage of it.

If I had any sense, I'd have pulled over in Andersonville and taken a snooze, but this is me we're talking about. The quiet was nice, however, so I decided to prolong it by continuing the ride through the streets of my old hometown, Oglethorpe, and neighboring Montezuma, which is about three times as big and has such additional features as chili cheeseburgers at Troy's Snack Shack and, well, the same stuff as Oglethorpe three times over.

I chose cruising my old stomping grounds for the peace and quiet — and because if I'm ever gonna figure out who I am or who I'm gonna be, I need to figure out who I was.

In Montezuma, I rode by the massive brick school where my parents went to high school — and where I went to elementary school and experienced my last brush with good grades and first brush with puppy love. (Somewhere after fifth grade, I got more worried about girls than grades and experienced little success with either from that point on.)

I thought I was riding by the school. When I looked to my left, it was gone without a trace. Just a giant hill of weeds. Only in that town could somebody steal a school and no one notice — or bother to tell me about it.

I rode by a distant cousin's tennis court where I was often humbled by the county's best tennis players, a group for which I fell short of qualifying by one good second serve. There were weeds there, too, and Prince rackets and Wilson balls had been replaced by Poulan saws and John Deere tractors.

I tried Oglethorpe. The water tower where I considered painting a cute blonde sophomore's name in 1988 until I remembered I was scared of heights was gone, too. Just more weeds.

And the old home, you got it — weeds were the only residents besides the two ghosts that roam it in the middle of the night. It needs painting, too. It's over 100 years old but probably won't see another 10.

It's pretty hard to get in touch with your roots when they're covered by weeds.

Bird brains

Whenever you hear a scream come from the kitchen, it's generally not good news. Never in my life have I heard "aaaayyeeeee!" come from the kitchen and heard it followed by,"Wow, that was one magnificent bowl of Spaghetti-Os!"

It's far more likely that a scream from the kitchen means that someone has either tried to frappe a finger or forgotten that the filling inside a freshly microwaved Pop Tart is roughly the same temperature as molten lava.

So, when I heard a scream emerge from the kitchen last Sunday, I knew it couldn't be anything good. And the scream was my wife's voice, which prompted the obvious question, "What is SHE doing in the kitchen?"

As it turns out, the problem was not that SHE was in the kitchen; the problem was that IT was in the kitchen. You never want an IT in the kitchen. IT could be a rat or a roach or even a snake. In this case, IT was a bird.

It's not the first time we've had a bird in the kitchen, but it's the first one that didn't come with mashed potatoes and four biscuits. It was a little bird, so I guess it couldn't carry the side items.

"Cool," I said after analyzing the problem. "But it'll take at least a dozen of those to fill me up. Hey, wait a minute! I asked for extra crispy."

I'm not sure why this bird struck such fear into my wife or why I ducked when it charged me. I'm not a birdwatcher, so I don't even know what kind it was. It was one of those birds with wings, beak and feathers, you know. Could be a brown thrasher. Could be a pterodactyl. I am reasonably certain it wasn't a penguin.

It took about eight hours to get this bird out of the house but only about a minute and a half to let all the air-conditioning out through the doors. The bird ignored the doors and had a lot of trouble grasping the concept of glass in the windows, which reminds me of the old saying: People who live in glass houses shouldn't own birds.

Mr. Bird was persistent, but I'm not sure persistently stupid is an asset. Eventually, with the help of Mr. Broom, Mr. Bird found the door. (I learned that trick from several old girlfriends.)

I guess it's only fair that the very next day, my son, Saylor, and I found ourselves locked out of the house when it was a mere 95 degrees. (I'm not sure how it happened, but I blame my son. I certainly couldn't do anything that stupid. No, not me.) Saylor was screaming "I want go inside!" and I was hollering "I want go inside, too!"

Unfortunately, the if-you're-stupid-and-lock- yourself-out key wasn't where I left it, and I had to walk with Saylor on my shoulders a quarter-mile to a store to use a pay phone and summon my wife home from the health club to let me in. I told her I couldn't find the stupid key.

"Oh, I moved it," she said.

"Thanks for telling me. Where is it now?"

"The birdhouse."

To get to his home, the bird had to fly through mine. To get to my home, I had to go through his. This can't be the "Circle of Life" Elton John was singing about. Or maybe it is. Maybe that's why I'm dizzy. Either that, or because I spent an hour outside in 95-degree heat trying to pick a lock with a buck knife.

Stormy weather

Unlike farmers and gardeners, I don't have a lot of stake in whether or not it rains. But, still, I hated those recent dry summers and am liking this one a bit more.

Rain is great, but I really love the addition of thunder, lightning and wind. My neighbor, who until recently had one of my trees lying in his back yard, doesn't like storms nearly as much — nor does my squashed fence or insurance agent.

Unless you get hit by a falling pine tree, nothing's better than cuddling during a thunderstorm — except maybe sleeping through a thunderstorm. That runs in my family. Once, during a tornado in Atlanta, Mom took me to a hallway, but Dad refused to get out of bed because the tornado was "good sleeping weather."

Maybe it's one of those weird things about growing older, but it seems that summer thunderstorms were more frequent and severe when I was growing up in Oglethorpe, Ga. You could set your watch by them. There was the 5:15 p.m. freight train and the 6:15 p.m. thunderstorm.

And almost all the homes in our neighborhood had wonderful, giant front porches for storm watching. Ours faced due west, perfect for watching the thunderheads build and the purple sky light up as the storm approached. A warm breeze would ruffle the azaleas, the sun would disappear and that smell of steam rising from wet asphalt would waft through the neighborhood and stir us from our homes.

Even Dad, who hit the recliner first thing after a long day at the paper mill, would spring out of the chair, grab his guitar and be on the porch before the first major thunderbolt rattled the windows of the now 100-year-old home, whose front porch was bordered by a horse and carriage shelter. The rhythm of the rain seemed to keep up with Dad's guitar playing, but the thunder couldn't drown out Dad belting out "Kaw-Liga," much to the dismay of me and our neighbors. (Really, Dad, Hank did a couple of other songs.)

Mom would peek out the door and tell me, "You're gonna get struck by lightning." Sometimes, this warning would be followed by the story of how one of her friends died in a lightning strike. Though Mom grew up in an even smaller town than Oglethorpe — Ideal — all of her friends died in some weird fashion: lightning, riding bikes with no hands, petting a strange dog, even forgetting to wait 30 minutes after eating before going swimming. As far as I know, Mom is the lone survivor among Ideal's cursed children of the '50s and '60s.

The storms didn't last long. They'd blow down a branch or two out of the live oak trees but rarely do damage. If anything, they seemed to make the neighborhood just a little greener and cleaner, except for Max, our wet bird dog.

I don't know which I miss most — the thunderstorms or the front porch. There's not enough of either in Columbus.

What would Red say?

It's looking more and more like there's going to be another baseball strike this year. What a country! Where else do millionaires go on the picket line to complain about the gross injustices they suffer?

But this isn't a sports column. I've written plenty of those during my days as a sports writer (1989-95). This column is about a man I knew simply as "Red."

It was 1994, and I was consumed with either putting out a sports section or building my house just outside of Americus, Ga. When summer came and the schools let out, I saw that as time to put the finishing touches on the house. The last thing I needed on my schedule was a baseball collectibles show at Georgia Southwestern College.

I put down my hammer, took a shower and headed out to do an interview with former Cincinnati Reds slugger George Foster, who was the main drawing card. George didn't show. I found myself chatting with Phil Dixon, an expert on the Negro Leagues. Beside him was an older man I didn't recognize.

We got to talking about Satchel Paige and what a shame it was that he didn't get the shot he deserved at Major League glory. He may have been the greatest pitcher of all time, Phil noted.

"Oh, yeah," the old man agreed. "He struck me out the first time I faced him, but I got a hit the second time up. Ain't never been prouder of a hit in my life."

It then struck me that this old man was a walking history lesson. I've never known baseball to be divided by race. My first hero was Hank Aaron, a baseball player who just happened to be black — no big deal. And Red Moore would have been a major leaguer, but "I was just born too early." He was considered the best fielding first baseman in the '30s and '40s.

If I'd been in his shoes, I'd have been bitter to have been denied a chance at Major League glory over something as stupid as racism.

I'm sure many Negro Leaguers were — and rightfully so. But Red wasn't bitter. In fact, he was downright happy.

He didn't get paid much, but he did get paid to play the game he loved. He saw his former roommate, Roy Campanella (then just 16 years old with the Baltimore Elite Giants), become a major leaguer and a Hall of Famer. Red had a successful professional life outside of baseball and a wonderful family. He had reasons to smile, but — gee whiz — he never stopped smiling.

Until I asked him about the looming strike threat of '94, which, indeed, came to pass. He was a member of the "million-dollar infield" with the Newark Eagles, but it was just a catch phrase and hardly the sum of their salaries.

"Greedy," he said. "Just greedy."

The players killed the '94 season and World Series but won the battle. A merely average player now is not just a millionaire, but a multi-millionaire. And they'll strike this year if they don't get even more.

It's been a long time since I heard from Red and a long time since I've met anyone who loved the game as much. But I know what he'd say today.

"Greedy, just greedy."

Shake your what?!

While riding down River Road with my son by my side, an Eminem song came on the radio. No great fan of this millennium's Vanilla Ice, I reached to turn the station, but something distracted me.

Saylor, who is all of 2 years old and 100 percent boy, was rocking back and forth in his car seat like some headbanger at an Ozzy Osbourne concert. "I like this song," he said.

I couldn't help but laugh. He could care less about his "Dragon Tales" tape and screams "Stop!" every time I sing in the truck (as do pedestrians when I have the windows rolled down), but Eminem comes on and he's happy.

As hard as it is to admit, I actually like this one Eminem song even though it's been overplayed by radio stations. (But what song isn't?) Still, once I got through laughing at my 36-pound headbanger, I began to worry.

After hearing Eminem at least twice a day while flipping through the stations, the last thing I need to hear at home is a 2-year-old singing, "It feels so empty widdout me." Fortunately, he hasn't picked up on the lyrics just yet. That's good, because Eminem ain't exactly Mr. Rogers.

If Eminem were to take over Mr. Rogers' neighborhood, the opening would sound a little more like, "It's a beautiful $#@&! day in the $#@&! neighborhood. A beautiful day to beat up a neighbor. Why don't you die, why don't you die, why don't you die, my neighbor. What up, little homeys and homegirls? Oh, what up, Trolley? You been where? The magical land of make-believe? You be trippin'."

Anyway, I know what kind of influence musical artists can have on kids. When I got old enough to buy my own tapes (yes, kids, before CDs there were cassettes), my idol was Prince, the guy (sort of) who got Tipper Gore riled up and led to all those "parental advisory" labels that doubled the sales of vulgar records and started a whole new industry. And the first concert I saw after getting my car at 16 was the Beastie Boys in Columbus, the one where they got thrown off the stage at the old Municipal Auditorium.

(They apparently broke the giant, inflatable organ ordinance. Maybe if it had been a kidney, they could have gone on with the show.)

Point is, with influences like Prince and the Beastie Boys, it's no wonder I turned out to be the screw-up I am today. And I was a teenager. If Saylor likes Eminem at 2 , I don't want to hear what he's listening to at 16. Then again, I'm an old dude now and no old dude really wants to hear what 16-year-olds listen to anyway.

And I'm not against rap or hip-hop. The Rayvon song "My Bad" just might be my new favorite song ever. ('Bout time they wrote a scorned-guy song.) Of course, when I think of rap, I think of Run DMC, Kool Moe Dee and Egyptian Lover. Yes, I'm old school. Very old. I guess I'm just a daddy and daddys are supposed to say things like, "We don't listen to that kind of trash in my home!"

Then again, that's the same thing my folks said about Prince and the same thing my grandfather said about the Beatles. Probably just made us love 'em more. Maybe I should call "Dragon Tales" trash. That "Shake Your Dragon Tail" song is just disgusting!

Tennis or football

When my son, Saylor, was born and weighed in at 9 pounds, 10 ounces, the first thing I thought was "linebacker."

He looked like a linebacker, too, especially after getting his head squeezed and shoulder broken after being determined to make his entry into the world the old-fashioned way, with a little help from a doctor trying to keep her C-section rate down to please her insurance company.

Of course, this came after all the mushy stuff and getting choked up when he first looked at me and I saw my eyes for the first time. But when they put him on the scale, it was time to start thinking about that first football season.

That's one of the many differences between me and my father. My father never cared about football. When I was born, he still thought he was going to be a preacher. He was concerned about what kind of morals I would have, what kind of contribution I could make to society — you know, junk like that. But I'm a Pigskin Protestant. Sunday, to Dad, meant church. Sunday, to me, means NFL doubleheaders.

Saylor was all of one day old when the first argument hit. Someone on my side of the family — which believes running into people at a high rate of speed in a legal effort to break their bones is a legitimate sport — asked when pee-wee football began. But his mom — whose family believes riding in circles at 180 mph is a more efficient bone-breaking sport — said, "No way he's playing football. Why can't he play tennis or golf?"

Tennis or golf? No. True, those were my sports, although I was slightly better in tennis than golf in that people didn't laugh hysterically when I played. It was more of a chuckle. But I was just 5-10 and 175 pounds in high school. If I had been what Saylor likely will be in high school — somewhere around 7-foot-4 and 450 pounds — I'd have played football and taken great pleasure in throwing kids around like rag dolls.

We eventually came to an agreement: I'll teach Saylor to play tennis, and he can continue with the sport if he wants. Meanwhile, if he decides he wants to play football (if he wants a car and an allowance, he will), his mother will allow it — so long as he plays a fairly non-contact position. I've convinced her that "linebacker" is a fancy word for "waterboy," so he may have a shot.

Of course, she's determined he'll play tennis. The other day she told him, "Daddy's gonna teach you to play tennis. Daddy used to be a good tennis player."

To which Saylor responded, "Daddy no play tennis. Daddy need to sit down and be quiet."

Good point. Daddy no play tennis since his car wreck, and Daddy probably does need to be quiet more often.

So, I guess it'll be up to Saylor. Hey, whatever gets him a college scholarship. God knows, if he inherits my scholastic abilities, there's no HOPE for us getting into college on grades alone.

My bet is on tennis because he not only inherited my eyes, but my wandering eyes. The day I saw Wendy Paulk in a tennis skirt, I decided to become the next John McEnroe. Growing up in the Anna Kournikova era, that boy may never touch a football.

I make a pretty good date

You don't really believe that women want those sensitive, nice guys they talk about on "Oprah," do you? I'm a 32-year-old sensitive, nice guy, so I know better.

Nevertheless, I found the perfect date for a 32-year-old sensitive, nice guy like myself — me. That's right: This past week, I went out on a date with me.

Fortunately, I didn't turn myself down when I asked myself out on a date — which is good because I don't handle rejection well. And let's face it — if a dork like me won't go out with a dork like me, what chance have I got?

I didn't have to get too dressed up, because I knew I wasn't impressed by that, nor did I have to splash on a bunch of stink good (cologne) because I was worried it might give me a headache. And the last thing I wanted was to hear me whine all night about how my stink good was making me sick.

I was a cheap date, something I kind of figured beforehand. When I suggested a $6 buffet, I readily agreed. I knew right away that I and me have something in common: The words "all you can eat" send my heart and stomach all a-flutter, and mine, too.

I was glad I didn't have to watch my date eat some dainty thing like a salad while I pigged out on fried chicken, mashed potatoes, meatballs and other healthy foods. I was a total pig, and I could have cared less. I wasn't even ashamed to burp in front of me. I was hitting it off with me from the start.

After dinner, however, I had to come up with an activity to keep the magic I had going with me. I couldn't take me bowling because it looks funny to be bowling only with me, especially when I try to give myself a high-five after a strike. A night of cuddling with myself in front of a movie at home sounded nice, but my DVD won't hook up to my dinky 13-inch TV.

So I suggested a movie — "Spider-Man." Granted, I had already seen it, and I had, too, but both of us agreed that it was a great movie. We also agreed that it was worth the $1.50 it cost to see it at the cheap theater. Unlike some other date where it might cost me the whopping $3 for two movie tickets, I knew that if I bought myself a ticket, I could sneak me in for free.

Any movie, really, would have been fine because it would be dark, and I knew that the date was going so well that I just might get frisky with me, though not in a Pee Wee Herman sort of way.

I guess if I did anything wrong, it's that I went too far on the first date. That's right: I took me home, had a drink or two, talked for a long time and then I woke up in bed with me the next morning. I knew that as wonderful as the night had been, it was time to call it off. It had gone too far, too fast.

I jumped out of bed and told me that I was going to take a shower, and if I wasn't out of that bed by the time I got out, there was gonna be trouble. Sure enough, by the time I got dried off, the bed was empty. I haven't heard from me since.

Oh well, I could have been my soulmate. Maybe I'm just afraid of commitment. Or maybe I know I can do better than me.

Way to go, ABC!

I was all set to rail against ABC's ridiculous series "The Bachelor" in this column and the shallow women on the "Pick me! Pick me!" bimbo parade when someone notified me that "The Bachelor-ette" begins in January.

I have no idea what "The Bachelorette" will be like, but it can't be anything like "The Bachelor."

In case you have any taste and did not witness this show, here's the premise: One good-looking guy with a high-paying job gets to date and pick a partner from 25 gorgeous women. These women — apparently not wary of a good-looking guy who can't find a decent relationship without the help of a major television network — are content to share him with 24 other women while he slowly but surely weeds out the losers.

I don't understand what kind of woman can feel any affection for a guy whose idea of sweeping you off your feet is giving you a rose and telling you you're a top-10 finalist. When I was single, no girl would have taken that from me without slugging me in the nose or laughing and saying, "Like there are nine other girls who'd go out with you."

Now, before I go any further, I must say that I do have way too much taste to watch "The Bachelor" on purpose. Every now and then, the newsroom TV "accidentally" wound up showing it — perhaps because several women here think the dude's hot. And we guys would have raised hell about watching this shallow junk TV if we didn't think it would have ruined our chances of seeing the "Victoria's Secret Fashion Show."

Anyway, Aaron finally proposed to the last woman standing after jilting some cute girl from Alabama. Congratulations, ABC. You took the mystery of love and narrowed it down to what it should be — a calculated science of elimination.

I can't believe this is ABC's idea of a "reality" series — one guy choosing from 25 women? C'mon! At least "The Bachelorette" is likely to be more realistic — one pretty girl hounded by 25 guys, which can be seen in Columbus bars on any given weekend.

I also can't believe that a guy with the money and looks of the bachelor would settle for a woman who would subject herself to this contest for his affection. I think if I were in his shoes, I'd want the kind of woman who throws rocks at "The Bachelor" contestants.

Of course, the networks never banged down my door to get me on one of these "reality" series like "The Bachelor" or "Who Wants To Marry A Millionaire?" They thought about it but didn't think "Who Wants To Marry A Moron?" would boost their ratings much.

I'm not sure "The Bachelorette" is gonna catch on like "The Bachelor" did. Although, it could be a lot bloodier. While the women on "The Bachelor" politely discussed their relationship with Aaron, the guys on "The Bachelorette" will be beating each other stupid because guys can't handle other guys cutting in on their women.

And while it's permissible in this society for a guy to see a whole bunch of women, ladies aren't entitled to see a lot of guys without gaining a reputation. That's not my rule, just a fact of life. However, if they change the name to "The Tramp," it could gain a few more male viewers.

Wackos multiply

Lately, the Raelian religious sect has stirred fear around the world with claims that a company it founded, Clonaid, has begun cloning humans. I'm not worried.

Why? Two reasons. One, because Clonaid sounds like something whose products should come in strawberry, lime and tropical fruit flavors. And, two, because the term "religious sect" is the media's politically correct synonym for "bunch of wackos."

Granted, a bunch of wackos can be dangerous (such as Waco, Heaven's Gate and al-Qaida), but the Raelians seem harmless enough. After all, they're hell-bent on creating life and not killing folks.

But before you go worrying about the whole human cloning controversy, you should know that the Raelians are led by a guy who couldn't clone a piece of paper with a Xerox machine — Rael.

Formerly Claude Vorilhon, he got the name Rael in 1973 from an extraterrestial named Yahweh Elohim, a supreme being who took Rael for a little ride in his spaceship. Rael even got to visit Elohim's home planet, where Rael got to meet Jesus, Mohammed, Buddha and Moses. It is unclear what the four told Rael, although some theorize it was "Dude, you're interrupting our Uno game."

Of course, skeptics persist and cite no evidence of Rael's regular encounters with extraterrestials, which include conversations via mental telepathy and annual rides on the spaceship. But it's not like you can get souvenirs on these spaceship rides, though some Raelians are said to wear T-shirts that say, "My leader went to Gamma Quadrant 5, and all I got was this lousy T-shirt."

Most skeptical are scientists who doubt that Clonaid has the ability to successfully clone a human. And, as of press time, no scientist had seen evidence of baby Eve, said to be the first human clone and an exact replica of her 31-year-old mother.

But I don't care anything about seeing the baby. I want to see the mother and see if she was worth cloning in the first place. Let's face it: If she buys Rael's story, she's probably not real bright, and the last thing this world needs is exact replicas of morons. We should clone important folks like Albert Einstein and Jimmy Buffett.

Actually, we shouldn't clone at all. It would take all the fun out of looking at a baby and saying, "Why, you're just the spittin' image of your mama!" And you couldn't yell at the kids and say, "Why can't you be more like your sister!"

I've thought about joining the Raelians but find their disapproval of nicotine, caffeine, alcohol and drugs disturbing. I must confess: I am totally addicted to Diet Dr Pepper.

If they can overlook that one little flaw of mine, I might join — but only if they let me go on one of the spaceship rides with Rael. And if it's not too much to ask, I'd like to sit on Elohim's lap and hold the steering wheel while he works the pedals.

But I better not load up on the Diet Dr Pepper before we head out. I hear there's nowhere to make a pit stop between here and Gamma Quadrant 5.

TV needs a reality check

Please, Mr. Television Executive Producer Man, stop with the reality TV already. From "The Bachelor" to "Survivor" to "Real World" to "Joe Millionaire" to "The Mole" to "The Bachelorette," I've had it.

For decades, television has been a form of escape. I'll admit it's always given us a window to the world with news, documentaries and sports coverage, but those real things are a far cry from reality TV. Besides, after presenting us with the real world, television used to whisk us far away to fantasy land.

It flew us via seaplane to an island where a man in a white suit (even after Labor Day) made dreams come true. It let Mr. T drive us around in a van while his A-teammates fired off millions of rounds of ammunition without killing a single person. It put us on a bus destined for a small town where the sheriff didn't carry a gun, nor did he need to. It sat us in the back of a brown station wagon with six kids who shared one bathroom without killing each other. How groovy is that?

It's not that I mind nonfiction television. In fact, if you took away Headline News, ESPN, GPTV, The Learning Channel and The History Channel, you could go ahead and disconnect my cable. I'd let you have the whole TV, but I need it to occasionally watch "Pee Wee's Big Adventure" on my DVD player.

But there's a huge difference between nonfiction television and reality TV. Usually, there's very little realism in reality TV. It's no more realistic than an astronaut frustrated because he has to put up with a genie who'll grant his every wish. What was Maj. Nelson thinking anyway? Who wouldn't want their own genie — especially if she looked like Barbara Eden? But I digress.

Nonfiction television has enlightened me and reality TV has frightened me, but fantasy television is why I cut the boob tube on in the first place. (And my college professor called it the boob tube long before "The Anna Nicole Show.")

I've gone through spells in my life where fantasy television saved my sanity. Thank God for Fred Flintstone after a trying day in junior high school. You decide which is more of a fantasy — that humans and dinosaurs could co-exist in Bedrock or that you're going to use algebra every day for the rest of your life. If I believed the latter, as my eighth-grade algebra teacher told me, I'd be hitting the cactus juice pretty hard these days.

Of course, I've thought about cashing in on the reality TV craze myself. I've patented two inventions. One is a mirror with TV dials on it. I'm marketing it as a reality TV show called, "The Private Life of Someone Who Looks And Acts Just Like You." The other is a window with TV dials called "The Really Real World."

I've also proposed some new reality TV series to ABC that are even more realistic than today's reality TV, including "Fred Balances the Checkbook" and "Battle of the Crocheting Irmas."

You want reality? Real reality? Here's an idea: Cut off the darn TV for a change. And if you find the real world hard to deal with, feel free to call me. I'll be in Mayberry. Have Sara ring me over at the diner.

Sleeping is for the birds

Over the past couple of years, a few buddies whose wives were pregnant have asked me if I had any advice for them. I've been a daddy for nearly three years, and I've been a son for 32 , so I have plenty of words of wisdom — or plenty of words anyway.

My No. 1 piece of advice for soon-to-be moms and dads: Go to sleep. Right now! It may be your last chance.

I knew when my son was an infant, this would be an issue and I was prepared for it. I'd hear a little whimper and stumble into the kitchen — and into a couple of walls along the way — and warm some formula. By the time I made it back down the hall to the bedroom, my son — convinced that we had forsaken him and were planning to never, ever feed him again — would be screaming like an air-raid siren.

But I didn't mind. The formula pacified him, and all was right with the world as I rocked him back to sleep. And I knew he wouldn't always be small enough to cradle in my arms, although as a baby Saylor was as large as most defensive linemen. It was a lot like rocking Warren Sapp to sleep.

I knew in a few months, I would win the war, and Saylor would appreciate a good night's sleep after a long day of crawling, drooling and pooping. I know I do.

Wrong!

Saylor's never really taken to the idea of sleeping. In a desperate quest for help searching the Internet, I read that a child his age needs about 11 hours of sleep a night. That boy hasn't slept 11 hours this year.

I think he may have a hearing problem. When I say, "Hey, Saylor, let's go nite-nite," I believe what he actually hears is, "Hey, Saylor, let's go sit on a cactus, light our toes on fire and listen to Zamfir, Master of the Pan Flute."

But the best thing about having a child with Saylor's hatred of sleeping is grandparents. A couple of weeks ago, we dropped Saylor off with the grandparents and took off to a nearby resort atop an itty-bitty mountain. With its heart-shaped jacuzzi tubs, the resort billed itself as a romantic retreat, but equally attractive was the prospect of up to eight hours of sleep — IN A ROW!

But at 4 a.m. each morning, deranged roosters began crowing. They crowed for hours until they finally woke up the sun. Then I'm sure they went to sleep all day convinced they dragged out the sun for all us humans.

The second morning, at 4:30 a.m., I braved the cold and went chicken hunting in the darkness. The roosters hid, shut up, and I nearly got frostbite crawling around the resort calling, "Here chicky chicky!" One woman slapped me. Then, seconds after I crawled back into bed, I'd hear it: Rah-rah-rooooooo. They didn't even know how to cockle-doodle-doo right.

Even the chickens are in on this conspiracy to keep me from sleeping. I bet Saylor holds monthly meetings with chickens, teenagers with loud car radios, barking dogs and telemarketers to discuss new ways to keep me awake.

Oh well. I may never sleep eight straight hours again. But when we picked up Saylor the next day, we went and ate the heck out of some KFC.

World's longest one-liner

So a priest, a rabbi, a nun, a Christian Scientist, a Southern Baptist, a Scientologist, a Hindu, a Freemason, a Buddhist, an atheist, an agnostic, a nihilist, a Taoist, an animist, a Chen Taoist, a Falon Gong follower, an Ascended Maser, a Baha'i , a Branch Davidian, a Heaven's Gater, a Zhong Gong member, a Seventh Day Adventist, a Mormon a Mennonite, a Universalist, a wiccan, a Swedenborgianist, a Quaker, a Sikh, a Muslim, an Orthodox Jew,

a Reform Jew, a Jehovah's Witness, a Naturalist, a voodoo priest-
ess, a Moonie, a humanist, a Yashuan, a Brownsville Revivalist,
a fundamentalist Christian, a Church Universal and triumphant
worshipper, the Pope, the Dalai Lama, the Karmapa Lama, the
Panchen Lama, the Reting Lama, a Methodist, a Lutheran, a Northern Baptist, a Christadelphianist, a Confucianist, a Concerned
Christian, a shaman, a fortune teller, a Hare Krishna, a polytheist, a
Raelian, a Family member, a Oneness Pentecostal, an Ambassador
for Christ, a member of the Corporation of the Presiding Elder of
the Apostolic United Brethren, a member of The Local Church, an
Associate for Scriptural Knowledge, a Rosicrucian, a Branhamist, a
Black Christian Nationalist, a Bet Hashem, a Chicago Bible Stu-
dent, a Penetite from Brother of our Father Jesus, a member of the
Church of Metaphysical Christianity, a worshipper of the Summit
Lighthouse, a Conneyite from the No Name Church, a Dawn Bible
Student, a member of the Foundation for Inner Peace, an Ontolo-
gist from the Emissaries of Divine Light, a believer in the Aum
Shnrikyo, a Psionic from the First Universal Church of God Real-
ization, a member of the Fifth Epochal Fellowship, an astrologer,
a member of the Nation of Islam, an asceticist, one of the Apostles
of Infinite Love, an Alawite, a Shiite, a Sunni, a Manifest Son of
God, a Syncretist, a worshipper from the Solar Temple, an exorcist,
a Doukhobor, a Sabellianist, a numerologist, an 11th Hour Remnant
Messenger, a neo-Nazi, a Demonologist, a Neoplatonist, a Kansas
City Prophet, a Kingdom Now Theologist, a polygamist from the
Kingston Clan, a Free Soul, a Traveler, a Servant of the Eucharistis
Heart of Jesus, a snake handler, a pagan, a resident of The Farm, a
vampire, a pantheist, a Peniel Pentecostal, a member of the Temple
Mount and Land of Israel Faithful Movement, devotees of Adidam,
a Promise Keeper, a cessationist, an Odinist, a Friend of Freedom,
a member of the World Message Last Warning Church, a member
of the Latter Rain Movement, a Discordian, a soldier in the Lord's
Resistance Army, a Rastafarian, a PTL supporter, a Breatharian,
a Calvinist, a creationist, an evolutionist, a Platonist, a Neoplatonist, a Garbage Eater, a Nuwaubian, a Jain, a Urantian, a yogi, a
Zen master, a Shintonian, an Episcopalian, a Hellenic Polytheist,
a relativist, a Peacemaker, a member of the Intergalactic House
of Fruitcakes, a Honohans-Sanpogyo foot reader, a resident of the

Dominion of Melchizedek, a Zoroastrian, a Primitive Baptist and a psychic walk into a bar.

Always skate forward

Is there anything more fun than ice skating? OK, that's a stupid question. Of course there is, like being massaged by a giant porcupine.

As I made my second-ever appearance on the ice two weeks ago, I realized ice skating is just a microcosm of my life: If I get overconfident, if I try to go too fast, if I forget to put one foot in front of the other or if I forget to face forward, I fall flat on my face. That, and I hear way too much Nelly in the background.

Until I attempted ice skating, ice hockey looked like a lot of fun to me. There was so much about it I liked, such as beating people up for no good reason. It's really not that much different than what would happen at some of those honky tonks back home if they froze over. And I still think I'd make a pretty good hockey player if I could get the other players to wait for me while I climbed off the ice every 25 seconds and if I didn't have to try to hit that little puck with a stick.

And while I still hate figure skating, I realize how hard it is. Yeah, I rooted for fresh-faced Sarah Hughes last year, but if the world of sports ends the sport of figure skating forever, it won't hurt my feelings. Any sport where ugly people aren't allowed to win once in a while just ain't fair — again, a microcosm of life, I guess.

Apparently, the career path chosen by Boom Boom Bechard and Sarah Hughes is not as easy as it looks. Nothing ever is. That's one lesson I learned. The other is to never burn bridges. I didn't learn that on the ice, but I was reminded of it coming off when a woman stopped me.

"Hey, Chris." I shook her hand, looked in her eyes and knew I was supposed to know her. "It's me . . ."

I met her about half my life ago when she was a skinny teenager hanging out at the bowling alley in Americus. She would harass me and my buddies on our weekly outings. Though I swore to my buddies I'd never give that aggravating little girl the time of day, we dated on and off for a few years. There was even a time when I figured we'd wind up married. But we never fell in love, and that's a good reason to NOT get hitched.

It was one of those rare situations where we both left the relationship with no ill will. I didn't want her to marry some loser so she'd regret losing me. She felt the same way. I can't say that about all my old relationships. But she and I did care about each other, and we cared enough to bury the hatchet.

As I remembered those days, I knew I'd better call my wife over for an introduction. Fortunately, I had told my wife about this old flame, and she knew she was one of the milder, not wilder, ones.

I could have burned that bridge in 1989. And if I had, she might have told my wife that I was a little geekier back then than I care to admit. She could have told her how heavily I drank as a teenager to cope with girls and school. She could have told her about that time I walked out of the bowling alley with my bowling shoes still on.

But she didn't — although, the look she gave my wife clearly said, "Congratulations on taming that one."

I guess I turned out OK. She did, too. It sure is a lot easier to face forward when those bridges aren't collapsing behind you.

Are you ready for kids?

How do you know when you're ready for children? Is it when you hear that biological clock ticking? Of course not. In fact, don't let anyone in our Homeland Paranoia Department hear that biological clock ticking or you may wind up contemplating that question in Guantanamo Bay.

Really, it's not that difficult a question. I can answer it for you — you're not. No, you're not. No, trust me. Here, take this handy-dandy little quiz and see for yourself.

1. My idea of typical dinner conversation is:
(a) Please pass the potatoes.
(b) Duck, honey! Here come the potatoes!
2. When I see "Teletubbies," I say:
(a) I'll never let my kids watch this kind of mind-numbing nonsense.

(b) Go ahead, Tinky Winky, numb my child's brain so I can rest for 30 minutes!

3. I've made room in the household budget for kids by:

(a) Tucking away $20 a week for the past 10 years.

(b) Taking compromising photos of Bill Gates and Michael Jackson.

4. Those grocery carts with the little cars for kids attached are:

(a) Kinda weird.

(b) Man's greatest invention since the wheel.

5. Poopee and wee-wee in the potty is:

(a) Where it ought to be, duh.

(b) Worthy of high-fives and hugs (except maybe at the office).

6. Eight hours of sleep is:

(a) Refreshing and gets me ready to face another wonderful day.

(b) Pretty good for a February.

7. My living room looks:

(a) Pretty typical with a couch, recliner, coffee table, TV and stuff.

(b) Like Baghdad will in a month or two.

8. Chicken nuggets from fast-food restaurants are:

(a) Loaded with fat and too unhealthy for children.

(b) What keeps American children from starving to death.

9. My idea of exercise is:

(a) Running laps around the track at Lakebottom Park.

(b) Running laps around clothing racks in Wal-Mart.

10. My carpet pattern:

(a) Is waves of slightly varying hues of one color.

(b) Is waves of drastically changing hues of various Hawaiian Punch flavors.

11. A child's hands are:

(a) Cute little tools to create works of wonder.

(b) Dirty, grimy, nasty little tools of destruction.

12. A child's nose is:

(a) So cute you just want to kiss it.

(b) So nasty and runny that you could power a town the size of Ladonia if you could dam up one nostril.

12. The joy of childbirth for a woman is:

(a) Experiencing every feeling that comes with bringing a new life into the world.

(b) Drugs.

13. The joy of childbirth for a man is:

(a) Sharing the experience with your wife.

(b) Knowing that your wife — and not you — has to push that thing out.

The answers are b, b, a, b, a, a, b, b, a, b, a, b and b — not necessarily in that order.

Legend of the fall

If I were Joshua Berger of Phenix City, I'd cross the Chattahoochee River and buy me a lottery ticket because I'd be feeling pretty darn lucky right about now.

I'd also make sure the next time I get a hotel room, it's on the first floor.

In case you haven't heard about the 18-year-old's misadventure during spring break in Panama City Beach, you obviously don't attend Smiths Station High School, where word of the senior's painful mini-vacation in Panama City Beach spread like a "Fight! Fight!" breaking news alert racing through a high school corridor.

"Yeah, everybody knows about this," he told me last week.

On March 25, Joshua, a Smiths Station senior, was playing cards with friends and doing the kind of things teenagers do in Panama City — no matter what their parents may think. Moments later, he was lounging on a poolside chair.

Sounds uneventful enough, huh? Then why were his friends panicking? Well, because Joshua didn't take the stairs or the elevator to the poolside chair. No, he took a short cut. He plummeted from the balcony of his fourth-floor room.

To hear Joshua tell the story, you'd think he fell 60 inches instead of 60 feet. And the events of that typical spring break night remain fuzzy. (Which I can understand; the trips I made to Panama City as a teenager remain a little fuzzy to this day.)

"I don't remember anything about the fall," said Joshua, who apparently grabbed at gutters and overhangs of the Mariner East Condominiums to slow his descent. "The last thing I remember was playing cards."

I'm not sure I'm falling for that one, no pun intended. (OK, pun intended.) You don't just go from playing cards to flying out of the sliding glass door, over the rail and onto a chair except in cartoons. No, this definitely has, "Hey, y'all, watch this" written all over it.

Joshua escaped this misadventure with only bruises. He was out of the hospital in two days. Last year, Brandon J. Schlosser fell from a second-story balcony and died when he hit headfirst.

"I'm pretty lucky," Joshua said. "I don't plan on doing anything like that again."

Lucky ain't the word for it. Folks don't fall 60 feet and live to tell about it very often. We're talking about the kind of guy who could be stood up in front of a firing squad and 30 seconds later announce, "You missed!"

Everybody's got a friend like Joshua. You remember that guy who used to drive 120 mph and live to tell about it. The guy who would play with rattlesnakes and emerge without fang marks. The guy who could go streaking in a blizzard and lose nothing of major importance to frostbite.

My cousin Keith was like that. In fact, on one Panama City trip, he safely climbed from balcony to balcony at our six-story hotel like Spider-man with a beer gut, or more like Peter Porker. However, I could fall off a bar stool, land on a beach chair and still break my neck.

If you ever decide to go skydiving, mountain climbing or alligator wrestling, I'd suggest taking Joshua along for the ride as a good luck charm.

But I wouldn't play cards with the boy if I were you.

Whine of the wheels

Last weekend, my wife called me on the cell phone from somewhere on this side of Eufaula, Ala., and demanded that I go to Montgomery, find the head of the Alabama DOT and strangle him.

I explained to her that, one, I was a wee bit busy at work with this war thing; two, killing is frowned upon by law enforcement; and, three, after many road trips through Alabama I was pretty sure that there was no Department of Transportation and most of the high-

86

ways were old Indian trails.

"Perhaps I could go find the chief of the Pothole Authority and kill him for you," I suggested.

"Just be sure it's a painful, slow death," she responded.

She was about 5 miles from the city limits, and approximately 4 billion cars were trying to head south through Eufaula, most of them en route to Panama City for spring break. Traffic bottlenecked where it came into the historic district of the city, where the annual pilgrimage to the beautiful old homes was taking place. Cars stretched bumper to bumper from the Shorter Mansion to somewhere around Soldier Field in Chicago.

We both had to work that day while my 3-year-old son bopped around Lake Eufaula with his Granddaddy and cousins Zack and Ciara. I was still stuck behind a desk, and my wife, after working overtime, was stuck in a motionless sedan with her only entertainment other than a "Blondie's Greatest Hits" CD being our garage door opener on the visor.

"Cool!" she said as she found another match for the code on our remote opener. "Uh-oh. Somebody's in there."

"Do they look mad?" I asked.

"No, just real confused. This is getting ridiculous! I'm not even moving!"

"Oh, big deal!" I said. "The longer you take to get there, the more fun Saylor's having out on the boat. If you want to feel sorry for somebody, think about all those poor teenagers on their way to Panama City for spring break stuck around you. They should be working on their first hangover and in the early stages of a raging STD by now."

"Not funny! And I'm hungry."

"Aren't there some giant Pixy Stix left over from Saylor's birthday party in the back floorboard?"

No answer. A lot of shuffling sounds. "Woo-hoo!"

"Go easy on 'em."

"Too late!"

"You ate one already?"

"No. . . . Two."

"You know those are gonna make you . . ."

"Out of my way! Vrrooommm! (The car, not my wife . . . I think)

Hey, the shoulder of the road's in better shape than the highway! Arriba, arriba, andale! Watch out, trash can!"

". . . crazy!"

"You're such a sucker. I haven't even got the first one open yet. I gotta go. I'm losing service on the phone."

"All right, just don't call me if the Pothole Patrol busts you for DUIPS."

"What's that?"

"Driving Under the Influence of Pixy Stix."

In a couple of weeks, we're driving to Sea World. Actually, make that: In a couple of weeks, I'm driving to Sea World.

How to look this good

I've known few women who could get ready to leave the house in less than a half-hour. I've even known women who would spend an hour or two dressing, caking on makeup and doing frilly things with their hair simply because the cable guy was supposed to drop by at some point.

I can't bear to spend more than four or five minutes getting ready to head out for the day — and that includes showering, dressing and brushing my hair . . . if I get around to it. Usually I just run my fingers through my hair a couple of times and hang my head out of the window of my truck like a dog to dry my hair on the way to work. Several people in my neighborhood are convinced my wife is married to a Labrador retriever.

I know this comes as a shock to many of you who look at the picture of the guy above this column and say, "Wow, it must take hours and hours to look that good."

As hard as it must be to believe, I look this good as soon as I wake up in the morning. Some mornings I roll out of bed, look in the mirror and say, "Good morning, you handsome stud." Then I realize that I don't have my contact lenses in yet and am actually looking out the bedroom window. Then I hear a voice from the other side of the window: "Uh, I'm the cable guy. Somebody was supposed to let me in this morning."

When I finally do roll out of bed, it is literally a matter of minutes before I hit the road. Ideally, I'd like to soak in a tub of hot water for about two hours before I head out to work, but that would require getting up two hours earlier instead of hitting the snooze button 22 times. So, I stumble into the shower, which is almost big enough for Calista Flockhart, and put my face in the steaming stream of water. My wife invariably picks this moment to flush a toilet and turn it into a scalding stream of water. Fortunately, this saves time because you don't have to shave when burning flesh is peeling away from your face.

I use my wife's shampoo, which is something like Apple Coconut Possum Blossom, and then wash with a bar of soap the width of an index card. I've never actually seen a new bar of soap in my house. Sometimes my wife will admonish me drooling over some commercial with a naked lady lathering up. "It's not the chick," I'll say. "Check out that big ol' bar of soap. Mmmmm."

I towel off a couple of parts, spray on a little ozone-depleting deodorant, jump into some holy underwear, slip into my Levis and sneakers and throw on the last clean T-shirt in my closet. Then I stop at the guest bathroom and do the thing that wastes the most time in the morning — brushing my teeth. This takes too long because my dental hygienist made me switch to an electric toothbrush. She thought that would be better than the shock and awe approach I once used against my teeth.

I run my fingers through my hair, most strands of which are not even an inch long, courtesy of my coupon haircut. And I'm out the door and on the road with the window rolled down.

Five minutes, twenty-four seconds — a little slow today. I'd been out the door faster, but I couldn't find where the cable guy ran off to.

Hotels and motels

I've decided that for our next family getaway, we're just going to get a room for two nights at a nice hotel — anywhere.

I've always liked staying at hotels, probably because someone else makes the bed and I can run the air-conditioner at full-blast until I can spit ice cubes.

And it doesn't have to be a four-star hotel to satisfy me. I've stayed at the seediest motel in Panama City and been perfectly content. In one of those books that gives hotels ratings from one to four stars, it was rated a "black hole." The shower was as big as a middle school locker, and I slept with my head about 12 feet from the highway, knowing I was one drunk teenager away from being killed. And even though I was maimed by mattress springs, I believed it was $50 well spent — probably because the Gulf of Mexico was only about 50 yards away.

And I've stayed at luxurious hotels where I could scan the city skyline from above, where I could soak in a jacuzzi tub and where the room service prices would make even one of Mike Price's lady friends think twice before ordering.

During a recent trip to Sea World in Orlando, I realized my son feels the same way about hotels. When we headed home, Saylor wasn't as upset about saying goodbye to Shamu and his dolphin pals as he was about leaving our temporary home with the giant swimming pool and those cool, clean sheets. I didn't realize just how fascinating a hotel could be until I saw it through the eyes of a 3-year-old.

It took me back to those family vacations in the '70s. At home, Dad monitored the path of every kilowatt in the house and could feel our window air-conditioner unit sucking money out of his wallet. However, he would freeze us out of the hotel room on vacation. (Granted, after four hours of "Are we there yet? Are we there yet?" it may have been a ploy to get rid of us.)

Dad had it better than I do. Not only could Dad save money by taking the family to such luxurious hotels as the Dead Squid Inn (or something like that), but he could send my Mom out with my sister and me to the pool or beach. If I told my wife to take Saylor out to the pool while I napped in a frozen hotel room, she'd say "Excuse me?" and then shove an ice bucket down my pants.

Come to think of it, my wife sent me out with Saylor a good bit. I made all the ice machine trips that weekend. Saylor and I would ride the elevator to the fourth, the second, the sixth and seventh floors before we found an ice machine that would work. This was an adventure for Saylor who thinks an elevator is like a Six Flags ride and was amazed that we could actually get ice on demand —

unlike at home where my wife stores empty ice trays in the freezer.

I guess Sea World was kinda anti-climactic compared to getting ice, cool sheets, swimming in a heated pool and sleeping in the same room with the television.

Of course, the Dead Squid Inn had our hotel beat on one count — those vibrating beds. You could get a quarter's worth of heaven back then. Fortunately we had our own version:

"Here, Saylor. Here's a quarter. Now jump 'til Mommy and Daddy fall asleep."

Imaginary monsters

When I was kid, I didn't have an imaginary friend. There was this one imaginary kid in my neighborhood, but he didn't think I was cool enough to hang with.

I did get a sister when I was 5 years old, but I wasn't too excited and didn't want to talk about it. She's 27 now. I guess I should say "hey" or "welcome to the family" at some point. Nah.

So I was a bit of a loner — and have been ever since. And I've never had any desire for imaginary friends, although there is this one imaginary guy who hangs around downtown and offers me candy when I leave work.

My son is an only child — and judging by my net worth and net hours of sleep I've had since Feb. 22, 2000, he's probably gonna stay an only child. But don't feel sorry for him: He's got plenty of young cousins, and he's got a daddy who'd just as soon plop down and play with Hot Wheels cars as go earn some money.

(Of course, Saylor takes all the cool Hot Wheels and sticks me with some sissy Thomas the Train car. I'd complain, but my wife looks at me funny when I run to her and complain that Saylor won't play fair. Then again, she looks at me funny pretty much all the time — sort of a do-I-know-you look.)

But even when I'm not there or his cousins aren't around, Saylor's never alone. In fact, the poor kid hardly has any time to himself — especially now that he's got these 10 monsters hanging around with him.

That's right, my son doesn't just have imaginary friends, he's got imaginary monster friends. And not just one. No, he's got to have a whole posse of imaginary monsters.

At least, I think the monsters are imaginary. Saylor says they have yellow fur, pink faces, red noses and blue hair. It could very well be that these monsters are following us around all over the place and I just can't see them because I'm pretty darn nearsighted. I couldn't see a pink-faced, blue-haired monster if it was standing right beside me.

(YIKES! Honey, please don't sneak up on me with that stuff on your face while I'm trying to write.)

If they are real, they are either indeed monsters or a lame '80s band. I haven't asked Saylor if any of the monsters is named Boy George. If so, Saylor's buddies are gonna get the boot right in their "Karma Chameleon." I'd rather have Bigfoot in my house.

Fortunately, Saylor insists they are monsters, not Culture Club. We'll arrive at Saylor's day care every morning in the pickup, and Saylor will hop out and tell the monsters who hitch rides in the back, "All right, monsters, come on. Hurry up!" Then he'll hold his hand out and tell them, "We gotta hold hands in the parking lot."

I'm not even sure if it's legal to ride with monsters in the back of your pickup. They cracked down on that kind of stuff a few years ago. At least Saylor's day care is in Alabama, where I think it is legal to ride 10 or fewer monsters in a pickup so long as you stay off the interstate.

So, I guess the monsters can stay. They all seem to play well together. But if I hear Saylor lets them play with the cool Hot Wheels, I'm gonna accidentally leave the tailgate down on the way to day care one morning.

Don't be shocked

Every now and then, I change my answering machine message, mainly to deal with telemarketers. The last one let folks know I screen my calls to avoid solicitors, but anyone else should feel free to leave a message.

I closed this outgoing message with, "Please leave your name and number, and we'll return your call as soon as possible — unless you're a solicitor, in which case we don't want to talk to you."

It's only a little bit smart-alecky. I have far more smart-alecky messages to deal with telemarketers, including one that asks them to leave their name and number and a time when they can be reached during their dinner or while they're trying to sleep.

It's not that I hate telemarketers, only telemarketing. I've known folks who have had these tough jobs, and it's quite a grind. And, usually, it's legal, but so is passing gas in an elevator. What's legal and what's right are often two different things. That's why I wish it also were legal — or at least possible — to send an electric shock through the phone line:

"Mr. Johnson, this is Fred from United Turnip Distribution Technology Services Incorporated and have I got a deal for you . . . aarrrggghh!"

Oh, how I long for such practical technology. I guess in another day and time, I'd be the hillbilly rocking on the front porch taking shots with my 12-gauge at "revenuers" when they set foot on my land.

Only problems with my answering machine messages is that few telemarketers listen to them and they bug family members, friends or other folks who might have a legitimate reason to call me. I think most telemarketers only listen for the beep at the end of the message instead of the message itself. But, occasionally, I'll still get a message from a telemarketer that begins like, "I'm surprised you haven't returned my call about our offer . . ."

Gee, buddy, it doesn't take much to surprise you. If you want to be surprised, be surprised I haven't found your telemarketing office and wrecked it like Joe Don Baker in "Walking Tall III: The Consumer's Revenge."

Only once since I left the latest message has a telemarketer directly addressed it. I heard his brief response when I got home from a camping trip: "Oh yeah, well I'm a solicitor, and I don't want to talk to you, either."

You could hear him fumbling around on the other end of the line and slamming the phone down quickly before anyone could pick up. If I'd been home screening the call, I'd have picked it up and insulted him with something really clever like, "Oh yeah, well, your mama wears combat boots."

(Which I've never really understood, by the way. I personally think any mama that wears combat boots is one cool lady.)

Or I could have taken him off guard with logic. "Well, if you didn't want to talk to me, why did you call me, you freakazoid?" But logic was uncalled for, no pun intended.

It's too bad junk e-mailers and telemarketers are ruining two great communication mediums. Kinda reminds me of what Mom would say when I broke various expensive items around the house:

"This is why we can't have nice things!"

Any porch in a storm

Anybody remember the drought? From El Nino to La Nina to Christina Aguilera, I can't keep up with which weather phenomenon is dictating our weather these days, but whatever it is life sure seems back to normal with the daily afternoon thunderstorm.

But the drought had little effect on me. I still went swimming. I took a bath or two. I even washed the dog. Hey, wait a minute! I don't have a dog! That canine tricked me! Zoinks!

What I missed during those dry days are thunderstorms. There's just something about the rumble of an approaching storm that gives me goosebumps. Maybe I should have been a storm chaser.

Nah. Using radar and stuff to follow a storm is like stalking Mother Nature. Besides, I don't know how to read a radar or satellite images, though it became a lot easier after the government painted all those chalk outlines around the states so that you can recognize them from outer space.

I love thunderstorms, even though they haven't been kind to me or my neighbors since I've lived in Columbus. Several years ago, straight-line winds (otherwise known as a goal-oriented tornado) knocked down four trees in my yard, and last year a thunderstorm leveled a large pine tree in my backyard and nearly landed on my new neighbors as they were grilling out on their patio.

(Talk about a great way to meet your neighbors. "Hi, I'm Chris. Welcome to the neighborhood. Sorry we almost killed you.")

But storm chasers capture only the fury of a storm, not its beauty. There's magic in watching a thunderstorm roll in, unleash its power and leave you with an awesome sunset. And there's no better place to witness this than from our old house on Baker Street in Oglethorpe, Ga.

It seemed that a storm rolled through my hometown every day around 6 p.m., as regular as the trains pulling away from the pulp mill where Dad worked. I'd sit on the massive front porch and stare westward, while Dad brought his guitar out and serenaded the neighbors with the same three Hank Williams songs.

After the first lightning bolt, Mom would peek out the door and tell us how we're going to get killed like one of her friends. My Mom grew up in tiny Ideal, Ga., and witnessed hundreds of her friends die while doing such things as playing in thunderstorms, riding their bikes with no hands or hurling firecrackers. Her childhood was a lot like "Apocalypse Now."

The first giant raindrops would pound the asphalt streets and steam hovered around the ground like a scene from a bad horror movie. The clouds then bumped into each other and rattled the windows of our 100-year-old haunted house.

After the storm settled down, our bird dog would show up from God knows where to shake water onto us and then head out again.

And after the rain had rinsed off Oglethorpe, the only thing that could draw us away from the orange and purple sunset was the smell of fried chicken wafting through the screen door.

You know, they just don't make thunderstorms like they used to.

A little birdie

There are crucial survival skills a father knows from day one that he must teach his son — such as how to throw a curve ball, how to play air guitar and proper burping techniques.

But it's teaching the little things, the seemingly unimportant things, that separates an average dad from a great dad like myself. I'm this generation's answer to Ward Cleaver except somebody's got to die for me to wear a three-piece suit and I would never name my son after a goofy-looking woodland creature, such as a beaver or an SOA Watch protester.

My son, Saylor, can do everything your average 3-year-old can, meaning that he can recite the alphabet and scribble on the living room walls. He can tell jokes in which every punch line has the word "poop" in it and he can sing along with the radio. The latter is kind of cute until he gets stuck on a song like Kool and the Gang's "Get Down On It."

I know what you're thinking: "Wow, Saylor sounds exactly like my husband — except Ralph can't recite the alphabet." But Saylor still has plenty to learn — the little things. And hopefully he'll stop singing "Get Down On It" by the time he gets to high school.

The little thing we're having the most trouble with right now is indeed little — only a couple of inches long. But it sure can get you into a lot of trouble, especially when you're waving it around in a public place. Of course, I'm talking about the middle finger.

Now, don't get the wrong idea. It's not like Saylor just walks around and flips people off all day long. Sometimes he takes a nap. Besides, he doesn't even know he's flipping folks off. It's merely how he points.

And Saylor's a curious, talkative kid, so he's always pointing stuff out with his middle finger and asking about it or commenting on it. This is not much of a problem when he's pointing at an airplane (Delta hasn't complained yet anyway), but he gets some funny looks when he points at people in the mall.

"Look, Daddy, he got an Incredible Huck shirt on." The bird. "What that policeman doing?" The bird. "Daddy, that's a pretty gull." The bird, no pun intended.

Granted, there are plenty of gulls I've wanted to flip off, and I've certainly considered giving the finger at a couple of speed traps, but you definitely don't want to flip off any full-grown man wearing an Incredible Hulk shirt. Those are the kind of guys whose neighbors will be asked by TV news folks to describe him after he's arrested:

"He was a loner. He kind of kept to himself. If only that kid hadn't given him the finger and told him to 'Get Down On It.'"

"Thank you, ma'am. And did you witness that tornado last week?"

"Yes, it sounded like a freight train."

Saylor and I are working on pointing with the correct finger. Sometimes he'll extend his index finger and ask, "This one, Daddy?" So, he is physically able to point correctly. Still, his first impulse is to point with the middle finger. Until this phase passes, I might as well make the best of it — especially while I'm driving.

"Hey, Saylor. See that guy who just cut Daddy off? Do Daddy a favor and point at him."

Do right, y'all

One of the things I really hate about being part of the media is the steady stream of stories from the Mideast.

As the folks with whom I work can most certainly attest, I really hate to be a cynic. But there's never gonna be peace in the Middle East. As long as there are children seeing suicide bombers as heroes and being raised to believe that killing anyone in the name of God is a free pass to heaven and as long as the different sides hold grudges over millenniums, there's just no chance of it.

I realize it's supposed to be the Holy Land, but I think God (who I truly believe looks like George Burns) looks down at that area and just shakes his head in utter disappointment. When all these suicide bombers get to the pearly gates (along with folks like Paul Hill and Eric Rudolph who kill in his name), St. Peter's just gonna knock them in the head with a big ol' stick and say, "Dude, what part of 'Thou shalt not kill' didn't you understand?"

I guess no matter what religion you choose or are born into, you've got your own impression of God. My God ain't much into killing folks, nor is he into parading religious views around like Roy Moore or making silly rules like Saudi Arabia's Committee for the Propagation of Virtue and Prevention of Vice which recently declared Barbie dolls a threat to morality.

I seriously think that if he knew everybody was gonna twist the Bible, Koran and every other religious book around to meet their warped views, he would have just sent down a two-word Bible that simply read, "Do right." Of course, just as there's a King James version of the Bible and such, there would be various versions of this book, too. Down South, it would be, "Do right, y'all."

But of all the problem areas in the world, the Holy Land seems to have the highest concentration of hate and violence. And nothing's more repulsive to me than seeing some religious nut cheering because a 2-year-old got blown up on a bus. I think there's a special place in hell for those folks.

Any day now, there's gonna be this great heavenly message in the clouds that says: "New Holy Land — Belize." Or someplace like that. Maybe Margaritaville.

We need a Holy Land where there are no rocks to throw, only beach balls. We need a Holy Land where when people die, no one cheers; they simply drop by the funeral home and say clever things like, "Don't he look natural?"

We need a Holy Land where God could tell folks "do right" — and they would, without needing any explanation. We need a Holy Land where the background music is Jimmy Buffett and steel drums, not funeral marches.

We need a Holy Land where the only thing the customs agents won't allow you to bring in is your hate — for anybody or anything (except maybe snakes). A place where you're not defined by what you are, but who you are. A place where you're not judged by your clothes, but rather what's in them. Or maybe a place where you're not judged at all.

Then again, maybe God never intended the Holy Land to be a physical place or a state at all, only a state of mind. Whatever it is, the Mideast ain't got it figured out.

Best friends

Shane and I became best friends in the first grade. For the next nine years, we were practically inseparable.

I'm not exactly sure what brought us together at first. Perhaps it was our love of Marvel comic books or those games of "Logan's Run" on the playground. But I can mark the passage of my youth by the memories of our growing up together.

Shane had the coolest room. His dad was an artist and painted images of Spider-Man, the Hulk and Captain America as if they were crashing through his walls. My room was off-white. And he liked the way my mom cooked bacon in the morning until it was crispy, while I preferred the soft, greasy bacon his mom made in the mornings I woke up at his house. And he had almost white hair, while mine was brown. Other than that, we were way too much alike.

We both appreciated fine television ranging from "The Dukes of Hazzard" to "The A-Team." We both fell in love with Daisy Duke, but I called dibs. We spent many Friday nights waiting for "Friday Night Videos" to come on. That was back in the early days of music videos, and we had no MTV out there in the boonies. We waited weeks for the "Thriller" video to finally air. That was back in the early days when Michael Jackson was black — and cool.

Our musical tastes were similar, too, albeit similarly bad. We thought Men At Work were musical geniuses, as were Prince and Midnight Star. And we loved horror movies. The night we watched "The Exorcist" at his house, he swore he saw the little possessed girl giggling at the end of his top bunk. I was too busy hiding under the covers on the bottom bunk.

Racing go-karts through the boonies, hollering for the Dallas Cowboys, pouring cold water on girls who untied their tops while sunbathing at the city pool — we were partners in crime. (I'd reveal more of what we did, but I'll have to check the statute of limitations on some of it first.)

Then, in our sophomore year, we split. I don't remember the specific event that led to our big fight or really what was said. But it was all over in a flash. All I know was that Shane had pretty much decided I wasn't cool enough to hang with anymore. In all honesty, he was right, but I was too much of an individualist to be cool in high school.

I've had many people to call friends since then, but never another best friend. Really, not even a close friend since. I've spent many years building the walls around my island.

Speaking of islands: I was on Okaloosa Island in Florida recently with my wife, son and niece dining at a crowded bar and grill. We were in a tiny room on the second floor. A man and his wife and daughter were seated next to us.

Moments later, he said, "Chris!" It was Shane. We hadn't seen each other in about 10 years. We talked for a while, but he was dumbfounded by the odds of our being on vacation at the same time and next to each other in the same room of the same restaurant in the same Florida town.

Why we were thrust together again 18 years after we parted ways,

I have no idea. But we'll figure it out. We'll start with a tennis match soon. I gotta warn him, I'm no cooler now than I was in high school, but my first serve's better.

Bachelor for the weekend

Last weekend, my wife painted Atlanta red with some girlfriends while my son tromped around Providence Canyon with his cousins. That left me to do whatever I wanted for two straight nights.

Any fool in my shoes who had just gotten paid after another stressful week of work would have blown off some steam. But I'm not just any fool, and, besides, any fool in my shoes would look down at my shoes and say, "Dude, these sneakers have gotta be at least a decade old."

With the weekend to myself, I did what any 33-year-old, tired, married dad would do — pretty much nothing.

Sure, I could have rounded up some guys, had a beer or two and bragged about our glory days of sports and girl chasing, but I didn't have the energy to lie. My eyesight faded too early for me to be any good in baseball, and the only girls I ever caught probably had the same eyesight woes as I.

Besides, as Bocephus sings, all my rowdy friends have settled down. Paul's busy with his restaurant. Keith's married with two kids. I think Thad accidentally uploaded himself into a computer system. AIDS took Travis away nearly five years ago. And, even those crazy newspaper folks I've gotten to know over the past 14 years are becoming — gulp — semi-normal.

Granted, I did go crazy in a 33-year-old, too-lazy-to-leave the house sort of way. After work, I dropped by a convenience store and got a cold beverage (a 44-ounce Diet Coke) and some beef jerky. Don't underestimate what 44 ounces of cold caffeine can do after a half-dozen Diet Dr Peppers get you through a long day of work. I went wild.

First I did the dishes. They'd been piling up in the sink so long that the mold growing at the bottom was actually mature enough to hand me the dishes as I rinsed them off.

Then I plopped down in the recliner and gnawed away on my beef jerky while surfing the hundred and something digital cable channels. Because I was alone, I could eat the jerky the way it should be eaten: like a tiger, complete with the "arrghhhh" sounds as my teeth ripped at the dried-up meatlike product.

Still early in the evening, I cut on the stereo to enjoy those digital music channels. Usually, I have to wear the headphones and quietly mouth the words to classics like "Funkytown." But I pulled the plug on those phones and turned up the volume.

Not only could I sing along with KC and the Sunshine Band and the Bee Gees, but I also could disco dance on the sofa in my underwear. Occasionally I'd check out how extremely cool my reflection looked in the window before I realized the curtains were open and neighbors could check out how extremely weird I was, er, am.

I just got crazier — taking a hot bath, hitting my punching bag at 3 a.m., sleeping 10 hours and watching football. And beef jerky was the healthiest "food" I ate all weekend.

Of course, when anyone asked what I did all weekend, I simply responded "nothing." Then again, I bet if I told them I spent most of it disco dancing in my underwear, they'd probably quit bothering me with questions like that.

A few words to live by

Every now and then I get one of those e-mails full of inspirational sayings to get me through the day. It's usually sandwiched between an e-mail telling me how to make something bigger and an e-mail telling me how to make something else smaller.

But it's not fair for me to reap the rewards of all these inspirational sayings as I route them to the trash can unless I give something back. So, here are a few of my own sayings. Feel free to e-mail them around and inspire your friends and family.

• Friends are like sores. Pick at them and they'll hang around. Ignore them and they'll go away. Rub some greasy medication all over them and they'll go away faster.

• Jesus loves the little children — except Little Roy Snappleton III of 411 Maple Leaf Lane.

• Mama always said life was a box of chocolates. Mama wasn't all that bright.

• You can't teach an old dog new tricks. You can't teach a penguin to fly. You stink at teaching.

• When life hands you lemons, throw them at life while life's walking away.

• Give a man a fish and he'll eat for a day. Give a man some Cheetos and he'll eat for a day. Pretty much all man does is sit around and eat.

• Today is the first day of the rest of your life. Friday will be the last one.

• Beauty is in the eye of the beholder. Never mind, it's just an eyelash.

• I'll go the extra mile for you. I doubt even you can annoy me from a mile away.

• Some days, it just doesn't pay to get out of bed — especially if you're a hooker.

• Don't rob Peter to pay Paul. Rob Jerome. He's loaded.

• A teaspoon of sugar makes the medicine go down, but a shot of bourbon will shut 'em up all night long.

• Don't sweat the small stuff. Just don't sweat at all; you're starting to smell.

• Blood is thicker than water, but water sure tastes better after a long tennis match.

• Whistle while you work — one more time — and I swear I'm gonna smack you!

• The world is my oyster. Figures. I hate oysters. Why can't the world be my fried chicken?

• Charity begins at home. Go home and quit asking me for stuff.

• Behind every dark cloud is this big ol' lightning bolt just waiting to strike you in the butt.

• If the devil danced in empty pockets, my Levis would be the Sooouuul Train.

• The bigger they come, the faster I run.

• Laughter may be the best medicine, but morphine's gotta be running a close second.

• Sunshine on my shoulder makes me sunburned.

• Possession of enough money to get a good attorney is nine-tenths of the law.

• A picture's worth a thousand words — unless it's that picture of Madonna kissing Britney Spears, in which case it's worth only four: "I've had this dream."

• Never put off until tomorrow what you can trick somebody into doing for you today.

• Curiosity killed the cat. Come here, Curiosity! Here, boy! Bad dog! Bad Curiosity!

Seven hours in hell

During a recent three-day stay in Savannah, I found myself trapped in hell for seven hours. For those of you who've been told to go there but missed the exit, I'll elaborate.

My wife and I decided to abandon Savannah's historic district for a little while to get a simple burger or something for lunch before we blew our upcoming paychecks on dinner along the riverfront.

You can't get anything simple — or cheap — on the riverfront. The restaurants don't have burgers. They have "choice patties of ground Peruvian sirloin marinated in our very own secret sauce of worchestershire, soy and Castrol Syntec with a light sprinkling of peppercorn and cricket parts and served between two slices of pumpernickel bread imported from Statesboro."

The burger we were looking for was 99 cents of meat, bread and ketchup prepared by a chef who probably skateboarded to work.

We reasoned such a fine establishment would most likely be found on the other side of Savannah around Oglethorpe Mall. So, we mapped out a direct route through downtown, which was designed by James Oglethorpe, who apparently didn't drive a car. Downtown Savannah is a maze of historic squares, historic homes and random historic yield signs. Adding to the fun are art students on bicycles without brakes, darting out like villains in a video game. Getting across town was a lot like playing Pac-Man. And by the time we arrived at the mall, it was game over for the car.

Fortunately — or so I thought — the car conked out as we arrived at the mall and we left it for what was supposed to be a couple of hours (yeah, right) at a nearby repair shop. We figured we'd stroll around the mall for a little while, pick up the car and then park it for the rest of the trip. Instead, we were trapped at the mall for the rest of the day while they repaired everything on the car from the brakes to the flux capacitor.

(Hint: Never drop your car off with a mechanic hundreds of miles from home and tell him it's making a funny sound. That funny sound quickly becomes "cha-ching.")

The mall, any mall, is just no place to spend more than 20 minutes, much less seven hours. These are not my people. I don't buy overpriced CDs. I don't want any sales lady spraying perfume (or "stink good" as Grandma called it) at me. And I don't walk around with a cell phone glued to my head.

The only thing that kept me from going insane was the mall's massage chair. Other than the morons stopping to look at me as if I were a zoo exhibit, the massage rocked. You put in a buck, lay back and 47 burly men named Gunther beat you in the back with sledgehammers.

The next time my car decides to break down and spend the day getting a makeover, I hope it's along some quiet stretch of coastline where the margaritas are cheap, the massages are provided by tan young ladies and folks snooze on chaise lounges while their cell phones (with their dead batteries) melt in the trunk.

Those are my people.

Always on the go

Where I grew up, folks took life kind of slow. OK, extremely slow. Like a snail crawling through tar kind of slow. Like me in Algebra class kind of slow. Like 26,400 bps on the Net kind of slow.

Granted, my little hometown was a mere suburb of the big city of Montezuma, Ga., with its urban sprawl of darn near 5,000 people, so I guess we couldn't be expected to keep up the pace of those city slickers on the wrong side of the Flint River. But we did put up one traffic light just in case the Montezumans rubbed off on us and life got too fast in Oglethorpe, too.

I remember walking with Grandma down to the IGA on many summer mornings. She had a car, but the store was only a half-mile away. She figured such a short drive was a waste of gasoline.

And, along the way, we'd stop and talk to every great aunt and third cousin in Oglethorpe, which was virtually the entire population, not counting a handful of dogs who roamed the town unleashed. It must have taken two hours to get there and back. All that work, and then she had the nerve to make us eat some nasty vegetable like squash. Heaven help the poor little children like me who grew up in small towns without Chicken McNuggets.

I thought about those days while waiting behind three vehicles at an ATM the other day. The lady in front of the pack was making a deposit and apparently refinancing her home. The folks between me and her were waving their hands and banging their dashboards — you know, the kind of stuff that makes slow people even slower.

And I, too, was growing frustrated. I'm already mad that I can't even begin my ATM transactions these days without first telling the machine I'd like to do this in English. ("What country do you think this is?!") The last thing I need is a traffic jam keeping me from hitting that "fast cash" button and getting $20 to eat at a fast-food joint.

It was the latest in a string of slow encounters that day. It began at the grocery store, where I always pick the wrong checkout lane. There can be just one person in front of me at the grocery store and eight people in each of the other checkouts, and every one of those folks will be in their cars before me. The person in front of me is inevitably the one who argues about the price of her peaches, has to actually write a check (remember those?) and forgot to get milk.

Then, at the health club, there were too many people doing their butt exercises. No matter what machine I needed — lats, shoulders, hamstrings, you name it — there was somebody sitting on it. They often do these butt exercises while chatting with a person doing his arm exercises by leaning on the machine. Why can't they stay at home and sit on . . . oh, I don't know . . . perhaps a chair? These folks should make an exercise video: Buns of Still.

I wonder what Grandma would have said if she knew I was about to bust a vein because I was having trouble with my quick workout, my sprint through the grocery store and snatching my "fast cash." Actually, I know what she'd say if she were still here. She'd say I was getting too citified and that the faster I live, the sooner I'm gonna die.

"Oh, and eat your squash."

1621 revisited

As we prepare to welcome families into our home for a feast that will leave us thankful when they're finally gone until at least Christmas, this is the perfect time to revisit the day that started it all — the first Thanksgiving.

My ancestors came over on the Sunflower, which was a little party barge, complete with radio and beer cooler, that followed the Mayflower over to Plymouth Rock from the Old Country. At the top of our family tree is Cousin Eddie, who spent most of the voyage across the Atlantic jumping over waves left in the Mayflower's wake.

Cousin Eddie kept a journal that was handed down from generation to generation in my family and includes accounts of such historic events as the signing of the Mayflower Compact and the Indians' sale of Manhattan to the Dutch for just a few trinkets and Knicks season tickets. And, of course, it has the following account of the first Thanksgiving:

Hi. Cousin Eddie here. Me and the other folks around Plymouth had ourselves a big ol' meal last week. You see, Ebeneezer, Josiah and me scored big on our latest hunt. Killed a whole bunch of deer and wild turkey. Of course, if we hadn't killed off all that Wild Turkey, maybe Josiah wouldn't have fallen off the four-wheeler and broke his leg.

Anyway, we brought back all the dead animals, and the women folk — Sarah, Priscilla, Abigail and the gang — whipped up some side items, although Priscilla and Abigail got into it over the whole dressing or stuffing debate. "Getting ready for the Salem Bitch Trials a little early, ain't ya?" Abigail commented at one point.

We were gonna have a nice quiet dinner but then found out Jedediah invited the Indians over, too. He's been hanging out with the Indians a lot lately. I think he's having an identity crisis. Last month, he was running around with Old Mr. Samuel's slaves and asked us to start calling him "P. Doody."

Most of the Indians were pretty cool, but there's always that one you invite only because somebody's related to him and you'd feel guilty if you didn't. I didn't think Chief Full of Bull would ever get off that whole we-were-here-first, stop-calling-me-an-Indian kick.

But the food totally rocked, Pilgrim. Turkey, corn, potatoes and pumpkin pie. Of course, Prudence and her boyfriend, Crazy Jacob, got there late because they had to stop and buy a box of chicken fingers.

Anyway, we all went back for seconds and several of us had to kinda recline on the picnic table and undo those tacky Pilgrim belt buckles while we watched some Cowboys and Redskins throw this leather sack back and forth.

Meanwhile, the ladies cleaned all the dishes themselves and made plans to go shopping the next day, while the children played some popular games here in the settlement — such as marbles, leapfrog and Grand Theft Auto III.

When our dinner settled, Jedediah suggested we all go throw around a leather sack, too. However, the game ended far too soon as we realized that we were extremely white and British and the Indians all ran off when William lined up in the shotgun formation.

The snuggler's blues

When I sleep, I like to roll around in about four layers of linens and a few pillows until I wake up in the morning in a sort of cocoon.

It's a lot like that classic movie "Gremlins." Before I go to bed, I'm a cute little critter, but I like to eat after midnight and when I wake up in the morning and emerge from my cocoon of covers, I look like a creepy gremlin and have a similar attitude. And Phoebe Cates is there and still looks 16 years old.

Going to sleep for me is quite the production. Sometimes I lie in the living room and listen to jazz or my "sound sleep" tape. Then I crawl into bed in the wee hours of the morning. Problem is, I need tons of covers in which to snuggle up, and my wife steals all the covers before I get there. And while I may be a gremlin upon waking, my wife's a lot more like "Alien" if you shake her from her cocoon too early.

The best I can do is grip the 2 inches of cover she leaves me while I cling to life on the 2 inches of mattress upon which I'm allowed to rest. My only comfort is to throw my leg over the cocoon and snuggle up to it. My wife's asleep, so she barely notices — although she does keep having nightmares about a tree falling on her. But I've got to snuggle. I can't sleep if I can't snuggle.

My son will let me snuggle, but only if I get him a cup of juice and he gets to karate kick me every three seconds. It's a lot like snuggling with Jackie Chan — though I wouldn't have to take Jackie Chan to school in the morning.

But things have changed at my house. When my wife leaves for work and my son is settled at school, I have a new snuggling partner. I found her at the Wal-Mart SuperCenter a couple of weeks ago --- a body pillow.

Guys, if you don't have a body pillow, trust me, go get one. Yeah, it may sound a little sissy, but nobody's got to know. It's not like you'll have to write a newspaper column and confess all your sins. Here are some of the advantages of making a body pillow you're snuggling partner:

• Body pillows don't punch you in the ribs when you toss and turn or snore. Not that I snore.

• And body pillows don't snore, either. (Not that you do, honey. No. No way.)

• Body pillows don't ask you to walk around the house in your underwear looking for prowlers every time the wind blows a piece of pine straw against a window. (I personally think my wife just likes watching me walk around in my underwear — or at least likes watching me stumble into doors as I'm nearly blind when I'm not wearing contacts. Besides, what am I gonna do if I catch a prowler while in my underwear? Flash him? Then he could sue me for cruel and unusual punishment.)

• My body pillow cost $9.95 and hasn't asked me for a cent more in the entire time I've known it.

• If my body pillow gets a little fluffy, it doesn't ask me if it looks fat.

• The other night when I ate a bowl of leftover hot dog chili, my body pillow didn't say a word.

So, fellas, go get a body pillow while they last. Or, get to bed before 3 a.m. and you just might get to share the cocoon.

Jump! Jump!

It's been a few weeks since Christmas now, so most kids have pretty much put away — or in our case, left in the middle of the floor forever — everything Santa Claus brought them.

Few toys keep a kid's interest. OK, so you tickle Elmo and he laughs. You tickle him and he laughs. You tickle . . . all right already, I get it! Now, let's play Kick Me Elmo. Darn! He still laughs.

I had my share of similar dumb toys as a child. But a couple of gifts from Santa Claus endured — most notably my basketball goal and trampoline.

Dad set my basketball goal at about 10 feet but swore it was official height. I think he was merely trying to squash my professional basketball aspirations by proving that I would never, ever be able to dunk the ball like Dr. J.

My son, Saylor, got a basketball goal this Christmas, though it currently stands at only 5 feet. He hasn't seemed too interested in it, but I've had a lot of fun and discovered that if I were 11 inches taller than an official basket, I'd be worth millions in the NBA. And, unlike Shaquille O'Neal, I could still shoot a free throw.

Saylor has paid far more attention to what his cousins got from Santa, a trampoline. I can understand that. Of all my Christmas presents, even the official unofficial height basketball goal, none was more enduring than my trampoline.

Granted, by the time I finally got a trampoline, Santa was making me cut the grass and wash the car. Santa got that trampoline second-hand and even made me help paint it.

But it was worth it. I hit that trampoline almost every day for about nine years. Some days I'd just lie on it and soak up the sunshine. On rainy days, I'd douse it with dishwashing liquid and slide across. Other days, I'd push it onto my dirt basketball court so I could slam that 10 -foot goal. A couple of bounces, and I was Dr. J. Although, I don't think Dr. J ever gave himself a concussion by bonking his head on the bottom of the rim.

I bounced on that trampoline approximately 4,243,769 times, give or take a couple of bounces. Nothing really fancy. Just bounce, bounce, bounce, a couple of flips. Nearly every day for nine years.

By the time I was 18, the springs went and things began to sag. And the trampoline wasn't in all that great shape, either. But it was still strong enough to handle my baby sister and her little brat friends' bouncing. And, while my bounces made contact with the earth below, it still wasn't a bad place to curl up with a girlfriend on a spring day.

A few days ago, I saw a picture of folks training for the U.S. Olympic trampoline team. Really. Apparently they've had Olympic trampoline teams as far back as the 2000 Games in Sydney.

That's almost as silly as solo synchronized swimming, also an official Olympic sport. Who'd have ever thought that bouncing and/or swimming by yourself would qualify you as a world-class athlete?

I don't know all the official Olympic trampoline moves, but if they can bounce on a wet trampoline and dunk a basketball, it may be worth watching. And if they can figure out how to steal a kiss from Shannon Preskitt in between bounces, more power to 'em.

That's worth a gold medal.

For sale: glorious Georgia

It lasted only a few minutes before the folks at eBay either decided it was a joke or it didn't meet the high standards of the online auction site, but someone recently offered the state of West Virginia to the highest bidder.

Of course, this is a site that in the past has had such items up for bids as "jar of air from Woodstock" or "fossil turtle poo." I'm sure that jar of air was a little cloudy, and, quite frankly, I don't want to know what fossil turtle poo looks like — or fresh turtle poo for that matter.

But this little incident set me to wondering. It doesn't take much to set me to wondering these days. (Hmm, I wonder where I left the keys to the truck.)

Anyway, it set me to wondering how I would list the state of Georgia, my beautiful home state and the most perfect of all the states in the Union, if I were going to list it on eBay. It would go something like this . . .

Love the mountains? How about the beach? Big cities? Small towns? Have I got a deal for you! The Peach State, the Empire State

of the South, a.k.a. Georgia, is now available to the highest bidder.
Features include:

• A beautiful, unspoiled coastline free of strip bars, dance clubs,
tattoo parlors and high-rise hotels. And hurricanes only hit about
once a century.

• For those who prefer higher ground, Georgia features cute little
mountains from Pine Mountain to Brasstown Bald. And you won't
get killed in any avalanches. Although, you may be forced to do all
your skiing on pine straw.

• There are a few minor plumbing problems, most of which can
be traced to Atlanta and followed down the Chattahoochee. But
most of it flows just fine, as you'll learn if you bother to paddle the
beautiful, natural Flint River.

• You can indulge yourself here. There are plenty of places where
you can still get hamburger steaks smothered in gravy, cheeseburgers (including the bun) dripping in grease and virtually any animal
deep-fried. And Georgia's grandmas still know how to make biscuits and caramel cakes. (Note: This fact is not guaranteed beyond
the next 25 or so years.)

• This purchase includes sprawling Atlanta, which would be one
of the nation's most bustling cities if the traffic actually moved.
And, if for any reason you're not satisfied with your purchase of the
state of Georgia, you're welcome to keep Atlanta as our free gift.
But the nice small towns such as Hawkinsville, Hahira, St. Marys
and Dahlonega must be returned in pre-sale condition.

• Speaking of Atlanta, your purchase does not include the city's
sports teams, as many folks beyond this state's borders call the
Braves, Falcons and Thrashers their home teams. Granted, if you
try to claim the Hawks as part of your purchase, no one's likely to
notice, so, by all means, enjoy your NBA franchise. We're not.

By the way, bidding starts at a kajillion dollars. But you get what
you pay for. If you can't afford that, perhaps you could try to purchase a state more in your price range, like West Virginia.

Refill, please

There were a lot of mom-and-pop restaurants where I grew up, which was a little town surrounded by bigger little towns. Actually, most weren't run by moms and pops; they were run by moms and pops and sons and daughters and cousins.

I miss a lot of those places, though I've found a few good substitutes in Columbus and surrounding towns. I like that these folks don't wear uniforms. They don't have a standard "Hi, welcome to so-and-so's" line. When you walk in, you're more likely to get a "Hi, how y'all doin'? Y'all sit anywhere you want."

When you ask to substitute for cole slaw, they don't look at you like you've got three eyebrows and they can't remember if that's the way it's supposed to be. And they don't put weird things in your mashed potatoes.

On a recent road trip through middle Georgia and then the Pine Mountain area, I ate three straight meals at non-chain restaurants. (As a north Columbus resident, that's quite a feat for me these days.) At each spot, I asked for a Diet Coke and was given a 12-ounce can and a glass of ice — with no free refills.

OK, so mom and pop have their faults, I reckon. Problem is, a lot of these places are run by or handed down by folks from another generation. Most things associated with previous generations are big — big cars, big hair and even big wars. But when it came to soda, all they needed was a little bit of "Co-Cola." They thought 10 ounces of Coca-Cola in a glass bottle was heaven.

I'm from the little generation — little phones, little cars, little computers and little patience. We thought Grenada was a war. But we also grew up on the Big Gulp of Coke. Those cups grew with us, grew so quickly that cars' cupholders have always been a step behind. That's why we all have cola stains in our cars and why we have trouble squeezing into our little cars and trucks. We've got Big Gulps and Big Guts.

I've had Coca-Cola in those glass bottles before. And I remember grabbing empty bottles off my grandparents' front porch in Ideal, Ga., and walking a mile to redeem them "downtown" at Albritton's store. And I'd pick up a can of Prince Albert for Granddaddy and a pack of candy cigarettes for myself. And the 10-ounce bottle of Coca-Cola was indeed quite refreshing. But it left me longing for more. About 34 ounces more.

Granted, if I drank 44 ounces of regular Coca-Cola now, I'd be wilder than Howard Dean after the Iowa caucuses. But 44 ounces of Diet Coke or Diet Dr Pepper, and I'm content. Of course, that could be why I'm writing this at 3 a.m.

I'm really not asking for much, mom and pop. You can keep those tacky pigs on the shelf. You can keep those soap operas on the TV instead of something decent, like "SportsCenter." You can even get on to me on the odd chance that someday I don't clean my plate. But don't hold back on the carbonated caffeine. I've got to get my fix.

Fortunately, there are some folks out there with the right idea, and they collect a whole lot of my paycheck. Imagine, a mom-and-pop restaurant where they give you free refills and leave your mashed potatoes alone. Now that's heaven.

Macho, macho man

I'm not sure whether I buy all this mumbo-jumbo about guys having a feminine side. The way I see it, if you're a man, every side of you ought to be just oozing masculinity — but hopefully not all over the recliner.

I've always considered myself very NOT feminine. If you're gay or feminine or anything else I'm not allowed to make fun of in the newspaper, please don't be offended. While I'm not gay, more power to you if you are. I'm not homophobic. I even support gay marriage. Just be careful what you wish for, fellas. (Oops, hope my wife doesn't see that. Man, I wish my delete key worked!)

This whole feminine side issue came to mind a couple hours ago after I got out of my bubble bath and sat down to watch HBO's "Sex and the City." A hot bubble bath does wonders for the muscles after lifting a bunch of very heavy, manly sized weights at the gym. It's not like I'm wearing footies or anything. (My wife stole 'em.)

I'm obviously not gay. Now, I don't want to reinforce any stereo-types (that's Bravo's job), but I literally have three pairs of shoes. That is sooooo NOT gay or feminine, or so says a sick co-worker who proudly says she has 41 pairs of shoes as if that were an ac-complishment and not a disease. I have my sneakers, my casual leather shoes and my who-died shoes. And if someone were to notice my shoes and ask, "Hey, groovy dude, where did you get those cool, stylish shoes?" I could honestly say, "I have no clue. I don't even know who made 'em." Again, so NOT gay.

And if I accidentally look at a lady, I don't notice whether her shoes are stylish or cheap or if they even match. Straight guys just don't have the shoe-noticing or shoe-caring gene.

I must admit that I had a near-gay experience the other night while watching "Eyes Wide Shut" with Tom Cruise and Nicole Kidman. (By "with" them, I mean "starring" them. They weren't like sitting on the sofa. That'd be silly; that's where all the unfolded clothes are piled up.) Anyway, I noticed Tom Cruise is a good looking guy, while Nicole Kidman doesn't float my boat at all. Fortunately, I then saw "Vanilla Sky" with Tom Cruise with Penelope Cruz and was relieved to find that I much preferred Penelope. Whew! Not gay! That was close!

I've been paranoid since I bought a shirt last summer and was told by tactless colleagues that it was a "gay" shirt. How could a $4.99 shirt be gay? Fortunately a wise co-worker stepped in and informed them that it was not a gay shirt; it was simply that they weren't used to seeing me dress with any kind of style whatsoever. "Thanks, dude," I said.

Still, to be on the safe side, that shirt has not been worn since. It now rests in a small section of my closet I call "might be gay." It's right next to the "made the wife laugh" area, which takes up three-fourths of the closet.

So what if I like chick flicks and bubble baths? If that's enough to say I've got a feminine side, so be it. But if any guy checks out my feminine side, I swear I'll bop him in the nose.

Glad I got that cleared up. Gotta go now. There's a Valerie Berti-nelli movie on Lifetime.

No more worries, mate

I spend way too much time at 3 a.m. staring at the ceiling as I lie in bed. The room's pitch black, the night is silent and I can't even see the ceiling, yet I lie there with my eyes wide open.

I'm worried about something. I'm always worried about something. Nothing in particular, just something. It's just my nature. It's a family tradition on my mother's side. They worry about stuff until it kills 'em — which is completely different from my father's side where folks are care-free and instead eat themselves to death.

If you read my column regularly or by accident ("Wait a minute! This ain't George Will!"), I know what you're thinking: Gee, he seems so easygoing, whimsical and amazingly good looking. Well, at least one of those is true. I am, indeed, amazingly whimsical looking. But, I am also a worrywart.

I worry until I get so stressed that drinking an expresso and watching pro wrestling would actually calm me down — if I liked either of them. In fact, wrestler Randy "Macho Man" Savage could drink eight expressos and would tell me, "Dude, you're too intense, man! You need to calm down like me, man! Here, snap into a Slim Jim!"

I worry until I find myself staring off into space worrying about something as petty as global warming or what I'd do if I were attacked by a rabid ferret, and my wife asks the dreaded question: "What are you thinking?" Fortunately, after 12 years, she now takes my word for it when I say, "nothing." But now I'm worried about why she believes that so easily.

And I worry until I can't sleep. The reason I'm up right now is because I'm worried about why my son can't sleep. Maybe he's worried, too. What if Barney snaps and eats one of those annoying kids? Are Scooby Snacks Atkins-friendly? I hope no old man tries to play knick-knack on my thumb, my shoe or my knee, whatever knick-knack is.

There's nothing outside my worry realm. I even worry about things nearly 20 years behind me. What if I had studied harder in high school? What if I had studied at all in high school? What if I had stayed awake in high school?

More than anything, like most folks I worry about money. I know what it's like to go to the ATM and play it like it's a slot machine or something. "Come on, $20, fast cash, be there! Baby needs a new pair of shoes! Daddy needs a cheeseburger!"

I worry about my health, mainly because I don't share all my stress and worry with folks and let it eat me up inside. Speaking of health, do we really think we're ever going to cure another disease when there's far more money in treating diseases than curing them? Maybe the president should offer a $1 billion reward to anyone who cures a major disease.

And what if the sun just up and burns up tomorrow . . .

I can't take it anymore. As of this very moment, as God and all five of my readers are my witnesses, I give up worrying forever. I shall relax and live a care-free life forever more.

Perhaps now I can finally sleep. If the average pillow didn't have thousands of dust mites, including dead ones, maybe I could.

The real world

The line between fantasy and reality often gets blurry, even when you're an adult. But when you're 3 going on 4, it must be even harder to see.

Fortunately, adults can handle having reality thrown in their faces with grace, or at least resignation. Picture this:

You're Joe Schmo sitting at a bar, your beer gut hanging over your belt as if you're a marsupial who mated with a beach ball. A lovely young woman waves your way, and you raise your hand from your mug to wave back. Finally, after all these years, someone sees the real you. She sees past the beer gut, the receding hairline and the golf shirt you've worn once a week for five years. She sees past all of this to the real you. No, wait, she sees past the real you, through you, right to her friend who just walked in. Reality bites back. Again. Take another swig, Joe.

My son, Saylor, turns 4 today. For weeks, he's been dealing with the harsh realities of preschool life — cowlicks, buttoning his britches and the dreaded "bedtime." He takes it all pretty well in stride. But every now and then he trips over that blurry line between fantasy and reality, and that's when he gets upset.

I try not to point out that line unless he notices it himself. For instance, he had my wife dial my number at work the other night so he could "tell Daddy something."

"News desk, Chris," I answered.

"Uh, Chris, uh, Daddy."

"Hey, buddy."

116

"Look, Daddy, I can stand on one foot!"

"That's great!"

"Look, Daddy, I can hop on one foot!"

"Fantastic, buddy!" I tell a dangling telephone as he hops away, still chatting in the background. No sense bursting his bubble, I figure.

Other times he discovers those lines himself. My wife has twice caught him opening a book, setting it on the floor and jumping on it. Then he gets mad and shakes his fists. "Ooooo, I can't do it!" This is not some rebellion against reading or Dr. Seuss. He's trying to jump into the book, like the animated Stanley on The Disney Channel. He's finally figured out that he can't actually jump into a book unless he at least gets his own TV show.

I unwittingly brought him to tears recently while driving him to his Granny's house to spend the night. I told him I was going to take all his hugs and kisses home with me. I had no idea this little joke would devastate him. He started crying.

"But then I won't have any to give Granny!" he whined through the tears.

I relented, and we agreed that I could have one hug and two kisses to take home with me.

I didn't mean to make him cry, but after all, he had nearly done the same thing to me as we began the drive with my reinforcing why he should take his vitamins.

"Don't you want to be a baseball player when you grow up?"

"Noooooo!"

"A football player?"

"Noooooo!"

"How about a soccer player?"

"Noooooo! I just want to be like you, Daddy!"

I reckon that will change at some point when he realizes I'm quite the Average Joe, but there's no sense in bursting his bubble now.

Or mine.

City and country deer

Staff writer Bryan Brasher — who knows more about fish and deer than I do about Jimmy Buffett and "The Andy Griffith Show" (meaning a whole heck of a lot about them) — wrote earlier this month about an Auburn University project to study the differences between rural and urban deer.

If only Bryan had come to me about this story, he could have saved himself a lot of work and Auburn a lot of money. And Auburn needs the money because you never know when they might need to jet off to Northern Kentucky Tech and try to steal their fencing coach.

You see, I've studied this issue myself. I grew up tromping through the woods of my home county, where even the cities are rural areas. And now I live in Columbus and see as many deer as ever. I am well aware of the differences in city deer and country deer, such as:

• While city bucks have antlers on their heads, country bucks have antlers on their heads and a satellite dish on their rump.

• A baby city deer is called a "fawn," while a baby country deer is called "Junior."

• Bucks have antlers for the main purpose of fighting other bucks during the breeding season, although some city bucks have been known to simply hire a good lawyer.

• Country deer often can be found drinking from rivers, streams and lakes, while city deer sort through trash for half-empty bottles of Perrier.

• Country does are seasonal breeders (usually over a couple of months in the fall), but city does will breed all year long if you buy them a few margaritas.

• Both country does and city does have an average weight of about 140 pounds, but a city doe will lie and tell you it's closer to 120.

• Country and city bucks usually lose their antlers during the months of December or January. Country bucks usually find their antlers while looking for their socks, while city bucks usually find theirs while looking for the remote control between sofa cushions.

• All deer have at least two digits on their hooves, though city deer have an extra middle digit to communicate with drivers who nearly run over them.

• Country and city bucks' antler size generally peaks around age 7 or 7 . After this point, city deer are bombarded with e-mails slugged

"Get bigger antlers now with new miracle pill!"

• Deer eat most types of vegetation, but country deer deep fry their vegetation or cover it with gravy.

• Deer whistle and snort through their noses and communicate by stamping their feet, though city deer usually whistle and snort over a cell phone.

• By the time fawns are 20 minutes old, they can walk slowly. By the time city fawns are 30 minutes old, they can walk to the phone and order pizza.

• A country doe "goes to the bathroom" an average of 13 times in 24 hours, but a city doe may go more often if her girlfriends have to go.

• And, when shot with tranquilizer darts so they can be studied, country deer run about 40 yards and then plop down on the ground. City deer will sue.

Second time around

Most people don't believe me when I tell them that even after a dozen years of marriage, my wife and I don't argue.

But it's true. My wife simply explains where I've messed up, and I apologize profusely whether I understand or not — usually not.

Every now and then, however, I understand where I've messed up. This happened recently while watching an episode of HBO's brilliant "Curb Your Enthusiasm."

The main character and his wife were preparing to renew their wedding vows after 10 years of marriage, something the male lead was less than enthused about — particularly when his wife insisted that he included a promise to be with her eternally. He stressed that he thought he would be single again in the afterlife since it was only " 'til death do us part."

I was squirming in my recliner, knowing a salvo was about to be launched from the sleepy woman on the sofa.

"Would you want to renew our vows?" she asked.

"I would," I said quietly.

(Wrong answer! Proper answer to question is: "Boy would I! How romantic! Let's do it barefoot on a tropical beach! With rose petals everywhere!")

"You would?" she asked incredulously.

"Yeah."

"If you had to, right?"

"Uh, no. Um, your hair looks nice. Did you have it cut or dyed or fixed or something? That was a great dinner you cooked, by the way."

"What dinner?"

"You know, that dinner, with the meat and stuff — what was it, '98, '99?"

"Don't try to change the subject."

Of course, I would try to change the subject. Weddings just aren't guy things. (Although, those little cocktail weenies at the reception are, because those rock.) Guys don't fantasize about their wedding day. The wedding night, perhaps. The bachelor party, sure. But not the fancy-schmancy ceremony — and certainly not twice.

I'm not bashing marriage. It's the perfect way for a man and woman to spend their lives together — or a man and a man, a man and his dog, a woman and a woman, or a woman and Rosie O'Donnell, depending on which city or state you're in these days.

But these lavish ceremonies just aren't my thing. My ideal wedding would have been to elope to Jamaica or somewhere and get hitched on the beach in a few minutes and get on with married life. And it would have cost less than a typical wedding without getting Vasoline spread under my car's door handles.

But I never told my then-fiancee about my ideal wedding because I wanted her to have a church wedding and the flowers and dresses and cocktail weenies. I wanted her to have no regrets.

When I told her about my ideal wedding years later, she popped me on top of the head and asked me why the heck I didn't say something.

"That would've rocked!" she said.

At least if we do renew our vows — someday, maybe — we'll probably do it barefoot on a beach. I wouldn't want her to have regrets, again. And I'll pack some cocktail weenies. I wouldn't want to have regrets, either.

It's spring: Get your legs out

Apparently, I have seasonal affective disorder — which is just something else to add to my long list of disorders. I'd add it to my list, but I can't find it on my desk, which is in a constant state of disorder.

If you don't know what seasonal affective disorder is, well, that's just SAD. Basically, what it means is cold weather stinks and I wish I were wearing shorts.

During winter, I'm pretty much a grouch. That's why I'm surprised there's actually a Seasonal Affective Disorder Association, because the last folks I want to be around during winter is a bunch of grouches like me.

Actually, SADA is a wonderful organization that supports SAD folks like myself. For instance, here's a transcript of the last SADA meeting:

President: Winter stinks.

Vice-president: I know, and I hate turtlenecks.

President: You callin' me a turtleneck?

Treasurer: Shut-up! I'm trying to write this check out to the gas company. What?! A hundred and fifty bucks?!

Vice-president: I think I'll take a nap.

Fortunately, it's spring and I'm not SAD anymore. Now, I'm just jealous. Jealous, because students are out on spring break.

Spring break was always one of my favorite times of the year growing up. It marked the beginning of the end of the school year. And by the time I got old enough to be interested in girls (from fourth grade on, I think), it marked the time when those smooth, sexy legs quit being covered up by blue jeans.

Of course, it also marked the time when girls would start saying, "No, Chris! I don't want to see your 'smooth, sexy' legs! Who told you that you could wear shorts anyway? It's just April, you freak!"

I'm most envious of those kids old enough to drive to Panama City and cram eight people into a hotel room so they can afford to stay three or four nights and still have enough money for breakfast, lunch and dinner — or as we called it back then, beer.

In February, the old Hathaway Bridge on Highway 98 into Panama City was demolished, its steel spans falling into the water near the 3,000-foot-long replacement bridge. The photos moved on the wire, but few were interested around here except me and another good ol' Southern boy from Eufaula. There was something disheartening about seeing that old bridge fall into the water — even if we all knew it as the Bridge to Sin, or BS.

In the middle of winter, the last thing a SAD person needs to see is an old friend blown up and plunged into St. Andrews Bay. Except my old friend Sammy; he deserved blowing up.

Many kids already have crossed the new bridge to sin this year, and this week even more will (unless their parents read this). They'll bodysurf, skinny dip and bellyflop their way through the week while having the same thing for breakfast, lunch and dinner.

So, here's to spring and spring breakers. And here's to old friends: the sun, the Hathaway Bridge and my cut-off shorts. May you all never go out of style.

Shoes or something like it

Recently, I overheard a discussion between an editor and a reporter concerning a story about a public forum on proposed dress codes for Muscogee County schools.

A teacher at the forum made the comment that you can't run in Birkenstocks. That led to the obvious questions for the newsroom's most fashion-impaired employee, otherwise known as me:

"Where the heck is Birkenstocks, and why can't you run there?"

This nearly gave the newsroom's reigning shoe queen a heart attack because, apparently, Birkenstocks are shoes or something like it.

That's good to finally know in case my 401(k) manager suggests putting 20 percent of my contribution in Birkenstocks — as opposed to where most of my contribution goes now, Fallingstocks.

While the hyperventilating shoe queen was picking herself up off the floor, a colleague who sits next to me explained with a straight face that Birkenstocks was where Jimi Hendrix set his guitar on fire. The sucker in me responded, "No, I think that was Monterrey."

The shoe queen forced me to look at a Web site that sold Birkenstocks, which are kinda like sandals, I guess. All I saw was that they were selling for $99, which is more than I've spent total on shoes over the past three years.

The shoe queen also called over various members of her shoe court so they could point at me and express their shock and horror. You'd have thought I'd never heard of Coca-Cola.

However, the whole Birkenstocks Incident (as it has come to be known around here) did convince me that I could stand to purchase a new pair of shoes. While the shoe queen buys new shoes every couple of weeks, I buy them every couple of presidential administrations.

Once in the shoe store — which is so not my territory that I thought someone would ask for my passport — I noticed that the sneakers were mostly white. I had forgotten that sneakers don't originate in light brown.

Being a country bumpkin, I put on the sneakers right then and there in the store before I paid for them. I put my old sneakers in the new shoes' box. The lady at the register opened the box before I could explain and gave me a horrified look I hadn't seen since, well, the night before when I didn't know what Birkenstocks were. She threatened to call in a hazardous materials unit.

I must say that my new sneakers are surprisingly comfortable, but they are just too white. I feel like my feet are glowing and I can't stop glancing down at them.

But the best thing about them is that new shoe smell. Actually, I'm not sure if it's actually a new shoe smell or it's just that they don't smell. I was contemplating this at work with my nose stuck in the shoe when a co-worker asked what the heck I was doing.

"Research," I said. "I'm busy. Now, leave me alone."

"Don't worry."

The only thing that compares to the smell is the price tag: $29. No shoe in the world is worth $99 no matter what the shoe queen says.

Besides, everybody knows you can't run in Birkenstocks.

Learning from Lewis

As much as I dislike anniversary stories in the newspaper, allow me to be a hypocrite for just a moment. I can't believe how few in the media made note of what happened a little more than 10 years ago on March 20, 1994.

I was spinning wheels in my fifth year as an overworked sports writer. That particular day I was covering then-unknown Karrie Webb and other up-and-coming women golfers in a Futures Tour event just outside of Americus, Ga. Webb fell out of contention when a hog on a farm bordering the course squealed as she was making a crucial putt. Only in Americus can the gallery for a pro golf tournament be slaughtered for bacon.

But that was hardly the tragedy that day. When I got back to our tiny office, I heard that Lewis had up and died. Grizzard, that is. Though, to most Southern folks and especially Georgians, he was just Lewis.

It was hardly a shocker. He'd had heart problems all his life, wrote a whole book about it and had been hospitalized all that week. Still, it closed a chapter in Georgia's history, in journalism's history. And it opened one in mine.

I set a goal to follow in his huge footsteps someday. He came from a small town, like me. He began his career as a sports writer, like me. That's about where the similarities ended, but it was enough to get me started.

What I quickly learned, however, is that there had already been a Lewis Grizzard. And some readers have made that quite clear: "You're no Lewis Grizzard," one who hated me wrote. And, yet, one who loved me wrote, "You're my favorite writer, next to Lewis Grizzard, of course." Indeed, I'm no Lewis, but if folks are bound and determined to compare me to a person (beats one letter comparing me to dog poopee), let it be Lewis, for better or worse.

I've read his autobiography and several of his books and have decided the reason people loved him and still love him is not what they insist, which is: "He was so funny." His humor was often politically incorrect and more often gentle, but rarely was it knee-slapping.

No, he won readers' hearts with his curve balls. It was when they went looking for something funny and instead read about a dog, Catfish, who "up and died." It was when they read about Mama or Daddy or the college classmate in the lovely sweater on whom he had an unspoken crush. His ability to wax nostalgic or tug at the heart strings was unmatched.

And he shared his life, from his four marriages and his heart surgeries to his love of golf and Georgia football. He took his readers with him, from Moreland to Bermuda. He had his share of faults, and laid them out for the world to judge.

So, thanks for the memories and the example, Lewis. I hope Heaven's golf courses are all you imagined and you get to see the promised land by train. Give Catfish a pat on the head and tell your mama'n'dem I said hey.

Top 10 smells of summer

Summer's here! OK, it's not officially here, but only because we're waiting on the Vermonts of the world to get above 50 degrees. But as far as I'm concerned (which is all that matters), once the temperature hits 90, it's summer.

Summer's in the air. I can smell it. What I like most about summer — other than the fact it's not winter — are all the sweet pleasures for my olfactory system. And I've got to soak up such pleasures before my olfactories start outsourcing smelling duties or shutting down.

Anyway, here are the top 10 smells of summer in the South:

10. We'll start with the old favorite, newly mowed grass. I love this smell so much that sometimes I'll wander through my jungle of a front yard to my neighbor's lawn and take a whiff.

9. This is about the time I start thinking about playing tennis again. I've recently bought a racket and several cans of balls. For some reason, I feel compelled to stick my nose right there on the can when you open it for the first time. Since I haven't found anybody to play tennis with yet this year, my game is pretty much limited to sitting around and sniffing tennis cans.

8. I used to go to Six Flags over Georgia every summer, and every time it was about 125 degrees. You can almost smell the pavement melting — or maybe it was just the soles of my sneakers.

7. Everybody — except a few vegetarian wackos — loves the smell of dead animals on a grill. But what's strange to me is how the smell of lighter fluid getting a grill started lights up your senses,

too.

6. It seemed like every afternoon back home we sat on the front porch and watched thunderstorms roll in. I loved the smell of water steaming up from the street that had been baked in the sun all day long.

5. Chlorine itself isn't such a wonderful smell, as I've painfully learned from stupidly sticking my nose in a bucket of pool-cleaning chemicals. But just the hint of it makes me want to dive back into my old next-door-neighbors' pool back in Oglethorpe.

4. Speaking of water, what's really more summer than the smell of the salty sea? At least, I think it's salt. Maybe it's just dead fish and rotten seaweed.

3. I'm not the kind of guy to stop and smell the roses, probably because gardening just doesn't interest me and I can't tell a chrysanthemum from kudzu — except that kudzu's a lot easier to spell. Still, I like the smell of the blooming flowers and rich foliage as I walk and drive around Columbus or the countryside.

2. The sulfuric sensation following July 4 fireworks is almost as wonderful to me as the dazzling explosions themselves. It seems like I work every July 4 nowadays and I love to soak up the smoke as it drifts over the newspaper building. I hope it's not poisonous (the smoke that is, not the newspaper.)

1. And, by far, the winner is suntan lotion. I don't use it myself, for I am running a close second to Michael Jackson as the whitest man in America. But I have applied plenty of suntan lotion. And the fact that it brings to mind some of my favorite sights doesn't hurt its case for No. 1.

Those summer nights

Summer nights. Oh, how I miss 'em.

Don't worry. I'm not going to belt out that song from "Grease." Well, actually, I am. But, don't worry, because you can't hear it — unlike these folks fleeing the newsroom right now.

WHERE ARE Y'ALL GOING? I CAN'T PUT OUT A NEWSPAPER BY MYSELF!

Whatever. It's not like it's the first time I've sung "Grease" tunes in the newsroom. I do a mean rendition of "Sandy" that would make William Hung cry. Oh well, these folks just don't appreciate talent. I bet they don't appreciate summer nights, either.

One of the things I loved about summer vacation as a kid — before I was old enough for summer luvin' and having me a blast — was staying up as late as I wanted. Fortunately, we had only 13 television channels, so I rarely spent those nights in the living room. No, I went outside — midnight, 2 a.m., whatever — and enjoyed the peace and quiet.

OK, so maybe it wasn't so quiet. There were crickets and bullfrogs. There were frequent train horns and that low rumbling sound from the tracks a mile away. Once, I even heard gunshots shatter the silence when a fellow across the street got murdered. In all of Oglethorpe, where folks blocks away said "Bless you" when you sneezed, I was the only person awake at 4 a.m. besides the killers to hear it. At 12 years old, I got called into court to testify about it. My knees were knocking louder than those gunshots.

I'd lie in the ditch across from the kudzu patch and gaze at the stars. You didn't have to drive 20 miles out of town to escape light pollution. We had very few streetlights back home, and most of the ones on my street had been knocked out by my rock-throwing cousin, who was sort of a meaner version of Ernest T. Bass.

There were some nights and wee hours of the morning I would spend indoors, but they were far less memorable. About the only thing I remember is watching "Rat Patrol" and listening to our horribly outdated stereo and our lone eight-track cassette. If you only had "Greatest Hits of 1977" to listen to, you'd spend a lot of your nights outside with the bullfrogs, too.

I wasn't always alone late at night in my youth. My older neighbors next door had a paper route, and sometimes I'd join them. And sometimes their cute cousin would stay a week or two during the summer, and I'd chase her around the pool all night. Tiffany, too, liked to gaze at the stars. She'd look to the heavens and wonder things like, "Why won't this crazy country boy leave me alone?"

And my dad, who thought Oglethorpe was a city and too loud, would drag me out to the country every now and try to make me afraid of the dark with ghost stories around a fire.

But not even my dad — who always managed to get himself

"lost" in the woods after telling me those stories — could make me fear those wonderful summer nights.

However, I'm not nearly as fond of the headless man Dad said roams Church Street in Oglethorpe. Apparently, he's a night owl, too.

Thanks, heroes

On Tuesday, for the first time in many years, I visited my Granddaddy's grave.

I'm not the kind of guy to visit cemeteries and the graves of loved ones. I'm very spiritual, and I strongly believe in an afterlife, but I don't believe my Granddaddy's lying underground in Ideal, Ga. I don't even want to be buried. My family is well aware that I prefer to be cremated after I've donated what anybody needs. The Earth's overcrowded enough with folks that are still alive.

But, for several reasons, I felt compelled to visit the Ideal cemetery and the grave of Frederick Murph Dixon. It was the day after Memorial Day, and I had spent a week reading stories and downloading pictures of World War II veterans as the long overdue memorial to their courage was finally dedicated in Washington.

Granddaddy fought in that war. He fought that war for nearly 40 years.

I was his oldest grandchild. A fan of westerns, he christened me "Pancho" the day I was born and never called me "Chris." It was fine with me because even before I understood the historical significance of World War II, he was my first hero.

He never told me or his other five grandchildren the truth about how he lost both his legs. Sometimes they were shot off by German airplanes. They were even bitten off once by a crocodile in the Nile. There were a hundred different stories, and we believed every one.

It wasn't until he died in 1981 that I learned the truth in an old newspaper clipping. He was fighting in North Africa and his jeep hit a mine. He crawled back to fellow soldiers with one leg hanging on by a thread as he carried the other in his bloody arms.

Granddaddy didn't make many trips because of the aggravation of living in a wheelchair long before there were handicapped spaces and ramps everywhere. But shortly before he died, we brought him to Columbus for an Army reunion. It was my first-ever trip to this city. During that reunion, we met the two soldiers who saved his life.

According to them, they had little choice. When first they came across him, they didn't know if he was alive. If he were dead, they could have continued on without being separated from their unit. But if they took him back for medical care, their buddies would move forward without them. Granddaddy looked up and ended the debate.

"Y'all better put my $%&! on that $%&! truck!"

Sixty years ago today, Granddaddy most likely would have been fighting at Normandy. Instead, he was in Washington singing on a radio show to raise money for war bonds.

I didn't have to drive far out of my way to stop in Ideal the other day. I could have simply taken his picture — packaged with his Purple Heart — off the mantle in my living room and spoken to him. And it's not like I had a lot to say. He can see me. Hopefully he's proud. And we'll meet again. What's really to say?

Nothing, other than "Thanks, Granddaddy."

Considering how far out of their way he and millions of others went to save the world, I guess the Ideal cemetery's not that far out of the way after all.

Y'all fight it out

I'm a middle-of-the-road kind of guy. It's where my politics lie. It's where I played football as a child. It's where I found dinner while driving home last night.

Ha! Just kidding. We didn't ALWAYS play football in the middle of the road. Sometimes we played in the kuzdu patch across the street from my house.

I might be a Reagan Democrat. Or maybe I'm a Clinton Republican. Or am I a Clintgan Republicrat? I'm whatever hybrid political breed of person it is who wants the government out of his personal life and out of his wallet.

For lack of a better label, I guess I'm a moderate. Yes, indeed, I'm moderate to the extreme. I'm an extremist centrist moderate, which on the political scale is where IQs peak before they slide on their way left or right.

As a extremist centrist moderate, I'm kind of a hard guy to get riled up about political stuff. A lot of folks may find that hard to believe, including my parents, who got upset when I was 10 years old when I cheered in front the TV when President Reagan beat Carter — even though Mr. Jimmy lived over in the next county.

At least one of my old high school teachers would likely find that hard to believe, too. She tweaked the script of "Cinderella" for a drama class production and cast me as the anarchist looking to overthrow the royal family. My role was to pace back and forth with a picket sign during the ball, which was about the extent of my acting ability.

But living in the center of the left-wing and the right-wing extremists these days, there's not much reason for me to hold a picket sign anymore. Although, there's a protest brewing for the August Republican National Convention that intrigues me.

A right-wing group called ProtestWarrior (www.protestwarrior. com) is planning to protest left-wing protesters at the convention. That ought to be interesting — folks who don't know how to have fun vs. folks who often smell bad.

You don't see a lot of right-wing protest groups unless you perform abortions or are gay — or unless you try to marry a gay abortion doctor. But you see plenty of left-wing protesters who are anti-war, anti-corporate and anti-deodorant.

I'll give the left-wing protesters credit for being far more colorful than right-wing protesters. But many left-wing protesters — especially many of those kids who come to Columbus for the SOA Watch protest — just seem to be protesting because they enjoy the protest culture. It's kind of like a roaming Woodstock.

Then again, the right-wing protesters may be more stuffy because while left-wing protests are mainly just group whining, right-wing protesters have the far more serious task of condemning those who disagree to eternal damnation. You can't do that with a giant, rainbow-colored wig.

The only protesters I support are those who paint slogans on their bodies and run around naked. I'm a firm believer that people — especially Republicans and Eskimos — wear way too many clothes. So, if I ever did get inspired to do some protesting, it would have to be with a group that runs around naked.

I could ask what we were protesting later.

Putting the 'yup' in 'yupneck'

I never believed it would happen to me, but slowly and surely, I'm turning into a yuppie.

Yep, even me — a South Georgia boy with blue-collar roots, dirt between the toes, catfish in the fryer, mud on the tires and PBR still somewhere in my belly — can get himself yuppie-fied.

Oh, I've tried to pretend I didn't see it coming. And I've done my best to temper it and cover it up by describing myself as the world's first "yupneck" — half yuppie, half redneck. But I'm at least 60 percent "yup" now and growing.

It dawned on me today while I was cutting the grass in the front yard. This in itself was the kicker. I was cutting grass — not weeds, just ankle-high, soft blades of green grass. For years, my front yard's been the kind of place that Brer Bear and Brer Fox wouldn't dare throw Brer Rabbit because it'd be cruel and unusual punishment.

It wasn't the first clue, though. That came the other day when I told a yuppie colleague that my son was going to play soccer this year. Soccer wasn't a sport where I'm from. Soccer was something you did to a girl if she tried to kiss you on the elementary school playground.

When I informed this person about our family's soccer plans, she said I was going to become one of those stereotypical bad youth league parents yelling at referees and interfering in the fun.

As a sports writer for many years, I saw too much of this mess to participate in it. But the more I thought about it, the more I realized I was much closer to the political demographic "soccer mom" than to "NASCAR dad." Of course, I never got into auto racing, but if your first car was a '78 Celica that went from 0-60 in three days, you wouldn't be interested in racing, either.

Speaking of vehicles — score another one for the "yup" department. Sure, I drive a pickup now (albeit a Japanese one). Sure, I haven't washed it in four years. And, sure, I've got a seat full of cassette tapes (remember those?) by Lynyrd Skynyrd, Bocephus and Jimmy Buffett.

However, my truck lease is up in January and I'm gonna get — gulp! — an SUV. Don't worry, I'll get a little bitty one. You can't jump into this yuppie life with a big ol' Suburban on your first try (not that I could afford the gas anyway). But I plan to get all the fancy options — maybe even some of those fancy windows I've heard about that you can roll up simply by pressing a button. I'll believe that when I see it. What will they come up with next? Cars that work the gas and brakes themselves?

Here and now, though, I vow to never become 100 percent yuppie. I'll never get some noise-polluting machine to blow leaves from here to there. I'll never buy a bottle of Perrier while I'm still living in Georgia. I'll never pay $60 to watch a guy in a tux play a fiddle. And I'll never know — nor will I care — which vintage wine goes best with whatever dead animal's roasting on my grill.

But, please, let's keep this yuppie stuff between us. If the boys back at Booger Bottom Country Club ever get wind of this, they'll knock the PBR right out of me.

Ask Doc about it

If you've got the Sunday blues, ask your doctor today about reading Chris Johnson's column every week. Just one Chris Johnson column can provide up to 24 hours of relief from reality.

In the past six years, more than 23 people have reported positive results from reading Chris Johnson's column every Sunday. It's the No. 1 doctor-prescribed newspaper column in a two-block area of north Columbus, one block of which is covered entirely in kudzu.

So, don't hesitate. Ask your doctor today if Chris Johnson's column is right for you.

Warning: Chris Johnson's column is not for everyone. Those who are easily offended or walk around with constant frowns and spend at least 60 percent of their day complaining about the government (however warranted it may be) should not read Chris Johnson's column.

Contraindications: Do not read Chris Johnson's column if you are currently reading work by respected writers, real journalists or anyone who has won anything like a Pulitzer or Nobel Prize or has some wacky word such as "laureate" near their name.

Active ingredients: 25% baloney, 35% cynicism, 39% what happens to you when you sniff Elmer's glue throughout your first five years of school and less than 1% journalism. In lab tests, only minute traces of actual journalism were detected. In addition, use of the term "active" in anything related to Chris Johnson is questionable.

Proper use: Do not use Chris Johnson's column orally as anyone within earshot may ask you to "Shut the heck up!" Do not eat Chris Johnson's column or stuff Chris Johnson's column into any body cavity. It is harmless but, please, it makes the writer queasy just thinking about places his column picture could go. If Chris Johnson's column comes into contact with eyes, flush immediately with water (the eyes, not the column) and call your eye doctor — you need glasses.

Precautions: Do not use Chris Johnson's column for any educational purposes whatsoever. (Editor's note: Ha! Like that's gonna happen!)

Laboratory tests: Lab mice subjected to Chris Johnson's column looked very confused. Human testing has yielded similar results.

To report problems: If you have any questions or experience any problems while using Chris Johnson's column, don't call the writer because he'll deny any responsibility whatsoever and certainly hasn't proved too darn handy at answering questions around the newsroom, either.

Overdosage: Do not exceed your doctor's recommended dose of Chris Johnson's column. Excessive Chris Johnson column intake in a 24-hour period can result in uncontrollable urges to jab sharp objects into your eye sockets.

Side effects: Reports of people busting a gut are extremely rare. Common side effects include nausea, upset stomach, vomiting, depression, infertility, profuse sweating, chest pain, headaches, itching, aggravated hypertension, aggravation in general and excessive whining. Many of these effects are mild and can be treated by covering up the mug shot above while reading Chris Johnson's column.

Dirty birds and words

If you plan to send me any e-mail here at the newspaper, you'd better watch your mouth — or at least your fingers.

In an effort to protect us journalists' tender eyes and ears, the mysterious people in charge of our Internet have made sure that no dirty words get through our e-mail firewall. Maybe that's why I don't get nearly as much e-mail from readers as I used to. How I long for the old days when I could open an e-mail and be called a "dumb $#&@!-ing Southern $#&@!." And that was the fan mail. You should have seen the hate mail.

This e-mail filter thing may sound all fine and dandy, but it can interfere with getting the news out, especially when the big news is boobies. And I don't mean Janet Jackson, I mean the blue-footed booby which might now be found in the Chattahoochee Valley after hitching a ride with Hurricane Ivan. You may get lucky and see one, even without Justin Timberlake's help.

Staff writer Bryan Brasher is one of the best outdoors writers I've ever read, but he obviously has a foul mouth (or fingers) because twice in the last month he's e-mailed stories to the newsroom only to have them bounce back because he violated our content filter.

The first time was in a story about the lawsoot — uh, I mean lawsuit — against Phenix City's Continental Carbon. A witness had said that something could not be seen "with the naked eye." Sure enough, "naked" didn't make the cut. Maybe if it were the nekkid eye, it'd be OK.

Of course, Bryan's story about birds that could have been blown into the Valley by Ivan got bounced, too, because of the blue-footed booby. We finally got the story into the paper this past Monday and even ran a giant booby photo right there on the front page — something the tropical bird blamed on a feather malfunction.

This also could explain why no publishers have responded to the proposals I've e-mailed for my second book, "Buford the Big Blue-Footed Booby's Hot Stock Tips."

Ours is hardly the only business to have installed such filters to fight all the filth that clutters inboxes coast to coast. The by-product of all these filters is that perverted solicitations and crooked business schemes now misspell all the key words that might get their e-mails bounced.

Of course, the purveyors of filth on the Net will still corrupt our children. But instead of merely turning them into perverts, they'll turn them into illiterate perverts. The only thing worse than finding graffiti at nice places like the Riverwalk is when the vandals spell the F-word with just three letters. It's five, right?

Hopefully, someday we can at least divide the Internet into a dirty section and a legitimate section to protect our children. In the meantime, I guess we'll just have to keep our kids off the Internet. Fortunately, while we're figuring out this whole Internet thing, we can all be reassured that our kids are safe in their other activities — such as listening to hip-hop radio and watching cable television.

And, please, if I've offended you with the B-word this column, e-mail me to let me know. Be sure to include "booby" in the subject line.

Health coverage changes

First of all, I'd like to thank you for gathering today in the Dead White Guys Memorial Conference Room for this very important meeting.

Today we're going to discuss changes in the company's health insurance plan. I use the term "changes" in much the same way the company uses the term "efficiency," which doesn't sound all that evil but actually means "ways to make your life more miserable at a faster pace."

In 2005, you will still be able to choose the traditional plan or the green plan, but in our continuing effort to give you more choices we've added the chartreuse plan — or as the provider refers to it, the I-Wouldn't-Get-Sick-If-I-Were-You plan.

Before we continue, I'll present this line chart to show how health costs have affected our company. This sharp-rising blue line shows how much more it's been costing us to insure you peons. This plummeting red line represents the services covered. This stagnant green line shows how much we actually care.

Now, I assure you the company understands the health insurance

crisis. Why just yesterday CEO Wink Finklemeyer III expressed great dismay that massage therapy, for instance, is no longer covered under the My-Granddaddy-Founded-This-
Here-Company Plan. He has had to pay from his own pockets for the services of Trixie's Magic-Handed Geishas ever since that traffic accident in which he was thrown from the limousine's hot tub.

Well, as you can see, under the traditional plan, you'll still be able to choose any doctor and pay just 20 percent for any medical services with no deductible. All you have to do to get the traditional plan is pay this monthly amount here, which as you see you couldn't afford even if you were Mr. Finklemeyer's illegitimate child. Oops, sorry Jim. Didn't know you were in here.

Under the green plan, there is a mere $20 co-pay once you meet the $40,000 deductible. Granted, some medical conditions aren't covered — such as heart attacks, diseases, accidents, infections or anything that causes coughing, rashes, fever, sneezing, or sickness in general. However, on a positive note, you can see there's no longer a deductible or co-pay if you're hit in the head by a Death Comet.

Would it kill you people to show a little appreciation?! It's not like we have to provide Death Comet coverage!

Anyway, moving on. You'll notice the chartreuse plan is much cheaper, but any services must be provided within network, meaning either Dr. Ralph Fingersticker or Jim Bob's Family Doctorin' and Transmission Service.

Yes, Judy? Ah, that's a good question. Did everyone in the back hear that? Judy asked if we knew that Dr. Fingersticker died in 1935. The answer is yes, but he's the only doctor in town who's charges are "reasonable and customary."

By the way, the vision plan has not changed. The basic yearly exam ("How many fingers am I holding up?") is still absolutely free.

Thanks for coming. And if there are any supervisors in here today, please sign up on your way out for next week's seminar — "Motivating Your Peons More Efficiently."

Peaches & Peanuts

When the girl behind the counter at McDonald's yelled "Peanut!" last weekend and four people in the restaurant turned their heads, it should have seemed strange. But it didn't.

We had seen strange. We had seen strange on the MARTA train the night before. We heard strange at our hotel. And, this is Georgia, where Peanut's as common a name as Michael and Mary are elsewhere.

The guys and I have been meeting at the Georgia Dome for the high school football semifinals for about a decade now. We had a few weird experiences in the mid-1990s, but the last few years had been fairly noneventful. We made up for it this time.

I had two double beds at my hotel, so I offered my friend David a place to spend the night. To get back to the hotel, we'd have to take MARTA, which I assured him was perfectly safe.

As we waited at the Five Points station, a man was stumbling around and hollering "WOO!" at the top of his lungs. Somehow I knew this drug-impaired man would share our car. And he did.

What I didn't know was that David would strike up a conversation with Mr. Looney while we headed south toward College Park. David even helped the Mr. Looney understand how to use his own cellphone, so Mr. Looney could call folks and ask "Where you at?" at least 25 times. He kept trying to get someone to pick him up from a train station, but apparently none of his friends knew where any MARTA station was. If I had been Mr. Looney's friend, I wouldn't have known where a MARTA station was, either.

We desperately tried to keep from laughing, mainly because I didn't want to disturb Mr. Angry who had decided to sit next to me. But we couldn't hold it in when Mr. Looney stood up, only to be sent flying down to the floor when the train made a sudden stop. Mr. Looney's response? "WOO!"

It was just one of those nights. It was one of those full-moon nights, in fact, which I only noticed when we walked out of the station. "That explains it," I said as we hopped into the truck for the short ride to the hotel.

Mr. Looney wasn't the only one howling at the moon that night.

Peaches, and her many friends, spent all night long howling and screaming and cussing and slamming doors. At 3 a.m., I got out of bed and went looking for Peaches and her friends. I didn't know them, but I hated them.

I never found them, but when I figured out around 7 a.m. that Peaches was in the room next door, I began calling Peaches — and hanging up. Many times. I took the "do not disturb" sign off her door and threw it down the hall.

Even after we checked out, I called back often and asked Peaches if she was getting enough rest and if she had a good time. Problem is, she actually held up her end of the conversation, only occasionally asking me, "Who is this?" I wanted her to cuss and holler about wanting some rest.

David called her, too, and asked, "Remember me from last night?"

"Yeah," she said, throwing him off. He's been known to howl at the moon himself on occasion, but I don't think he was looney enough to howl with Peaches.

Then again, when the girl yelled "Peanut!" he did spin around awfully quick.

Honkin' big deal

As we pulled away from my in-laws' house in little ol' Preston, Ga., last week, my wife honked the horn. I thought nothing of it, but it threw my 4-year-old for a loop.

"Mama, why you honkin' at Granny and Granddaddy?" he asked. It was one of the many moments I've looked at my son and thought this boy has been in the city way too long.

We explained that it was just a friendly goodbye honk, but it didn't really register with him. He just sort of shrugged and made another note for his future therapist.

Honking your vehicle's horn seems like such a simple thing, but a honk in Columbus or Atlanta is completely different from a honk in Preston or Possum Holler.

Where I'm from, when you hear a horn blow, your first instinct is to spin your head around and wave because it's obviously somebody you know saying "Howdy!"

In the city, your first instinct also may be to wave — but only with a single finger. Whoever's honking is not just saying "Howdy!" They're saying, "Howdy, moron! The light's been green for two seconds now!"

There have been a few times in Columbus when I've gotten a friendly honk. But folks are a lot slower to react to those in the city. You know how it goes:

HONK! Ok, chill, dude. I can't make these 37 cars in front of me go any faster. HONK! HONK! I'm not going to give you the satisfaction of being acknowledged. HONK! HONK! HONK! All right! That's it! Oh, hi Christina. Back at ya! HONK!

There weren't many non-howdy honks back home, but there were a few. There was the "hey, cow, get out of the road" honk; the "my brakes went out again" honk; and, of course, there was the "hey, dude, bring the ferry over here so I can cross the Flint River" honk.

My first car, a '78 Celica, had a horn that worked only when you turned the wheel all the way to the left. So I couldn't even honk to tell a cow to get out of the road. The best I could do was drive in a circle around it and annoy it. And when you drive a little bitty '78 Celica, annoying a cow is not a good idea.

And annoying is exactly what those little cars' horns were. They didn't honk. They beeped. Fortunately, car makers have moved away from that in recent years because a beep just isn't very effective at conveying to the other driver your opinion that he or she is a complete idiot.

With a stupid AM radio and a nonfunctioning air-conditioner, the Celica's horn wasn't worth fixing — unless I could have gotten some really cool horn like Bo and Luke Duke had on the General Lee. But I couldn't afford a cool horn like that. I couldn't even afford horn like Fred Flintstone had — a bird with a string tied to his tailfeather.

In the nearly eight years I've lived and worked in Columbus, I've done my fair share of honking. You know who you are — you with the cell phone glued to your head, you pulling out of you parking space before looking back and you sitting in the middle of a major intersection after running a red light to join a line of cars that's not moving. HONK!

But I'm definitely more honkee than honker. If you don't believe me, you should see me dance.

What's Chris watching?

Twenty years ago, I had a tiny black-and-white television and 13 channels. I'd stay up into the wee hours of the morning watching shows like "Rat Patrol" or those late Braves games from the West Coast on TBS.

I wasn't picky then. Now, I have digital cable with more than 100 channels, not even counting the music channels. Now, I'm picky. Bruce Springsteen once sang of this problem in his song "57 channels (and nothing's on)." I know how he feels. Let's take a quick spin through my channels and see if anything's on.

Click. Click. Click. Ah, the weather. This music rocks! OK, local forecast's over. Let's see who the weatherperson is. Geez, is this lady constantly pregnant? Where's Kristina Abernathy when you need her?

Click. Click. Oh, great! Reality TV. Beautiful women so desperate for a relationship they'll let a man take them and others for test drives. Click. The pompous, greedy guy with bad hair show. Click. And, of course, my 4-year-old's favorite show, "Fear Factory." He likes to watch the eating segments and tell us how he thinks he's going to throw up — but, "don't change the channel!"

Too late, boy! Click. The news — or rather what it's become today, the things you want to hear network. Click. Oh, that's much better, the things I want to hear network. If only everybody would watch my network all the time, folks wouldn't be so narrow-minded.

Click. OK, can't go wrong with sports. Poker?! These aren't athletes! These are fat guys smoking cigars! Click. Let's try the travel network. Poker again?! Click. Well, at least I know what to expect on the religious channels. What's this? "The Rev. Ike's Poker Challenge"? Good grief!

Click. Well, here's an actual sport. I didn't know the Falcons were playing a 2 a.m. game today. Wait a minute! This is the 1978 playoff loss to the Cowboys. Or is it the 1980 playoff loss to the Cowboys? Why don't they just call this the Salt In The Wound Channel?

Click. The horsepower channel. Vehicles going fast in circles. Vehicles going fast straight. Vehicles making noise and crushing other vehicles. If my car knowledge reached beyond knowing where to put the gas in, maybe I'd care.

Click. Click. Spanish television. I don't know what they're saying, but these folks on this soap opera are seriously upset. No, wait, they're just ordering pizza. I'll give them this: These ladies ain't ugly. A little intense, yes, but definitely not ugly.

Click. Movie channels. I love a great movie, but is "Smokey and the Bandit 2" really a classic? Part one, sure, but this stinks. Click. A movie I've seen 20 times. Click. Ah, the excuse to show people naked movie channel. Now, this is really disgusting. That girl and that girl and that midget and that donkey ought to be ashamed of themselves. I'm too disgusted to even change the channel.

"What are you watching?"

"Oh, hi honey." Click! Click! Click! Click! Click! Click! Click! "Um, 'The Rev. Ike's Poker Challenge'."

"I didn't know you liked cards."

"Me, either. I mean, uh, yeah boy!"

On hair and hickies

I have had the same hairstyle — if you can really call this a "style" — since about 1985. That's when I ditched the bowl-style haircut started by my mom and visited a stylist.

My "stylist" back home was Miss Susan. Miss Susan was the sweetest lady in the world, but it took her about a half-hour just to get to me and another half-hour to actually cut my hair because Miss Susan could talk. Unfortunately, she couldn't talk and cut hair at the same time, which is a good thing because she had a tendency to kind of flail her hands around while she related the latest gossip — or as she called it, "news".

But I managed to deal with the painfully slow haircut process back then because everything back home was a little slower than elsewhere — except for Troy's Snack Shack, which could whip out a 25-cent hamburger in 25 seconds. Besides, Miss Susan always did a pretty good job — except for that one subpar effort that came on the heels of her finding hickies on her daughter after a party at my house. You live and you learn — and your hair grows out.

And my hair grows out fast. But now that I live in the bustling metropolis of Columbus, I'm citified and don't have time for gossiping hair-cutters. That's why I go to those strip-mall, discount, coupon-offering hair-cutting places these days. I'm in and out in a few minutes, and if their daughters have hickies on their necks, it's not my problem.

But I must admit that I'm getting a little tired of this hairstyle after 20 years. Granted, there was a brief flirtation with a mullet in the 1980s, but my hair would curl up in back and leave me looking less like a cool rocker and a lot more like Gidget. And a couple of years ago I had it shaved pretty close because I was too lazy to brush it. But, for the most part, I have this same lame haircut longer than I've had a driver's license.

So, recently, I decided that I would grow it out, maybe something Beatle-esque or even Fabio-ish. I plopped down in the chair with my coupon in hand and said, "Don't shave it. Just trim it a little with the scissors." Of that request, all the stylist heard were two words: "shave it." Zip! One swoosh and no mop top for me.

I just shrugged it off. When you're 34 and still have all your hair, you don't dare complain about the way it's cut. You're just happy it's there. But you don't want to shave it all off, either, because it might stay that way — forever.

I don't mind having extremely short hair. It's more aerodynamic, dries faster and doesn't really need brushing. But short hair has its drawbacks, too: It's put a crimp in my plans to become a soap opera star or television news anchor.

I wonder if Miss Susan would have listened when I issued a plea for a new style. Probably not because it would have taken quite a while to relay all the news I've missed in the last 15 years or so since she last cut my hair.

Then again, there hasn't been too much news from back home in the last 15 years — although I hear Troy's went up to 35 cents on the burgers.

When spiders get loose

Central High School senior Victor Cross is the state of Alabama's high school nominee for the national Prudential Spirit of the Community Awards for his study of the effects of alcohol on spiders' web-making ability.

Of course, what began as a science fair project wasn't merely for the benefit of the spider community. By showing how alcohol impairs a spider's ability to spin a good web, Victor hoped someone, even if it were just one person, would get the message about how alcohol impairs a person's ability to drive a car. The differences between the soberly made webs and the drunken spider's webs are striking.

It's a unique look at a serious issue. Victor's the kind of kid who always whipped my butt at the science fair — probably because I always started my science fair projects about 7:45 a.m. the day they were due. When the judges came by my booth (where my project was to prove that it was scientifically impossible to guess which number I was thinking of between 1 and 10) they were rather unimpressed. "Guess what grade I'm thinking of between E and G," my teacher would say.

It wasn't my fault. Science wasn't my best subject. Nor were math, history and literature. I was OK in English, and I rocked in typing. Maybe it's because all my science classes were in the morning half of school and they required actual thinking — something I still don't allow myself to do until at least noon.

I showed plenty of interest in science after school. While most kids were glued to their Ataris in front of the living room TV as soon as school let out, I was outdoors conducting various scientific experiments. You may have read my well-known article in the March 1983 edition of South Georgia Science Journal titled: "Cherry Bombs and Frogs — the Art of High-Speed Dissection."

So, it's not that I have no interest in science. Why, just the other night I lay down on a sleeping bag out in the country, looked up into the universe and wondered: What the heck are all those shiny thingies up there and how come there are none of those twinkly doo-dads in Columbus skies?

And Victor's project just got me more curious about the effects of alcohol on spiders, so I took his idea a step further as I rounded up dozens of spiders by promising to buy them drinks at a downtown club. The effects of alcohol on the spiders' behavior was astounding:

The brown recluse came out of its shell and even sang "Copacabana" during karaoke. The granddaddy long legs told us war stories. The wolf spider wouldn't stop drinking and eventually went home with some ugly female spider with just seven legs. And the black widow kept pinching me in the behind, which I thought was cute until I got home and realized my wallet was gone.

The effect of alcohol on the tarantula was hardest to gauge, so I let him sit in my lap and steer my truck as I drove toward home. However, I realized that he, too, was drunk when he whipped us into the parking lot of a Krystal at 2 a.m.

Chinese make a mean Jeep

My niece, Bailey, recently turned 5, and, to celebrate, my 5-year-old son turned her birthday party into a scene from "The Dukes of Hazzard." Or was it "Smokey and the Bandit?"

The foundation for this thrilling party goes back a few months ago when I helped a jolly ol' elf put together one of those little motorized Jeeps. Like everything else I tried to put together in the month of December, this Jeep was made in China, home of America's economic recovery.

The instructions for the Jeep apparently were written by Chinese people, too, and their English skills fell somewhere between Tarzan and Ozzy Osbourne. They didn't have mere subject-verb agreement problems — their subjects and verbs were in an all-out war.

But there was one thing all-American about the folks who half-assembled this Jeep in China — they must love NASCAR because this Jeep's got more power under the hood than Dale Jr.'s No. 8 car and probably would win more races this year.

I think a 5-year-old is too young for one of these motorized toys. Actually, I don't think they're good for any kids. Call me old school, but I still think a kid should have to pedal their vehicles. But Bailey's not much for physical activity, and she has learned to drive the rocket-powered Chinese Jeep quite well. She keeps a wary eye on other traffic (such as dogs and cats), can carefully steer around fixed objects and knows when to take her foot off the gas and put it on the brakes. In essence, she can do what most Columbus and Phenix City drivers can't.

Saylor, on the other hand, has lived in Columbus all his five years, and it shows in his driving ability. We were all sitting around chatting in my Mom's back yard while Bailey was taking Saylor on a tour of the grounds. I trusted Bailey, who even made sure Saylor was wearing his seat belt. But at some point during the ride, Bailey decided to let Saylor have a turn at the wheel.

Because Saylor hasn't grasped such concepts as steering, this may not have been the wisest decision of Bailey's young life. But it's one she won't make again.

When I first noticed Saylor driving the Chinese Jeep, he had a huge smile on his face. For a moment, I thought maybe I shouldn't be so old school and should give him a chance to speed around our back yard in his own rocket-powered Chinese Jeep. Then I thought, maybe he should steer around that massive charcoal grill. Then I thought, gee I hope that falling grill is not going to catch the back deck on fire. Then I thought, surely after knocking over that grill he'll let off the gas pedal before he hits that stump. THUD! OK, maybe not.

I ran to him, expecting to pull him from the stalled Chinese rocket-powered Jeep and wipe his little tears away and calm him down. He wasn't crying, but he did need calming down because he couldn't stop laughing. After I pulled the Jeep away from the stump, he took off again and nearly decapitated himself and Bailey on a trampoline before I could yank my little Bo Duke from the driver's seat.

I guess the boy's ready for Columbus traffic now. All he needs is a cell phone.

Hangin' at the swamp

I don't like being the center of attention. Fortunately, being the most average white man in America, rarely am I even noticed.

However, I got plenty of attention last weekend as we began our spring break with a trip to Wild Adventures, just outside of Valdosta, Ga., where I spent my first couple of years in the newspaper business.

The town sure has changed since the last time I visited — a little over five years ago, when I went down to help a cousin add a room onto his house and then hang out for a barbecue at his cabin on a gator-filled lake. I told Saylor about my last trip just after I had given him a good laugh on a ride called "The Swamp Thing" at Wild Adventures.

"You were still in Mama's belly then," I told him.

"Did she eat me?" he asked.

"No, but if we run out of cash buying $2.75 Diet Cokes, we may have to eat you on the way home."

Since he figured he'd been eaten by my wife five years ago, perhaps I was wrong to put that image in his head and given him one more thing to talk to his therapist about 20 years from now. But, after all, the kid made a point of laughing at me just minutes earlier.

He's about 46 inches tall, which means he's about 2 inches too short to ride most coasters. But he had to be only 45 inches to ride The Swamp Thing even though it was bigger and faster than one we had gotten kicked off of earlier because he was an inch too short. It was also an inverted roller coaster, meaning you dangle in a seat and ride under the tracks.

This would scare most 5-year-olds, but Saylor has lived with me long enough that nothing scares him anymore. And the ride lasted way less than a minute. But when it was over, the fun was just beginning.

Saylor was riding alongside my wife in the car behind me and a 10-year-old girl who was more scared of me than the alligators underneath the coaster. And she would grow more scared because our lock-down bars would not unlock when the ride stopped. Fortunately for the girl, my wife found a way to get her bars up. My wife then tried in vain to free me, for six or seven seconds before giving up and leaving me dangling there.

"Where are we going?" Saylor asked her as they walked down the exit ramp to get a better look at my predicament.

"We're going over here so we can laugh at Daddy," she explained.

And they did.

Meanwhile, the dozens of people stuck in line for The Swamp Thing weren't so happy that this 30-something kid helpless kicking

his feet back and forth was delaying the ride. I even got some help-
ful advice from a few 8- to 10-year-olds, such as, "Hey, mister, just
push it down, then push it up. Geez!"

I got tired of waiting for the maintenance folks to free me, so I
finally Incredible Hulked my way out of the contraption, probably
doing several million dollars worth of damage in the process because I noticed no one riding in that car the rest of the day.

I guess I should have stuck to the lesson I'd learned many years
ago while skinny dipping in Town Creek back home: Never leave
anything dangling around a Swamp Thing.

Leave my undies be

Many months ago, I mentioned in this space that I like for my
underwear to match what I'm wearing on the outside. To this day,
I still hear, "Dude, I so did not need to know that." And you don't
even want to know what kind of comments I get when I wear a
brown shirt.

But you'll be relieved to know that I'm no longer matching my
underwear to my shirts and ascots. It's not that I've become less
fashion conscious — which many folks I know would claim is
impossible. The problem is my underwear are disappearing at an
alarming rate.

I'd put a few pair of underwear in the washer, and only a couple
would emerge from the dryer. Some days, I've grabbed the first
thing that looked like my underwear only to realize they belonged
to my 5-year-old son. You'd think the Scooby-Doo all over them
would have tipped me off — especially since I'm more of a Spider-
Man undies kind of guy.

I pondered the mystery of the vanishing underwear (which I think
was Hardy Boys book No. 58). Could it be some overzealous female fan of my newspaper column raiding my underwear drawer? I
asked my wife if this were possible, and I'll be sure to report on her
response just as soon as she stops laughing.

I called my wife at work the other day to ask if she knew where
any of my underwear might be.

"Oh, I know where some are right now," she said.

"What about my socks?" I asked.

"Yeah, I know where a pair of those are right now, too."

I may be no Frank Hardy, but I began to slowly piece together the mystery of the vanishing underwear.

I don't remember agreeing to any of this while taking our vows 13 years ago. I don't think that "to have and to hold" means that she gets to have and hold my underwear. Who knew I needed a prenuptial agreement to protect my Fruit of the Looms?

An old friend told me before I got married: "Don't forget, Chris, once you get hitched, what's hers is hers and what's yours is hers." I figured that rule applied to movie popcorn, towels and toothpaste, but not underwear. Of course, when the old friend told me this, he was wearing a T-shirt that read: "Be alert — the world needs more lerts."

This is one of those many marriage things that doesn't go both ways. I don't go looking through her drawers and 12 acres of closet space when I run out of underwear. Sure, I'll put on her high heels and dance to disco music at 2 a.m. a couple nights a week, but no way am I wearing women's underwear.

I don't even know how to operate half of the stuff women wear. I couldn't open a bra clasp with an instruction manual. I used to carry a chain and combination on my bicycle, but now I just keep a bra on the handlebar in case I ever need to protect my bike from thieves. Maybe that's why people look at me funny on the Riverwalk. Oh, heck, that could be any number of reasons.

Well, at least now I know what Jimmy Buffett was singing about in "Pencil-thin Mustache:"

Now, I'm getting old, don't wear underwear,

I don't go to church, and I don't cut my hair.

He was coming off a divorce about that time. I bet his first wife still had all his underwear.

5-year-old logic

When you have a 5-year-old boy, you never know what's going to come out of his mouth. When he hears a dirty word in a popular song or even a kid's movie, I have to hope it doesn't stick in his brain — right between some bad knock-knock joke (Tom Sawyer who? Tom Sawyer underpants.) and the location of that knight he allegedly swiped from my chess set.

Every now and then, he starts a sentence that freezes you in fear. His latest pet phrase is "What the . . .?" He doesn't finish it, just says "what the." He picked it up from "The Incredibles," a great movie for kids and adults in which the main character starts but doesn't finish that question either. Of course, the first few times he started to say this, we had no idea what was coming or where it came from.

And kids usually save the most embarrassing phrases they've picked up for places such as the line at the grocery store. That's when they'll finish "what the . . ." and everyone turns and glares at you for being the worst parent ever — the kind of thing we also would do before we had kids, the same way we thought we'd never be chasing our children through clothing racks or pulling them out from under tables in restaurants.

For those of you who don't have kids, it's gonna happen to you someday. For those of you who say your children don't do that, you're lying. And for those of you whose children really don't do that, well, I don't like you anymore.

Fortunately, my son, Saylor, no longer hides in clothing racks and limits his table ducking to only a couple of restaurants whose service is too slow for his limited patience. But we still have to watch his mouth.

The problem is that a 5-year-old has a limited understanding of what is an appropriate comment in public. We were sitting in a barbecue restaurant the other day and a rather large man walked by our table.

"Mama, Daddy, look," he said. "That man's got a big belly!" Of course, he says this while pointing at the man with his middle finger, which he still prefers to his index finger — not the best way to identify a large man you just insulted.

He doesn't know it's wrong to point out folks' physical flaws. For his sake, I hope he learns it before he gets married and gets the dreaded "Does this make me look fat?" question. If he doesn't learn it by then, I'll make sure our wedding gift to him is a sofa bed.

But we don't just listen to the boy out of fear that we'll have to cover his mouth before he can finish "what the. . . " We listen because we love him and because we just might learn something.

We were sitting at a restaurant (no, we never cook, though we do occasionally microwave things) and were admonishing Saylor for messing with a sore on his face. We decided to go straight for the heart, warning him that his girlfriends Kayla and Pricilla wouldn't think he was cute anymore.

"Kayla and Pricilla love me the way I look," he said matter-of-factly. "And I love me the way I look, too."

Maybe we should talk less and listen more. Somewhere between "Tom Sawyer underpants" and "what the . . ." could be something worth hearing.

Memories roll from the rubble

When I go back to my hometown, I expect to see a few more symbols of my younger days fading away.

Oh sure, some things never change. I still want a nap after getting a bellyful at the Mennonite restaurant; Troyburgers are still cheap and fast; the star of our high school girls tennis team 20 years ago still looks like a teenager; and T-Bone still hangs out at the corner store chewing on a piece of grass and talking about doing some work. I'm not sure T-Bone actually works, but he can talk about work as well as anyone.

And even the things that are supposed to change — such as the local newspaper in the box outside the corner store — don't seem to change much. The big headline my last trip home was "Gator spotted near Booger Bottom." Same ol' Booger Bottom. Probably same ol' gator.

But seeing things and people fading away can put a lump in my throat.

The historic house I once called home now has a window busted out, probably by its ghosts to keep the air flowing through. The tennis court on which I must have spent a thousand afternoons has lawn tractors parked on it. Most of the people I loved and even the people who annoyed me have long since fled and faded away. They now live from coast to coast — that's right, from Georgia's west coast on the Hooch all the way back to the Atlantic Ocean.

But one image jarred me on this last trip home even more than the collapsing homestead. The skating rink, at which I learned to skate counter-clockwise and to French kiss clockwise, is virtually gone. What had been born as a textile mill must have died via atomic bomb. It's now little more than rubble.

But in its heyday (the mid-'80s), it was a happening place to be for a kid not yet old enough to drive but too old to stay at home and watch "Friday Night Videos" or "Night Tracks" on Ted's Superstation.

It wasn't nearly as nice as the skating rinks around here. There was no smooth concrete, only the sanded wooden floor that my Dad had put down. When you got going fast, you sounded like a train speeding down the tracks toward that pulp mill south of town. And the video games weren't even as nice as you can get on a cell phone these days.

But I didn't go for the roller skating or the video games or the pool table. I went for the girls. For about three years, couples' skates and stolen kisses behind the Ms. Pac-Man machine constituted my love life.

And you definitely had to steal kisses because the folks who ran the place would put the smackdown on anyone caught tongue wrestling. It's probably because they had a beautiful daughter, and they got paranoid if she disappeared from their sight for more than eight seconds. Do you know how hard it is to steal a kiss in eight seconds, even with Ms. Pac-Man's help? I finally gave up on their daughter and instead fell for their niece. I have no idea why they didn't like me.

I'm sure some fella finally corralled their daughter for a lifelong couples' skate. I hope she was worth the smackdown he must have gotten.

Relax behind the wheel

I can't do it much these days with gas prices at such astronomical levels (up to about five Troyburgers a gallon last time I checked), but I sure enjoy getting out on the open road, even an interstate, and just driving to clear my mind.

Ah, yes, here I am, cruising south down I-185. I'm going right at the speed limit. I'm in no hurry. It doesn't get much more relaxing than this, especially with Norah Jones serenading me from the CD player. Yep, nothing could bother me now.

"HEY LADY, PICK A LANE! DO YOU NEED ALL THREE?"

No deadline pressures out here on the road. No phone ringing. No computer telling me an unexpected error has occurred. Unexpected, my rear end. I expect my computer to crash at least once a day. But nothing unexpected out here on the interstate, or even here as I exit on Manchester Expressway or Mr. Big Volume Way or whatever it's called now and come up on Armour Road.

"GEE WHIZ, PEOPLE, CAN I PLEASE GO NOW? SIX PEO-PLE RUNNING A RED LIGHT? Y'ALL KNOW RED MEANS ONLY FOUR MORE CARS HERE IN COLUMBUS! ARE YOU AN OUT-OF-TOWN SHERIFF?"

This air-conditioner feels so soothing on my face as I savor the soft tones of Miss Jones, but I think I'll roll the window down and let a little fresh air in. That should make this ride even more relax-ing.

"DADGUM! WHAT THE HECK IS THAT RACKET? MUST BE P. DOODY OR NILLY OR KOOL MOE COOL J CUBE T! HEY, BUDDY, I'VE GOT ABOUT 20 JIMMY BUFFETT CDs HERE IF YOU WANT SOME REAL MUSIC!"

Maybe it's the scenery that makes this drive so relaxing. Few cit-ies our size spend more money on aesthetics as we do. Downtown's really coming along. It'll be nice when they get through with it, even though all the money barons and power brokers have hogged the riverfront. Maybe Phenix City will wind up with a more quaint, more fun riverfront like Savannah.

"HEY, BUDDY! WHY ARE YOU THROWING YOUR CIGA-RETTE BUTT ON MY STREET? IT'S YOUR TRASH — DEAL WITH IT!"

As much as I enjoy just being alone in my SUV and cruising around, I also enjoy people watching. You've got all sorts of folks downtown, though seeing all these businessmen in uncomfortable ties and businesswomen in uncomfortable shoes makes me ap-preciate being in a tank top and sandals. Just makes me even more relaxed.

"LADY, COULD YOU JAYWALK ANY SLOWER? THE WORLD DOESN'T REVOLVE AROUND YOU, YOU KNOW!"

This peaceful ride has made me about as relaxed as I can be without falling asleep. So I better head home and take a little nap before I run over somebody.

"DUDE! IT'S A TWO-WAY STOP, NOT A FOUR-WAY! I'VE GOT THE RIGHT OF WAY NO MATTER HOW TIRED YOU ARE OF WAITING!"

So, if you need to relax, forget meditation or a glass of wine. Instead, try a little cruising. And you'll be calm, cool and collected like me.

"HEY, MORON! THE BLINKER'S NOT THERE FOR DECORATION! USE IT!"

Peace out.

Fear and loathing on U.S. 82

My latest mini-vacation was supposed to be a complete non-adventure — four days and three nights of complete relaxation on St. Simons Island. However, I had to face two of my greatest fears en route to my favorite spot in Georgia.

I don't enjoy the long drive from here to St. Simons, and I wish U.S. 82 bypassed the cities of Sylvester and Tifton. And Tifton to Brunswick is one brutally flat, boring stretch of road where there are grocery stores in singlewide trailers, where some churches still handle snakes and where it's not unheard of for a sheriff to go to jail for running a cockfighting ring.

So, the only thing that beats speeding through this area as fast as possible is breaking up the drive. We did this just outside of Waycross at the Okie Dokie Swamp, which is what my 5-year-old calls one of Georgia's natural wonders. Here, I'd face fear No. 1.

No, it's not gators. I saw plenty of those back home on the Flint River. There's very little difference between an alligator and a fallen tree limb, though I have been charged at by one mama gator who didn't like me taking a close look at her babies. Snakes, however, give me a severe case of the heebie-jeebies.

I was taking my son to the bathroom when I was frozen in my tracks by a rather large black snake lying right at the entrance to the men's room. I could tell by its head that it was nonpoisonous. I don't care. That doesn't make it non-creepy.

But my son is still at that stage where he thinks I'm a brave man who can fix anything and face any danger. (He's about 10 years away from the stage where kids think their parents are morons.) So I boldly stomped at the snake to drive it away while praying that I would not reveal my cowardice by wetting my pants. I survived, though I checked every stall for any of its buddies. I also relayed the experience to my wife as she emerged from the women's bathroom — as if she needed one more reason to avoid public restrooms.

About an hour after leaving the Okie Dokie Swamp, I faced fear No. 2 — the Sidney Lanier Bridge over the Brunswick River near St. Simons. Well, I'm not afraid of bridges in general, but heights bother me. And this bridge carries vehicles 203 feet above sea level so that ships can pass underneath on their way to port.

It's a beautiful bridge, though it would be a lot more beautiful if I didn't know that part of it collapsed during the early stages of its construction in 1999, injuring two workers. And my sadistic unconscious self took advantage of that fact as I got to the top of the bridge by resurrecting a tune from my childhood: London Bridge is falling down, falling down, falling down. This is the same unconscious self that likes to toss a snake into my dreams every now and then.

I don't exactly fear heights, but I do fear falling from them, especially if I'm falling onto those snakes swimming in the Brunswick River.

No wonder I needed three nights on the island and a few frozen drinks to relax. Most of all, I just needed to stick my feet in the sand. Ah, sea level. You can't beat it with a stick.

A pageant worth watchin'

I don't remember the last time I watched the Miss America Pageant or Miss USA or Miss Universe or even the Forestry Queen and Pine Princess pageant back home. And it's not just because I'm scared I'll get smacked in the back of my head by my wife (though I am).

Maybe it's because the women look kind of the same to me — classy and beautiful, but still the same. I got a little bored with it all. But that could change in January when the pageant moves to CMT, Country Music Television.

The pageant was dropped by ABC because it wasn't exactly a ratings bonanza. It's unlikely the pageant will even stay in Atlantic City. But I think this is a great opportunity to infuse some life into the event — and with it on CMT, a little country attitude and Southern spunk.

First, we must pick an appropriate location. Atlantic City certainly doesn't fit with a country Miss America. It needs to be somewhere on the Redneck Rivera, as my English 201 professor referred to the Florida Panhandle. He also referred to me as "the redneck." Maybe he thought I owned the place or something. Anyway, Club La Vela in Panama City would be well-equipped to host such an event. Although, closer to home, Booger Bottom Country Club wouldn't be a bad spot, either.

And the evening gown competition has got to go. I know women care about these outfits and stuff as do perhaps some fellas up North (you know, anywhere above LaGrange). But it's time we Southern boys had a say. And I think we'll be happy if the evening gowns are replaced by halter tops and Daisy Dukes. And no high heels. Only bare feet.

The talent portion is wide open. With the exception of opera, violins, mime or singing anything like Celine Dion, anything goes. And though violins aren't allowed, fiddle-playing contestants are welcome. Other possible talents include water skiin', wrasslin', cow tippin', deer skinnin', rock skippin' and mud boggin'.

The interview wouldn't focus much on contestants' aspirations for world peace or healthy children or anything like that. Questions to be posed would include: Hot enough for ya? How's your mama and them? How 'bout them Dawgs? What's your favorite Burt Reynolds movie?

I don't guess there's much need to tinker with the swimsuit competition. Although, I think it would be a little more interesting if each contestant were given $30 and told to find themselves a swimsuit at Wal-Mart that's at least one size too small.

And that whole "There She Is, Miss America" song is definitely a no-go in a country version of the Miss America pageant. I'm open to suggestions, but I'm leaning toward Mel McDaniel's "(Lord Have Mercy) Baby's Got Her Blue Jeans On." But if the winner gets caught bra paddin', "Your Cheatin' Heart" is an option.

On my short list to host and/or judge are George Lindsey, Sonny Shroyer, Dolly Parton and Charlie Daniels. However, if none of these folks are available, I'll gladly volunteer. Oww! Sorry, somebody just smacked me in back of the head.

Panama City Beach grows up

Panama City Beach is obviously working to shed its image as a party town whose economy once revolved around drunken, sex-crazed teenagers and college students. High-rise condos are going up and dance clubs are going down.

Why? Because those drunken, sex-crazed teenagers and college students are now tired thirtysomethings with headaches. And the last thing we, um, I mean they want to do at the beach is to hang around a bunch of folks acting the way they did in the '80s and early '90s.

I'm not saying whether this transformation is good or bad, but I've got to say it works for me. Now, to help you make your decision, I've compiled this handy-dandy guide to the new Panama City Beach. Here's what's in and what's out:

Out: Hotel names such as Dead Squid Inn and Seaweed Motel.

In: Condo names such as the Utopian Sunrise Towers and Gargantuan Albatross.

Out: Emergency call — "Hey, 911, my friend Bubba's all liquored up and says he's gonna jump into the pool from the 11th floor!"

In: Emergency call — "Is this the locksmith? Yes, my fool husband's out there trying to get in the car with a coat hanger!"

Out: $3.99 all-you-can-eat stale pizza.

In: $26.99 all-you-can-eat various things that crawl on the dirty ocean floor.

Out: Beautiful babes strolling the beach in hot pink bikinis.

In: Cute little girls jumping into the shallow end of the pool in their SpongeBob SquarePants swimsuits and floaties.

Out: Making a beer run.

In: Making a Noxzema run.

Out: Souvenir orange vests from working a day with the sheriff's department.

In: Souvenir t-shirts that read, "My Grandma went to Panama City and all I got was this lousy t-shirt."

Out: "The Redneck Riviera"

In: "Coney Island South"

Out: Kissing people you don't know because it's fun.

In: Kissing people you don't know because you forgot where you put your glasses.

Out: Long-legged women wearing too-short shorts.

In: Hairy-legged men wearing too-high socks.

Out: "The sun's going down — it's time to party!"

In: "The sun's going down — it's time for bed."

Out: Funneling beer.

In: Funneling Pepto Bismol.

Out: Driving 1 mph on the strip.

In: Driving 10 mph on the strip with your blinker on the whole way.

Out: Dropping lines at Club La Vela.

In: Dropping lines in St. Andrews Bay.

Out: Wet t-shirt contests.

In: Wet t-shirts drying on the balcony.

Out: Go-Kart racing.

In: Golf cart racing.

Out: Makin' whoopee behind the sea oats.

In: Makin' breakfast with the Quaker Oats.

Out: America's most beautiful beaches.

In: The world's most beautiful beaches.

And, after all, what more do you really need?

'Hello, this is Billie'

When I hear the terms "steel magnolia" or "Southern belle," there are plenty of Southern ladies, real and fictional, who come to mind.

But the first one who comes to mind is Billie Slaton.

Every small town in the Deep South has its own Mrs. Billie. You know how she spoke. You remember her well-kept house and manicured garden. You remember her pew in church or where she sat in the choir.

There was no shortage of steel magnolias in my little hometown of Oglethorpe, Ga., but Mrs. Billie reigned above them all. The only magnolia that stood taller was the gargantuan magnolia that shaded our entire backyard and a couple of neighbors' yards.

I never saw Mrs. Billie when her makeup and hair wasn't perfect — and I'd be surprised if anyone outside the Slatons' Victorian house ever did.

Speaking of that Victorian house, it was one of those where you probably weren't supposed to touch anything, though she never told me not to. I guess that was just understood. Heck, even their daughter's playhouse out back was perfectly kept. I decided I'd better not touch anything in that playhouse, either.

There was one time, though, that Mrs. Billie took a 9-year-old boy into her home even though he was covered in blood after running into a speed limit sign while riding his bicycle in front of her house. She took care of him until his folks could run him down to the doctor's office to get his head stitched up.

I've still got the scar on my forehead. I swear I never saw that speed limit sign coming.

More than anything, though, Mrs. Billie was remembered for having the sweetest Southern voice ever. It was so sweet that if you talked to her for more than five minutes, you'd need an insulin shot.

But people did so love to hear her slow, Southern drawl. OK, not so much people as men. I'd say her voice was sultry, but I'm afraid I'd go to hell for saying such filth about a true Southern lady. But I do know that men would call up the local Farm Bureau office just to hear her answer the phone, "Hello, this is Billie." The 10 seconds it took her to speak those four words were plenty to satisfy the men who would call and sometimes hang up.

I can relate somewhat because there was once a woman at the Associated Press office in Atlanta who took high school football score reports on Friday nights named Karen who had a voice nearly as sweet as Mrs. Billie's. It might have been unprofessional, but when

I was the sports editor in Americus I was sure to call in my five schools' scores one at a time.

And I suspect that voice is the reason Mrs. Billie probably had a little trouble getting into Heaven last week after she died of cancer. Oh, I'm certain she eventually got in, but I'm also certain she was delayed at the pearly gates as she had to repeat her name over and over while St. Peter pretended he couldn't find it.

"Why, St. Peter, is there some kind of problem?" Mrs. Billie likely asked.

"No, ma'am. I just wanted to hear you say 'Hello, this is Billie' one more time. You can go on in."

Quarter for your thoughts

When I get home from work, the first thing I do — after making sure there's no boogey man in the garage — is toss my keys on the kitchen counter and empty my pockets. Everything in my pockets goes into the penny basket by the refrigerator.

That means the penny basket gets hit at the end of the night with a couple of paper clips, a gum wrapper, a receipt from my favorite barbecue joint, a good bit of lint, a Tic-Tac (which is scary because I haven't bought Tic-Tacs since 1997) and, of course, coins. The coins are mostly pennies.

There's often a nickel or two, maybe a dime, sometimes even a Canadian penny. And, on good days, there's that most precious of coins — the quarter. Oh, maybe a quarter doesn't mean all that much to you, but it does to me, and not just because our economy's not quite as strong as it was in, oh, say, 1707. A quarter has always been so much more than just 25 cents.

When I was a kid, it was a game of Pac-Man, Donkey Kong or Centipede down at the Suwanee Swifty. And quarters were hard to come by in my house growing up. Thank goodness the boys next door had a paper route and kept on their kitchen table a massive stack of quarters from newspaper boxes. Anytime they headed to an arcade, they just scooped up a couple handfuls on the way out the door.

It must have been nice to grow up so rich. If I scooped up a quarter on the way out the door at my house, Dad would have called a family meeting. As a young teen, a quarter could determine who kicked off first in the daily backyard football game. As a high-schooler and college student (and I use the term "student" loosely), the ability to bounce it from a table into a shot glass could determine who would throw up in a few hours.

In Panama City, that same game of quarters could determine who wound up nekkid. And I could ring a shot glass from across the hotel room, which meant I usually stayed clothed, greatly reducing the number of people throwing up.

Through 1994, a quarter would get me the best greasy burger on the planet at Troy's Snack Shack. Then the flood came, washed away the menu board, and they raised the price to a whopping 35 cents.

When I got my first newspaper job — a part-time gig paying minimum wage — a quarter found in the floorboard of my Celica or in between the sofa cushions could make the difference in my meal. "Woohoo! I'm having cheese on my burger tonight, baby!"

When I got my first apartment, quarters became precious. Without them, I'd have been washing my clothes in the sink, which would really have ticked off the roaches who thought my sink was a water park.

Even today, I can't walk out the door without rummaging through this penny basket looking for non-copper coins. Who needs pennies anyway? They just cover up real money like quarters. There's nothing more aggravating than having to dig through $76,923.42 worth of pennies to get to — yes, at last — a quarter as I head out the door today.

Oh sweet! There's a Tic-Tac, too!

Great news from Hell

Hi! Satan here. I know you're used to Chris Johnson filling this column space with his gobbledygook every week, but I've got something to say and I've possessed his body for the next couple of minutes.

We demons and devils don't do a lot of possessions these days, but boy did we have some fun in the old days! Unfortunately, it all seemed kind of silly after that "Exorcist" movie back in the '70s. Besides, that movie scared the heaven out of some of our younger demons.

And possessions can get messy — you know, being inside a human's body and stuff. Speaking of which, if you run into Chris Johnson when this possession's over, tell him to lay off the greasy food. Man, it's yucky in here. So I'll make this short and sweet.

I just wanted you all to know that I've turned over a new leaf. As Satan, I've gotten a bad rap over the past few millenniums. I mean — dadgum — we're talking one little apple, people. Since then, I've behaved myself better than half the players in the NFL. They get suspended for a game or two and I'm down here for eternity.

Fortunately, it's not nearly as hot in hell as it used to be. Who can afford the heating bills these days? You'd think with all these Islamic terrorists streaming into hell on a daily basis that I could get some kind of break on oil prices, but nooooo. So I really don't want to hear that whole "hot as hell" comment anymore.

If you think I'm looking for a little sympathy, well, you're right. Folks, I have seriously mellowed over the eons. I'm hardly ever throwing temptation in anybody's face. I didn't even have anything to do with that whole Olsen twins countdown. Really, other than an occasional election and book burning, I hardly ever meddle in your business.

For instance, notice how Franklin Graham and some other evangelicals have called Hurricane Katrina a punishment from God. That's right — an act of God. Not a single person has said I had anything to do with that hurricane. I never mess around with the weather. Heck, I like beautiful, sunny days as much as the next demon.

I'm sure you think that I just sit around hell and torture folks like Hitler and Timothy McVeigh, but you're wrong. That's all delegated now. And it's not nearly as crowded here as you might think. Eternal damnation is soooo Old Testament. I haven't seen a homosexual here in decades. Truman Capote wandered in one day, but he was just lost. But a word of advice: I wouldn't kill anybody in God's name — he's still not too keen on that.

You know, I don't need y'all to worship me. I just want y'all to lighten up. I've changed, I tell ya. I do yoga. I've been to three Tony Robbins seminars and completed the Dale Carnegie course. I avoid red meat. I listen to a lot of Yanni and Kenny G. I don't even use aerosol deodorants. I'm not your father's devil.

And, quite frankly, I find those sports team names like the New Jersey Devils and Warner Robins High School Demons a little offensive and insensitive.

So, all I'm asking is that you give the devil his due. Thank you for your time. . . .

Whoa! That was weird!

Coins in the fountain

I've wished on a few falling stars. I've felt like a winner when I came away with the biggest part of a wishbone. And over the course of my life I've tossed a few bucks down wishing wells and into fountains. But I never took any of it too seriously. At least, I don't remember taking any of it too seriously.

I did get a serious spanking many years ago when a couple of my cousins talked me into going on a free dive in the Macon Mall fountain. Hey, why wish for money when you can just dive in and scoop it up?

But my 5-year-old son, Saylor, takes wishes seriously. We'll often give him a couple of pennies — which he thinks is real money — so that he can toss them into a fountain and make a wish. He'll hold the penny with both hands, clenching his fists as he pulls the penny toward his chin as if he were praying. He'll close his brown eyes tightly and whisper to himself before flinging the coin into the water with a great, hopeful smile.

They are usually simple, silly wishes. Simple and silly are the key adjectives in his world right now. He's wished for a dog, of course, but I prefer to bring as few pets into the house as possible. (It's for the animals' sake. I think I'm the only person who ever killed their pet rock.) He's wished that dinosaurs were alive again — but only the nice, plant-eating ones. He's wished we could live at the beach, leading me to ask for a penny from my wife so I could add a little extra wishing power on that one.

He's convinced that someday, somehow, one of those pennies will be money well spent. With his latest coin in the fountain, he's made a believer out of me, too.

In Saylor's first five years, he's known Daddy as the sleepy guy who staggers out of bed to take him to school in the morning but is not at home five nights a week. Five nights a week, he's gotten no bedtime stories, no night-night kisses and no tucking in from me. Five nights a week, I've been putting together the front page of your newspaper. He understands that Daddy works nights. Until now anyway. Now, I've landed a day job at the newspaper.

I got a sneak peak last week of what this new schedule will be like as I was granted a one-day turn on the day shift. I surprised Saylor by coming home early. We read books. We played cars. We wrestled. I tried to figure out his kindergarten homework. He explained it to me. I tucked him in. I told him a bedtime story. I kissed him night-night.

All that, and I still had time to exercise, catch up on some sports scores, write on the same old unfinished novel and have a little quiet time. I was almost like a normal person — well, about as close as I can be.

The next night, it was back to abnormal. My wife and son went to supper at a restaurant without Daddy, who was putting the front page together again. My son begged for and received a penny to toss into a fountain on the way into the restaurant. He clenched the coin, whispered to himself and hurled it into the fountain. My wife asked what he wished for.

"I wished Daddy could come home early every night," he said softly.

Sometimes simple wishes aren't so silly after all.

Speaking of kids . . .

Since the year 2000, I've asked a lot of questions I never imagined I'd ever ask. That's when I began making statements that never before seemed necessary. That's the year I became a parent and began uttering such things as:

• Believe it or not, there's a lot of food that doesn't come in the form of "nuggets."

• Oww! Why is there a T-rex in the bathtub?!

• Do not put your finger in there! (This applies to many situations: light sockets, pet stores, other humans, you name it.)

• That's enough ketchup. Really. That's plenty. Stop! Well that's just great! See what happens when you don't listen to Daddy!

• No, I don't know who's in charge of scooping up Clifford's poop.

• Now, why do they have to use that kind of filthy language in a kids movie?!

• What do you mean you didn't feel like wearing underwear to school today?

• Because you're only supposed to wear Band-Aids when you've got a boo boo. These things cost money; they're not fashion accessories.

• What does it mean he's on yellow?

• Honey, relax. It just does that sometimes when you wake up. It doesn't mean he's gonna grow up to be a pervert.

• I'd climb up in that thing and find him, but I'm scared I'd get stuck.

• Sorry, sir, but let's face it — if he says you've got a big belly, you might wanna lay off the all-you-can-eat buffets.

• Can we please eat at a restaurant that doesn't have a playground?

• Didn't I tell you to go before we left the house? (also applies to wives)

• Where did you learn that word?! Well, haven't I told you not to listen to what Mommy says when she's driving?

• The floor is not a dirty clothes hamper! (also applies to husbands)

• Use your napkin, not your sleeve. (also applies to husbands)

• Your shoes are perfectly adequate even if they don't light up when you walk.

• Yes, your goldfish is in heaven. No, snakes don't go to heaven. Ants? I dunno. Let me get back to you on that one.

• It's not "deck the halls with holly jolly." It's "deck the halls with boughs of holly." (This is a recent addition.)

• We've bought 300 pairs of little socks — how is it that not a single one in this house has a mate?!

• Get that finger out of your mouth; you don't know where it's been. Now give the finger back to whoever you got it from. That's not what I meant by "give the finger!"

• How come you won't drink water in a restaurant, but you'll drink it in the swimming pool?

• Doggone it! I've already seen this episode of "Teen Titans."

• I don't care if it is just a toy gun -- don't point it at other cars on the road. Well, OK, point it at that lady on the cell phone, but just for a second.

• You know, "Shrek" was a lot funnier the first 200 times.

• Yes, that's pretty amazing. You can flush it now.

• Of course Daddy doesn't have any underwear with Scooby-Doo on them. That would be silly. Daddy's a grown-up. Daddy's under-wear has SpongeBob on them.

CJ's Choke-n-Puke

From the crackdown on trans fats and the bans on smoking here and there, it seems the government is awfully worried about our health these days.

I guess that's a good thing, especially here in the South, where a lot of folks think recreational activity is sitting in a RV in the infield during a NASCAR race while lifting beers. (Not me, of course. I'd much rather have my workout by lifting beers at an SEC football game.)

I'm not saying the government is misguided here. Trans fats are definitely evil, being linked to coronary heart disease, diabetes, prostate cancer, athlete's foot, excessive ear hair and acrophobia.

But if we cut out all trans fats, all us fat Americans might lose too much weight, and that could throw the Earth's entire rotation out of balance. We don't need a wobbly planet. We might get demoted from the solar system like Pluto.

And what about the folks out there who want to eat or smoke themselves to death? And what about those poor souls who want to eat and smoke themselves to death? Don't they have rights, too?

Woody Allen once said: "You can live to be a hundred if you give up all the things that make you want to live to be a hundred." I understand completely.

Granted, I don't smoke, and I'm glad I no longer taste cigarette smoke in Columbus restaurants anymore. But God knows I've tried to eat myself to death over the past thirtysomething years, and there's a darn good chance I'll eventually succeed at doing just that.

It's not all my doing, of course. I grew up in and always will live in the South, where we've figured out how to fry everything from turkeys to cheesecake. And I had a pair of Southern grandmas who'd say things like, "You're only gonna eat one piece of pie? Eat the whole thing! I made it just for you!"

To which I'd respond with the health-conscious reply, "Okie dokie!"

But I'm not the only one who grew up with Southern grandmas, the kind who'd rub trans fats right on top of biscuits as they were baking. I'm not the only one who knows the joy of four double chili-cheeseburgers from Troy's Snack Shack in Montezuma, Ga.

And that's why I'm announcing my new venture today. I hope to open CJ's Choke 'N' Puke as soon as I can get financing beyond the loose change I've found in the backseat of my SUV. Here's my pitch to potential investors:

At CJ's Choke 'N' Puke, we'll never cut out trans fats. In fact, our No. 1 combo is the Triple Trans Fatburger topped with bacon, cheese, chili and a fried egg. And don't forget about the Southern-fried meatlike nuggets served with a small cup of pure trans fat for your dipping pleasure.

And feel free to light up at CJ's Choke 'N' Puke. And bring the kids. Yeah, I know you're supposed to be over 18 to enter a smoking restaurant, but we'll just say we thought they were short for their age.

We'll also sell cigarettes at CJ's Choke 'N' Puke, including the new brand CoughinUp, which guarantees lung cancer on the first smoke, so you know it's good. And every kids meal comes with a free pack of candy cigarettes.

I know, it's a great idea. But, please, don't everyone call at once.

Feelin' hot, hot, hot

In the mid-1970s, I got awfully worried about climate change after a couple of alarming articles by Time and Newsweek. I read these intently between watching episodes of "Sesame Street" and trying not to wet my pants.

Of course, the climate change paranoia during those days was about "global cooling." I hate cold weather, so "global cooling" was awfully alarming to this little kid (maybe that's why I wet my pants). Whether it meant as little as an extra month of wearing Toughskins jeans or the extreme of living in a Georgia igloo, I was 100 percent against global cooling.

So, I spent many an afternoon cranking up Dad's old trucks to spew as much carbon monoxide as I could into the air. I also set a lot of things on fire (leaves, Grandma's wigs, Garden Valley, etc.) and stressed out the family cow so it would get gas and release more methane into the atmosphere. Thirty years of hard work paid off as I managed to reverse the global cooling trend into global warming.

Unfortunately, global warming has got a lot of folks upset, especially scientists, many of whom gathered in Paris this past week to officially express great alarm about global warming. You never know what kind of crazy stuff a bunch of scientists will come up with when they get together and mix chemicals and mix drinks.

Last time a bunch of scientists assembled, they demoted Pluto as a planet --- which is ludicrous because thousands of science fair mobiles created by sixth-graders nationwide have proven that Pluto is definitely a planet . . or at least a little rubber ball.

I am sick of scientists, environmentalists, Antarcticans and the like dissing global warming. Quite frankly, I'm all for it, especially after the chilly mornings of this past week.

One of the so-called negative effects of global warming is that Antarctica and Greenland are losing ice. Big deal! The convenience store down the street from my house will give you all the ice you need for free. A 1,255-square-mile ice shelf broke off from Antarctica in 2002 and disappeared in 35 days. If I were an ice shelf, I'd leave Antarctica for warmer latitudes, too. And recent NASA

data shows that Greenland is losing 53 cubic miles of ice each year
— twice the rate it was losing in 1996. The biased data, of course,
doesn't account for the opening of Freddie's Frozen Daquiris that
opened in Nuuk in 1996.

Another so-called negative effect of global warming is the rising of the planet's oceans. Most scientists (Pluto killers) believe
the oceans will have risen anywhere from 20 to 55 inches by the
year 2100. So what? Granted, it'll be kind of aggravating to have
to don scuba gear to get down to Savannah's River Street for a
frozen drink from Wet Willie's, but I ain't gonna be here in 2100
anyway.

I want to see the ocean's rise a lot faster than that. I wanna see
FEET, not inches. The more it rises, the closer the beach is to my
house. Sweet! And that old briar patch on the family homestead
back home could become valuable beachfront property someday.

I'm not saying you've got to buy a big ol' gas guzzler, but if
you've got a dairy cow, I'd appreciate it if you'd stress it out with
some unrealistic milking goals.

Manly, manly man

Do you make "homophobic" remarks to your gay co-star on your
red-hot TV show? Do you get drunk and blame Jews for all the
world's problems? Do you hurl racial epithets at rude hecklers as
you perform in a comedy club? Having an affair with your cam-
paign manager's wife? Have you lost your congressional seat over
lurid online conversations with teenage boys?

Fear not. There's a new cure-all out there in America, and it's
called "therapy," derived from the Latin words ther, which means
"fixes," and apy, which means "dang near anything."

It works for disgraced politicians, diarrhea-mouthed stars and,
now, fallen-from-grace religious figures. Heck, I've even tried it a
few times over the years, but I've never been honest with a therapist
because then they'd know I was crazier than an earthbound astronaut who likes the feel of wet diapers.

The latest advancement in the field of therapy is the three-week
program that turned disgraced evangelical leader Ted Haggard from

a part-time homosexual to a full-time heterosexual.

"He is completely heterosexual," the Rev. Tim Ralph of Larkspur, Colo., told The Denver Post. "That is something he discovered" during three weeks of intensive counseling overseen by Ralph and three other ministers.

Now, this is not the first program to turn gay people straight or to help them "discover" their heterosexuality, which, fortunately, I was able to "discover" on my own at age 6 when I saw Jessica Lange being manhandled by a manly, manly ape in "King Kong." I know some of you may be skeptical about these programs that turn gay people straight, so here's a demonstration of how it works:

Straight officer: You're not gay, Billy.

Billy: Um, yes I am.

Straight officer: No you're not.

Billy: OK, fine, whatever you say! I'm not gay!

Straight officer: See, I told you.

Unfortunately, it wasn't that easy for Mr. Rev. Haggard, who needed three weeks and four ministers to get straight. A glance at the notes taken by the four ministers reveals glimpses of the great transformation:

Week 1: Ted admits problem. Agrees to listen to country music. Easing him into it with mildly hetero Rascal Flatts. Taught him how to crush aluminum soda can in hand. Ted still saying "excuse me" after burping, even when no women are present.

Week 2: Much progress made. Convinced Ted he's Merle Haggard's cousin. Crushed aluminum beer can on forehead, though he cried afterward. Successfully burped without saying "excuse me" and even announced what part of lunch the gas came from. Agrees to cut down on visits to gay prostitutes.

Week 3: Ted's finally straight. Listened to a lot of Willie, Waylon and Bocephus this week and learned to play "East Bound and Down" with his hand in his armpit. Crushed Sherwin Williams paint can on his forehead and laughed. We're convinced Ted can be released into the wild.

If therapy works that fast for Ted, imagine what else it can do. Maybe if the planet Earth would just check itself into rehab, it could kick this global warming habit once and for all.

Quest for Stepford children

Going all the way back to the dark ages when I was in school (the 70s and 80s), we've been seeing reports about how America's students lag way behind the students of other industrialized nations. I didn't buy those reports then and don't buy them now.

You think kids in other industrialized nations are smarter than ours? Ha! They think soccer is football! What little morons!

I don't believe American kids today are dumber than those of the previous few generations, nor do I believe high test scores and knowledge are synonymous. But I do think the adults of today are more paranoid than their predecessors. And adults definitely have more nerve as they call kids stupid and then ask them to fix their computers and program their TiVos.

Every time these reports come out, our panic-stricken, paranoid public cries about how our schools have failed. They cut out PE and recess. Politicians (now there's some smart folks to follow) demand test after test in the name of accountability and pray that there's a spike in the scores during their term so they can act as if they had something to do with it.

The public cries for same-sex schools. No pass, no play! Orwellian school uniforms! Vouchers! They even blame Coca-Cola and Doritos in the vending machines. They keep slamming their hand down on the panic button, and the scores keep falling.

The latest panic button calls for longer school days. The average American kid spends 6.5 hours in school, less than in most nations that think soccer is football. The paranoia patrol is now pushing for eight-hour school days.

Are y'all kidding me? Are we going to sap all the joy out of being a kid? Again, thank God they didn't come up with this when I was in school.

I wouldn't have been able to stand getting home from school at the same time my parents were getting home from work. Those couple of hours I had before they got home were precious. That was when I learned important life lessons --- such as how to run a down-and-out, how many times you had to blow that whistle to summon Goldar on "Space Giants," how to French kiss and how to lie about having done your homework.

There was time to take my dog Riley to splash around Oakley's Pond, time to lie in the grass and watch clouds float by, time to practice free throws on my dirt basketball court and time to play Evil Knievel on my bicycle.

Imagine sending kids to school all day in winter, letting them out about the time it gets dark. Isn't winter depressing enough with just a couple hours of daylight after getting home from school. And in this town, how would we ever fit in baseball with eight-hour school days?

Do I think kids might learn more test-worthy items in an eight-hour school day? Yes. I also think they'd learn more science, math and history if we dressed them alike, sent them to same-sex schools and kept them in individual learning cages for 24 hours a day. But there's more to life than school, tests and misleading statistics.

Ain't it amazing that when grown folks try to fix today's "dumb" kids, the first thing we do is tear down the very education system that made us such geniuses?

Put me in, Coach

When I was a sports writer, I swore I'd never be like some of the youth league parents I saw at games, berating their own kids and others, cursing the umpires and being jerks in general.

Of course, I saw these same kind of parents (and I use that term loosely) at middle schools, high schools and even colleges, but it was most disturbing when the behavior occurred around younger children.

However, now that I'm a parent of a little baseball player, I've got to remind myself every now and then that there are enough jerks in the world.

Now, I would never yell at another parent's kid. And I would never complain about officiating or umpiring. After spending seven years covering sports, I realized that 999,999 times out of a million, umpires and referees are doing the best they can. Sure, they make mistakes, but they don't cheat. Get over it, folks, calls generally balance out in the end.

But I do find myself wanting to push my son to play the doggone game like Willie Mays. Unfortunately, Saylor's biggest accomplishment in his first year on the baseball field has been learning how to spit. OK, well, he's not doing that so well, either, as the damp front of his jersey would indicate.

The kid's not a natural, but he's having fun. Although, I think he'd have more fun if the coaches spent an entire 2-hour practice focusing on spitting.

Yet I find myself wanting to yank the bat out of his hands and swing it for him every time he swings with his arms locked like he's a turnstile. I want to hold his glove hand for him so he doesn't yank it out of the way, which has led to a bonked head and a bloodied nose even before the first game. I long to push him in the back as he lollygags down the first base line. I keep hearing that "Lollygaggers!" speech from "Bull Durham" echo in my head every time he connects on one of those swinging bunts and runs to first base in slightly under two minutes.

But I think twice and hold back because I know that there's a fine line between being supportive and pushy when you're trying to motivate a just-turned-7-year-old.

Besides, what I think I'm learning about being a baseball dad is that it's not so much that I long for him to succeed as it is that I want to be in those size 2 cleats. And maybe it's because I got cheated in baseball.

When I was 13, my baseball career ended because I thought I completely lost my mediocre talent for the game. Always a third baseman, I was moved to the outfield where balls fell around me left and right. I'd go to bat and missed 20 pitches before miraculously connecting.

I would later find out it wasn't my talent but my eyesight that had vanished. My love for the game, however, never faded.

I still spent many a spring afternoon playing baseball with neighborhood boys and ghost runners in the kudzu patch and spent many a summer night alone in the backyard, hitting pears for home runs over the neighbors' fence.

So whether you're an Atlanta Brave, Columbus Catfish, CSU Cougar, Northside Patriot or the last draft pick for a coach-pitch team, all I ask is you love the game that I still miss so much today. And if you don't love the game, at least learn to spit properly.

Feast for the senses

Ain't a whole lot I like about fall, and there's hardly anything of note about winter. I reckon if I could throw some snowballs or go skiing more than once every 36 years, I might feel differently. But there just ain't enough sunlight, and it's only cold enough to be aggravating — in the South anyway.

But in spring and summer, I come alive. The world comes alive. It's a feast for the senses. The caress of the slightest warm breeze can carry a wave of memories. One bird can sing you back 25 years. Smoke wafting from a neighbor's grill can reunite you with folks long gone. When I think of spring and summer, I can taste, smell, hear, see and touch memories.

The greasy good aroma of fried chicken signaling the final stages of a touch football game and the call of "Supper!" officially ending it. The strangely enticing aroma of asphalt melting under your feet at the amusement park. Inches-deep Town Creek rippling over your toes. Lightning bugs illuminating the backyard. A final bell signaling the end of school.

The moist smell of thick steam rising from your street after a brief June shower. Croaking bullfrogs along Buck Creek near your campsite. The way everything, even the tops of Coca-Cola cans just removed from the cooler, smells like fish when you're fishing. The sweat on your forehead almost freezing after you run inside and stick your face right in the flow of the air-conditioner resting precariously in the window.

The smell of suntan lotion as your toes dig into the cool bottom sand during a stroll along the beach. The glistening bodies covered with that coconut flavor. The hum of a plane following the coastline carrying a banner with giant red letters advertising a local seafood joint's early bird, $14.95 all-you-can-eat special. The seagulls squawking for you to toss that piece of bread. The lifeguard's piercing whistle.

The creak of your great aunt's front porch swing that's generated a "you're gonna make that thing fall" warning for 15 years. The red dust kicked up by a passing pickup as you walk down a dirt road that's been two weeks without rain. The tinny music from the ice cream truck a block away sending kids sprinting for money. The sulfuric sensation from Fourth of July fireworks. Strumming Jimmy Buffett tunes on the front porch.

Freshly mowed grass. Buzzing bees. Marco! Polo! Sunburn. Sneezing. Kites flying. Beautiful legs. Not-so-beautiful legs and love handles. Music from a passing convertible. An approaching thunderstorm rumbling. Ants joining your picnic. That (hopefully not poisonous) whiff of a just-opened can of tennis balls. The thud of a crashing front porch swing.

And, best of all, there's no one yelling at you for writing something with 31 sentence fragments.

I don't get handbags

Perhaps I've been a little out of the loop on handbag fashions — and, really, any other fashion — but I had no idea how much handbags can cost. Not until my handbag-addicted editor Pork Chop left me a handbag story to edit before she left for vacation.

I think she was just being cruel, knowing how much I hate all things "fashionable" that she and the other conformist suckers fall for. Either that, or she was just plain unwise. Why would you want me to edit a story about handbags? That would be like asking Larry the Cable Guy to handle your brain surgery. Until I edited that story, I thought Oscar de la Renta was just that guy who fought Floyd Mayweather Jr. a couple of weeks ago. Apparently he makes pricey handbags, too.

I thought an average handbag was worth about $3, and a really fancy, schmancy one --- the kind you women notice and we guys don't --- would run up to maybe $50. Wrong! Designer handbags can cost $2,000 (as much as my first car, a '78 Toyota Celica) and up. And, unlike my '78 Celica, they don't even come with an AM radio or a permanent cigarette odor.

Who are you trying to impress? It's not guys, because I've got news for you: Guys don't notice your handbag . . . or your shoes, in case you were wondering. Any real man will take a barefoot country girl over a high-heeled city lady any day.

A hot chick with a $10 handbag and $10 shoes may be jeered by her own gender, but we guys aren't going to have a problem with it. Those chicks in dirty magazines don't even carry handbags — or so I've been told.

Poor Pork Chop — who owns more handbags than I have articles of clothing, counting socks and all — is always bringing in new handbags for my female co-workers to gush over. While the ladies act like it's different somehow from every other handbag, I try to offer genuine observations, such as: "Wow! It has handles and everything! And you can put stuff in it."

And you ladies can't win with your own gender when it comes to handbags and shoes anyway. If you buy some cheap handbag, they're gonna make fun of you when you walk away. And if you land a real winner with a $4,000 receipt, they'll find something else bad to say about you when you walk away. "What was she thinking with that blouse?!"

At least we guys are honest when we say, "Yep, looks like a handbag to me." That's about all we're qualified to say about handbags.

We're even scared to touch a handbag. When my wife tells me to get something out of her purse, I gently probe around as if I'm a member of some purse bomb squad. God only knows what's in those things.

And you wives can be so insensitive, making us hold your pocketbooks for you. What if another guy walks by? We could get kicked out of the Man Club. That's why we hold it disgustedly with just the tips of our fingers as if it's covered with poop or something.

I guess what I'm saying is a handbag is a handbag and is never worth $2,000. Save the money for something truly important, like a new set of golf clubs.

Skeeters!

Everybody's always focusing on the negative aspects of droughts. But droughts have their good points and it's time we gave droughts their due.

Now before any of you folks who make your living with the help of rain — farmers, umbrella makers and rain dancers — go throwing anything at me for defending the drought, just remember I don't make the rain. That's somebody with a far greater power than me: Kurt Schmitz, the weather man at WTVM. So, if you don't like the weather, go throw something at him, preferable during the 6 p.m. newscast; it'd be a real ratings booster.

I read this week that the drought has severely affected the mosquito population in Georgia. I can tell you're surprised: "He can read?!" By "affected," I don't mean Georgia's mosquito population is having to restrict when they water their itty-bitty lawns or take shorter showers. I mean "affected" as in there aren't nearly as many mosquitoes as usual. Usually at this time of year there are so many mosquitoes buzzing around that the top-selling fragrance of Axe body spray is Off.

I must point out at this juncture that the aforementioned mosquitoes shall be henceforth referred to as skeeters. Sorry to switch in midstream like this, but I had to clarify early that I was talking about those annoying little bugs and not the 47 beer-gutted guys around the Chattahoochee Valley who go by the name of Skeeter. Those Skeeters don't bite, unless you try to cut in when they're dancing with Wanda Mae while jukin' on a Saturday night. And if you don't know what "jukin' " is, then don't worry about it because you probably won't be bumping into any human Skeeters.

I'm all for this skeeter shortage. Those blood-sucking little critters carry all sorts of bad diseases like malaria, West Nile Virus and hypochondria. I caught a severe case of the latter last year and missed a whole week of work.

Of course, in today's paranoid America, even skeeters are worried about disease. One landed on me the other day and, before biting me, asked: "Have you traveled to Europe since 1980? Have you had any tattoos or piercings within the last year? Have you had sex with a prostitute? Do you have her number?"

If I had known about all those diseases when I was a kid, I wouldn't have flexed my muscles when skeeters sucked my blood. Certainly I'm not the only person who liked to watch them fill up too quickly with my blood and then be too full so that I could watch them get too full to fly away and then squash 'em. A lot of my boyhood friends got their thrills killing deer and doves, but I was an insect hunter. Unlike my friends, I never froze my buns off while skeeter hunting. Some of my old friends are completely bunless now.

Some skeeters got me back when I was a sports writer in Valdosta, Ga., and had to cover baseball games in Clinch County, a bullfrog's hop from the Okefenokee Swamp. The skeeters down there were so big, I first thought they were buzzards. I slapped one and it slapped me back.

Don't attack my kayak

Alligators rarely pose a threat to people. When alligators do decide to taste test humans, it's generally the result of human stupidity. That's why, as a stupid human, it's not a good idea for me to mingle with the creatures.

But being a stupid human, I do it anyway.

I've never been scared of alligators until recently. When I was a kid, I saw plenty slide into the Flint River in Macon County when we'd pass them in our fishing boat, and they never bothered us. And the one time an alligator lunged at me, it was because I was checking out her kiddie gators down at the Okefenokee Swamp. Apparently mama gators are a wee bit protective. Lesson learned.

But on a recent kayaking trip down the Chattahoochee River from Hatchechubbee Creek Park to Lakepoint near Eufaula — a little over 16 miles according to Google Earth — I learned a few more lessons about alligators.

The main lesson is that alligators are attracted to yupnecks (half-yuppie, half-redneck) in red kayaks. Maybe I looked like a giant chili pepper floating down the river. Or maybe some other bozo in a kayak has been feeding the little dinosaurs. Whatever the reason, I had brushes with at least six alligators, including a 10-foot monster.

I like alligators, as much as you can like something that looks like it just waddled out of "Jurassic Park." But I don't like getting too close to them while kayaking, mainly because my butt is right there at tooth-level for a swimming alligator.

I understand they're territorial and prefer to stay away from humans. So do I. That's why I was confused when two of them decided to follow me for a while, including the 10-footer. Generally, I bop along around 4 mph. But after that 10-footer tailed me for about 100 feet, I think I hit 60 mph. I passed somebody on a Sea-Doo. It was the most impressive paddling this side of Marv Albert. But paddling 60 mph is hardly what my lazy behind had in mind when I put in at the mouth of Hatchechubbee Creek. What I had in mind was floating . . . and snoozing until it was time to steer again.

(By the way, I really, really like the word Hatchechubbee. I'm pretty sure it's an old Native American word, and I'm pretty sure it means something dirty.)

I discovered something else that day: I can talk to animals, just like Dr. Doolittle. Granted, they can't talk to me, but that's not the point. The point is that I was able to conversate with that 10-foot dino:

"OK, OK, I'm leaving. Trust me, you don't want to eat me. I'm terribly high in cholesterol. Ask my doctor. You think Quarter Pounders are bad? I'm 195 pounds. Do you know how long it would take to swim that off?"

When I made it to Panama City Beach a couple days later (by car, not kayak), I resisted the urge to buy the gator tail special at Schooner's. I figure no gator has bitten me yet, so maybe I should return the favor.

Fizzy math

Numbers scare me. As a writer, I'm convinced numbers are from the devil and words are from God.

I'm about to reel off some scary numbers, so close your eyes if you can't handle it: 666, 13, 5,762 and 1, which is the loneliest number that you'll ever do. I can attest to that, because I've done number 1 in some lonely places — especially during long road trips on rural roads. In fact, I hear it's the loneliest number since the number 2. I'll take Three Dog Night's word for it.

You can uncover your eyes now.

During a recent outing to one of Columbus' 532 basic bar and grill restaurants, I noticed another scary number on my bill: $4.38. That's how much it cost for two soft drinks. Granted, they came with unlimited free refills if you could ever find a waitress, but I'm not sure even my caffeine-addicted self can drink $2.19 worth of

Diet Coke in one hour.

And this was a fairly run-of-the-mill bar and grill chain. This wasn't some hoity-toity restaurant full of pretentious people in uncomfortable clothes. The folks eating here seemed fairly normal.

Perhaps this restaurant has its Diet Cokes blessed by the pope or Dr. James Dobson. Maybe they spiked it with Jack Daniels without telling me — in which case I guess it's a pretty decent price. Or maybe it's imported from some far-away land such as France, Australia or Atlanta.

Something has to explain why this establishment charges a buck more than most fast-food joints. And very few mom-and-pop places charge more than $1.50 for a soda. Most are in the $1 range. Maybe mom and pop grow Diet Cokes in their backyard.

I continued my research into cola economics at a convenience store, which is now a misnomer since there often are 12 people in line trying to buy lottery tickets. I went to the cooler and found a 20-ounce Coke Zero for $1.39. Again, way overpriced in my economics-challenged opinion. But then I turned around and saw a 2-liter Coke Zero for $1.19.

Of course, the 20-ounce was cold and the 2-liter was not, and a 2-liter bottle doesn't fit all that well in the SUV's drink holder. But that 20-ounce doesn't taste nearly as good when you think you've been suckered. Maybe its because 20 is more than 2, or was when I was in school . . . before New Math. I bet I'd have to take out a loan to get 350 milliliters of soda.

Makes me wonder how much I spend on soda between restaurants, the drink machines at work and the confusing inconvenience stores. Let's see, 5 x 65 cents x 365 x $1.39 x 26 x the square root of pi. Good grief! I spent $12 million last year alone!

Oh well. Perhaps I should go cold turkey on caffeine for the hundredth time. But it tends to give me awful headaches after a day or two without caffeine. And the last time I tried it, my boss Pork Chop called me "Mr. Grumpypants." And in a hostile work environment where bosses carelessly hurl brutal insults like that, you need your caffeine.

Hangin' with Fred

Many folks are excited about "The Simpsons Movie" that just came out, but I think I'll be content to wait for it to hit TV.

D'oh'nt get me wrong. I like "The Simpsons." I like "King of the Hill" and "South Park" too. I just don't plan my day around seeing the shows. Heck, I sometimes go a year or two without seeing an episode.

Besides, they'll always pale in comparison to "The Flintstones" for me. It's not just because "The Flintstones" were all over TBS when I got home from school for years and years. Mainly, it's because I kinda like the way of life in Bedrock, much more than Springfield or Arlen, Texas. If I could jump into a cartoon, I think it would be "The Flintstones."

I think "The Jetsons" had a lot going for them, too, with all the modern conveniences and such. Plus, George Jetson had a smokin' hot wife. (I won't say anything about daughter Judy because I don't know if she's legal yet.) But I wouldn't want to live in an era where robots play football. The steroid era we live in now is bad enough.

But I'd fit right in if I bought one of those little stone houses on Cobblestone Way near Fred and Barney. I'm not sure I'd like working at the gravel pit. Perhaps I could score a job at The Daily Granite. And, after work, I'd definitely hang out with Fred and Barney. They're much more fun than Hank Hill and Homer Simpson.

They were always going bowling, shooting pool or playing golf and still found time to lie around in a hammock between two palm trees or hang out with the fellas at the Water Buffalo Lodge and guzzle cactus juice. Man, that's the life.

And despite the fact that Fred and Barney never seemed to have a lot of money, rarely spent any time at home and weren't much to look at, they did pretty well in the wife department. Betty and Wilma ain't half bad.

Best of all, they got to walk around barefooted everywhere, even in formal occasions. That would be awesome — well, except when you had to throw those soles down on the road to stop your 10-ton, stone-wheeled car. I think if I were in Bedrock, I'd make a fortune selling brakes.

There is one thing I'd definitely have a problem with, though: the dinosaurs. I realize they are awfully tame and hold down a lot of jobs other folks wouldn't want, but I don't like the idea of having a carnivore for a garbage disposal. What if you have to dig a fork out of the drain? And there's no way I'm flying Pterodactyl Airlines. I'm scared of heights.

Hopefully, the segment of creationists who think the world is 5,000 years old and that humans and dinosaurs lived together don't take "The Flintstones" as historical fact.

I don't think if humans and dinosaurs lived together that humans would be riding around on them. They'd more likely be hiding in caves. And you'd think they have noted it somewhere, like in one of those cave drawings: "I freakin' hate dinosaurs!"

Well, I gotta go to dinner. For some reason, I've got a hankerin' for a slab a ribs that could knock a car sideways.

Roaming the streets

This past week, I had the opportunity to chat with some middle school kids, a couple hundred actually. They were stressing out about research papers, and part of my job was to calm them down and put it in perspective.

So I thought back to my middle school — or junior high, as we called it — days and nearly had a panic attack. That's when I truly began to hate school. Never really got over that. That's when I went from being the gifted kid to the kid with a lot of potential. I had a lot more potential than I had A's on my report cards.

I'm still thankful there was no HOPE Scholarship when I was growing up because my parents would have killed me. I wouldn't have qualified. I was perfectly happy with having loads of untapped potential. When my parents and teachers would ask me if I were happy with just getting by, I'd say "no," but the true response would have been, "Yeah, pretty much."

But during junior high, I was hating school and still stressing about grades. It was a lot easier hating school when I was in high school and college and didn't care about my grades. But, in junior high, I wasn't merely burdened with potential. There were expectations. And when I didn't meet expectations the first time, I panicked.

I ran away from home.

I wrote a note to my parents on the dry-erase board explaining that I was a great big failure and that they'd never have to see me again.

Being a runaway on the streets of my hometown was a little different than if I'd lived in L.A. or New York City. With just over a thousand residents and just one traffic light, Oglethorpe was a wee bit smaller.

I wandered the streets. I snoozed under a tree. I fished at Oakley's Pond, but caught nothing. I'd lie down and hide in the kudzu when a car came by. I waded through Town Creek, which when I lived at home I was prohibited from visiting . . . but did anyway. I was free to do as I pleased on my own.

Oglethorpe's economy wasn't the best for an 11-year-old child of the streets. The biggest industry in town was a Suwannee Swifty convenience store and Ms. Susan's hair-cuttin' and gossipin' shop. I wasn't good in math, so I wouldn't be able to work the register at the Suwannee Swifty. And I couldn't wash hair or anything at Ms. Susan's because secrets didn't live long there.

I grew hungry, lonely, depressed. I began to think that maybe bad grades weren't the end of the world and that my folks might not kill me after all. They might sell me to the circus, I reasoned, but not kill me.

Then it struck me — the smell of fried chicken coming from at least a dozen old houses. I'd had enough of going hungry. Enough searching in vain for work. Enough hiding. Enough lack of fishing success at Oakley's Pond. Enough skeeter bites. I finally made the decision to go home and face the music.

Two hours as a runaway in Oglethorpe can sure put things in perspective.

Where Skeeter used to live

I recently heard a co-worker who's lived most of her life up North — which, to me, is any place above LaGrange, Ga. — turn just a little bit Southern.

She's lived most of her 25 years in Wisconsin and California, where most folks talk funny — that is to say they don't have a proper Southern drawl as every self-respecting human should. I eavesdropped as she explained the location of something by saying something to the extent of "where Skeeter used to live."

How Southern is that? That's a clear diversion from cheesehead to cheese grits. The fact that she actually knew of someone named Skeeter is Southern enough. Why, if she'd have also known a Peanut, Bubba, Junior, Smitty and Jimmy Earl, I'd have given her Georgia Peach status right there on the spot --- despite the fact she'll never turn in her high heels for proper Southern girl footwear: bare feet.

But more Southern than knowing a Skeeter is knowing the proper way to give directions down here. She jumped straight to advanced Southern direction giving by using something from the past or long gone as a reference point. Back home, it's expected that turns are pinpointed by where Uncle George used to live, where the water tower used to be, where Cletus flipped his truck or where they found Billy Ray's foot after the accident.

She skipped right over the basic courses — such as simple geographic directions. No, not north, south, east and west. I mean up yonder, down yonder, back yonder and over yonder. If you don't know those, you ain't got a chance of finding where the water tower used to be.

And don't even think of annoying us with exact addresses. We used a post office box back home in Oglethorpe, but certain businesses would bug my Dad for an actual street address from time to time, as if the person delivering anything to our house wouldn't be a sixth cousin on my Grandma's side or something. He got tired of coming up with different fake addresses and finally just decided we'd be 404 Baker Street forever more.

We're not into highway numbers and real street names. By the time we learn the important ones, like Fourth Avenue or the Beallwood Connector, they change it to something else. Then they scrambled the exit numbers after it took me 30 years to learn 'em. I knew to get off I-75 at Exit 45 for years when I'd visit family in Warner Robins. Now, I only know to exit when I see the place where the nekkid ladies dance. That's cool when giving directions to Bubba and the boys, but it's a little uncomfortable when Granny's explaining where to turn for the revival.

By the way, if you want to see my old falling-down house at 404 Baker Street, just turn left at the old Lions Club where Old Henry used to wave at passing cars, take a right where my Grandma used to live, turn left just past where the water tower used to be and stop at the old haunted Jolly House where they cut down the biggest magnolia tree there ever was. If you get to the smooth road, you've gone too far.

Better fill up before you leave Columbus, though, because it's waaay over yonder from where Skeeter used to live.

The lost children of Ideal

About an hour or so east of Columbus is the little town of Ideal, Ga. It's a quiet community of just over 500 folks living in old homes tucked away among rolling hills and tall pines. It's been called "the only Ideal city in Georgia" and was once featured in one of those "Beef: It's what's for dinner" television commercials.

It sounds like a gentle little community, but the name Ideal hides a horrific history, and I'm not talking about the time my granddaddy blew up the town's only movie theater with dynamite as he tried to make a World War II movie a little more realistic. (Some Ideal folks still refer to it as the first movie in America with Surround Sound.) No, I'm talking about the legendary lost children of Ideal.

My mom grew up in Ideal and saw hundreds, no, thousands of children die in unusual circumstances. I know because any time during my childhood when I got a little adventurous on my bicycle or played with dangerous objects, Mom explained how one of her childhood friends died doing exactly what I was doing at that moment. My poor mother barely had time to make friends before they fell out of a tree or got fatally dizzy on a merry-go-round.

I admit there was a time in my life when I doubted Mom's stories and wondered if it were some elaborate lie to keep me from getting my head busted open (to no avail, I might add). After all, I'd never seen these kids of whom she spoke buried in the town's main cemetery where many of my Albritton and Dixon relatives rest in peace.

So, last week, I went on a trek. I tromped through the woods until, finally, I stumbled upon a graveyard of kid-sized headstones that had long since been overrun by kudzu near Whitewater Creek. I examined the hundreds of marble testaments to the dangers of kid-dom. I owe my Mom an apology for ever doubting the stories of:

Jim Bob Snuckerton, who was riding his Huffy without using his hands and lost control of the bike, sending him tumbling down Clyde's Cliff like that "agony of defeat" guy from "Wide World of Sports" and ran head-first into a freight train.

Mary Sue Thornberry, one of the first children to die of radiation poisoning when her face melted off when she sat too close to the TV.

Sammy Snodgrass, who sank like a rock to the bottom of the ice-cold city pool when he waited a mere 28 minutes (not 30) after eating before going swimming.

Eddie Earl Eaton, strangled to death by an innocent-looking garter snake.

Francine Festus, whose feet rotted off after she got dew poisoning from walking through the grass barefoot one morning.

Billy Joe Rabbitt, who literally exploded right in the middle of Albritton's store after he didn't have a bowel movement for a full week because he was too scared to use the bathroom at summer camp.

And, most tragically, Augustus Applewhite, who survived childhood only to become the ugliest man on the planet after he frowned and his face froze that way. He died old, but unhappy.

Cute stars

There was a time in my life where I thought I'd never tire of conversations about pretty girls. That time was roughly from age 5 to 37.

But, now, I could really use a break from it.

I'm not talking about a group of guys at the bar making lewd comments about scantily clad women or office gossip about the new chick in accounting. No, I'm talking about neverending talk of Hannah Montana, JoJo, Ashley Tisdale and the Cheetah Girls (and, no, those aren't dancers in Atlanta). And the talk is not from a group of guys. It's from my 8-year-old son.

Saylor is obsessed with cute celebrity girls. I don't really get it, perhaps because stars and celebrities have never been my thing. Granted, I did write a love letter to Jessica Lange when I was 6 years old and that giant ape ran off with her. (Still haven't heard back, but keep your fingers crossed for me. Don't know whether she'll check "yes," "no" or "maybe. My wife's hoping she 'll check "yes." I guess she doesn't want to be the only one to make that mistake.)

There were a few other celebs who floated my boat. Dawn Wells from "Gilligan's Island." Lisa Bonet from "The Cosby Show." Even Tuesday Weld from "Dobie Gillis." And my next-door-neighbors and I used to fight over "Charlie's Angels." Thad was happy with Jacklyn Smith, and I was thrilled to wind up with Cheryl Ladd. Not sure yet how poor David got stuck with Kate Jackson.

Speaking of fighting, the first girl I fought over was Heather Hobbs, who was a celebrity in kindergarten as the winner of the county's Pine Princess Pageant. My cousin and I got sent home from vacation Bible school for fighting on the slide. On the surface, it merely seemed a matter of it being my turn to slide, not his. But we both knew deep down it had more to do with his cutting in on the love of my 5-year-old life.

From Heather on, I was far more fascinated with real local starlets more than those Hollywood chicks. There was Angela in third grade, who ruined my handwriting by tempting me to break my pencil point repeatedly so that I could walk by her desk on the way to the pencil sharpener. In fifth grade, it was Robin Vaughn. She was a tiny, delicate, blonde-haired girl whom I felt like I had to protect. Per the cliche, I'd carry her books after school. In junior high, it was Stephanie Wigglesworth, who on top of having a sexy last name was the first to start wearing training bras so we could pop her straps.

In high school, it was all those cheerleaders who wouldn't give me the time of day: Jenny, LeeAnn, Mary Ellen, Heather (yeah, same one), Rebecca and Becky and the cast of thousands of cheerleaders across the state who didn't exactly swoon over dorky tennis players with ugly cars. Of course, over the years, they somehow went from dream girls to real humans and, in a few cases, old friends.

I wonder if Saylor will ever know the fun of worshipping local starlets as opposed to the Hollywood chicks. He does claim to have a girlfriend in his class, but I get the sense she's just a stand-in until Hannah Montana calls. Just as long as he doesn't bring home one of those Spears girls, I guess all will be OK.

Where are you?

It's been a little over a year since we ditched our traditional land-line phone to go all cell all the time. It's saved money and made life simpler.

We're hardly the only folks to do it. The younger generation can't exactly grasp the concept of why anybody would have a land line in the first place.

The phone world has certainly changed a lot for me since I was a boy in the 1970s and a teenager in the 1980s.

In the 1970s, all I remember using are those old rotary phones. And at my house and my grandparents' homes, there was just one phone. One person could hog it for hours. Didn't really bother me because I didn't spend a lot of time on the phone then . . . or now for that matter. About the only time I'd have to talk on the phone in the 1970s is when my mom would call me to the phone with an order like, "Come tell Aunt Gladys thank you for those Spider-Man Underoos she sent you!"

That was always embarrassing. Although, I must say that those suckers have sure held up through the years. Must have been made when we actually produced things in America. They're a little snug-ger now.

One of my grandmothers lived in a tin house down a dirt road. I'd say it was the boonies, but you had to walk for miles just to get to the boonies. And in the boonies and those remote areas surrounding the boonies, they had a lot of party lines. And the only folks invited to the party out there were a couple of old ladies who fussed any-time I picked up the phone.

"Hold on, Bertha, somebody's listening to our conversation!"

And today's kids will never know the joys of those phone cords that were about 40 feet long, but only about three inches long when they inevitably got all twisted up. And you had to do that trick where you held the phone by the cord and gave it a spin. After about 500 revolutions, the cord was 40 feet long again. Of course, those long cords decapitated and strangled thousands of kids running through houses in the '70s.

Then came touch tones, which were fun to play with and see what kind of tunes you could create — at least until your dad roared into the living room with the phone bill in his hand wanting to know who's been calling Goran in Czechoslovakia.

But the cell phone has brought the biggest change for us. The best thing is that we don't have to call 47 people to tell them when we're heading out of town. In fact, now when people call, the first thing they ask is, "Where are y'all?"

However, it definitely beats coming home from a weeklong vacation and finding an answering machine blinking 88 times, striking fear into you until you hear 87 ways you could consolidate your debt.

Possum Holler High Class of '88

Twenty years ago, I graduated from Possum Holler High School. At least, I think I did. They're supposed to mail me one of those diploma thingies any day now.

I remember my graduation night like it was yesterday. Wearing that weird gown. Marching around. Wait a minute! That WAS yesterday. But my graduation was a lot like that, too, except it had long, boring speeches.

But there was a twist that night on the speeches. Naturally, the valedictorian of the class, Brenda Sue Thornwhistle (who scored FOUR digits on her SAT) got to give the main speech. But in an effort to be fair and balanced, the school also allowed the dumbest kid in the senior class, Snake Snodgrass, to give a speech, too. Snake was one of my best friends and sent me a copy of the speech that he still has posted on the wall of his isolation cell today:

Parents, teachers, fellow students, administrative types and extinguished guests. I ain't never done much speakin' before exceptin' when they ask me how I plead. But it is an honor to talk at you on this suspicious occasion.

When I was a freshman at Possum Holler High School nine years ago, I never would have believed that I'd be standing up here tonight in one of these girly outfits and a square hat. But to you younger kids out there, which purty much includes every student and half the faculty here, allow me to be an inspiration to you. With a little hard work and a decent lawyer, you, too, can get one of these here pieces of paper that says you done got learned something.

I would especially like to thank my parents, Miss Ellie Snodgrass and either Jim Bob Jenkins or Jesse Earl Larue. Or any one of those Durham Bulls who stopped at the diner on their way through town in August 1961. I do have one hell of a curve ball.

To my fellow students, let us not forget the good times we've had together at Possum Holler High. School daintzes. Football games. The club meetings . . . which reminds me I need to give a shout-out to the Disciples of Satan and y'all don't forget we got a meeting in the graveyard after this here ceremony.

And let's be thankful for the learning we got here and carry it through our lives. And I'd sure as heck hate to think I spent three years in Algebra II for nothing.

We may have made a few mistakes along the way. Setting fire to the auditorium in 1984 certainly comes to mind. But whether we got detention or probation, our stumbles of yesterday paved the way for the giant steps of tomorrow. Yeah, I know, I'm deep, ain't I?

And, finally, I want you teachers to know that we may make fun of you from time to time, maybe shoot a spitball or slash your tires, but we truly appreciate you. I'd especially like to thank Mrs. Tallulah Louise Templeton for inviting me to stay after class to "dust the erasers." Until then, I thought that had something to do with chalkboards. I'd like to ask Mrs. Templeton to stand up for a round of applause, but I'm afraid she might trip in them leg chains.

Thanks, y'all.

Summer meals

My dad and I have differing views on a lot of things — religion, politics, television, humor, music, clothes, relaxation, work and fun to name a few. Those last two — work and fun — he can even put together. Which is just sick if you ask me.

But in few areas are we more starkly contrasted than in our food tastes. In his business trips across North America, he's been taken to a lot of local yokel restaurants to sample the area's fare. If it's walked on the ground or sprung from it, he's eaten it and probably liked it.

I, on the other hand, have all the advanced taste buds of a 12-year-old boy. My favorite world-class chef is Chef Boyardee. Let me tell you, that man can box up a darn good pizza.

When summer rolls around, I start to get cravings for the kinds of foods that would get me through those June and July days when I was on my own for breakfast and lunch until school started again.

Breakfast was generally a non-issue as I slept in during the summer when I could. Besides, breakfast was an awful lot of work — sorting through all that whole grain junk to find every marshmallow in a box of Lucky Charms can wear a boy out.

But, come lunchtime, I needed something more hearty than food from a box. Yep, it was time for something from a can. And no one can whip up a bowl of Spaghetti-Os like Chef Chris Boyardee. See, anyone can heat up some Spaghetti-Os on the stove or in a microwave, but real chefs like me spice it up a little. That's the way those uppity chefs do it in places like Italy, France and Possum Holler.

Before heating up the Spaghetti-Os, I'd search through the fridge. I could usually find some hot dogs. I wouldn't bother to cut them up into neat little circles. I'd just bite little chunks off and spit them into the bowl of Spaghetti-Os. What? It was going back in my mouth anyway!

I'd find some bologna and rip a couple slices into little pieces and toss them in. A little Spam leftover from the last time you had a fried Spam sandwich? Mix in a little of that, too. Add some of those Kraft singles and sprinkle some black pepper on top, and you've got yourself a meal fit for a 12-year-old king.

You can't eat that good canned food every day, though, or you'd get spoiled. So I'd balance that delicacy with such other healthy lunch options as Pop Tarts (with cheese melted on top), frozen pizza (with extra cheese), a half-box of instant mashed potatoes (with cheese), mac-and-cheese and grilled cheese sandwiches. And, some days, I'd just eat some cheese and cut out the middle man.

Dad, meanwhile, hates only one food in the world: Spaghetti-Os. Won't touch 'em. The man will eat things that would make a bottom-feeding catfish vomit, but no Spaghetti-Os. Must have seen me adding the hot dogs one day.

How to meditate

Everyone should practice meditation. I say practice because it takes a while to get good at it. With enough practice, you can reach such a state of relaxation that they have to call a coroner. That's one of the reasons I'll never vote for a Democrat for coroner. When somebody comes to pronounce me dead, I want them to be extremely conservative. As conservative as Dick Cheney's and Pat Robertson's love child.

Meditation has enormous benefits. It eases stress. It can lower blood pressure. It has even been known to bring peace between striking unions and management. No, wait, that's mediation.

I learned the art from the most enlightened man in all of Possum Holler, the Bubba. Bubba Turkleton. He was once Jimmy Earl Turkleton and heir to great riches in the form of Turkleton Towing & Transmission Repair but left the family business to seek enlightenment and from then on was known as the Bubba.

Some folks can tune out the world more easily than I, so I don a pair of headphones and listen to the meditation-assistance musical track on my MP3 player. It's all sorts of various tones allegedly scientifically designed to stimulate various brain waves. It's labeled "Meditation 1," but sometimes I don't advance it far enough through the "M" songs and wind up meditating to "Man of Constant Sorrow" from the "O Brother, Where Art Thou?" soundtrack, and that just gets me down.

But when all goes right with my meditating, I can really clear my mind. I'll demonstrate. I just hooked up these little Electronic Brain Wave Monitor Thingies ($19.95 at Wal-Mart) to record my every thought. Pay attention. Here's how meditation should go:

OK. Sit on the floor. Cross your legs. Well grab your leg and pull harder. You're comfortable now, Chris. Listen to the sounds and go to your happy place. The beach. Listen to the waves. Quit imagining girls in bikinis. Imagine a few seagulls flying by. Great! Now why did you have to imagine it pooping on you?!

Whatever. Clear your mind. And ignore that. Ignore what? That itch. The one in the middle of my back? Yeah, that one. OK. Just imagine nothing. Just space. No worries. No problems. Like the doctor's bill on the counter the insurance refused to pay? Yeah, like that. OK, I can't take it anymore. MUST SCRATCH! OK, do it and come back to nirvana.

Ahh, that's better. Relax. Be one with the universe. Repeat your mantra. Don't get no haircut from a bald-headed barber? No! Beg forgiveness, not permission? Oh, never mind. Is that a faucet dripping? Forget it. Just relax. Find your soul center. No, I think that's a kidney. There. Now, go deeper. Into a trance. Deeper, deeper, deeper. ARRRGHHH! CRAMP! CRAMP!

And that's how you meditate. Good luck.

Quarter life

While sitting at my desk at a cabin in the boonies a few days ago, I noticed that one of several quarters lying on it was dated 1970, the year I was born. Unfortunately, my first thought was that's one old quarter.

I don't like the new quarters. They all still have that same lady with the big nose and wig on front, but I find myself turning over these new quarters to see what state they represent. I don't know why it matters. Maybe I just have a hard time thinking a Vermont quarter is worth as much as a Georgia quarter. I'm pretty sure the Vermont quarter is worth just 22 cents. And then there's the Florida quarter, which I resent getting in years when the Gators beat the Dawgs.

I held onto the 1970 quarter for a couple of days, mainly because I was out in the country and miles away from any vending machines to feed my caffeine addiction. Much like America's dollars go to feed its oil addiction.

Besides, I felt like the 1970 quarter and I needed to catch up with each other, talk about old times and share the story of our journeys before I shoved him in a slot in exchange for a Diet Dr Pepper.

My story wasn't nearly as interesting as Mr. Quarter's. I'm not much for traveling. If I never leave the state of Georgia again, I won't consider that much of a tragedy. Although, I do like to get down to Lake Eufaula a good bit, and I consider crossing the Vandiver Causeway from Georgetown to Eufaula overseas travel. I've been as far west as Seattle, as far north as Detroit and as far south as Miami.

But Mr. Quarter has been everywhere.

He left the U.S. Mint and headed straight to Reno where he played the slots and lost. Spent days in the darkness before being freed and taken to Omaha where he helped Mrs. Gladys Thornwhistle do a load of laundry. His story went on and on.

A Coke machine in Toledo. A pool hall in Buffalo. A close encounter with a train while lying on the tracks in Newark. A game of Donkey Kong in Paducah. A little extra for that sugary-sweet Hooters waitress in Valdosta. A game of quarters with some teenagers in Panama City Beach. A full year in a fountain in Portland. Five pieces of gum at a Dallas 7-Eleven. And, somehow, finally, from my pocket to a cabin in the boonies. Actually, you have to drive about 7 miles from the cabin just to get to the boonies.

Mr. Quarter has been there, seen that, bought that. He's met thousands of people. I try to stay as close to home as possible, and the very thought of thousands of people makes me want to hide somewhere in the boonies.

And, yet, Mr. Quarter and I have come full circle since 1970. Sitting there in that cabin, 38 years later, we're both still worth about 25 cents.

Pen to paper

In my haste to get my pokey family — especially the pokey 8-year-old — out of the house last Friday and moving toward a freezing cabin in the country, I snatched up my laptop case, not knowing it was unzipped. And not knowing I'd grabbed the wrong end.

Everything spilled out. I shoved the computer, the mouse, the spell-checking elf and everything else I saw back into the bag.

Late the next afternoon, I got everything out to do a little leisure writing. Everything, that is, except the power cord that was obviously still in Columbus. I purchased the cheap laptop in an online auction, and it has no battery. It's useless without the cord. My wise son, with whom I'd had a blast all day hiking and flying a kite, suggested that it was divine intervention — that God took the power cord out so that he and I could spend more time together.

I don't think God was meddling in my computer bag, though I've no doubt Satan logs onto my work computer on a fairly regular basis. Heck, he writes half my columns for me. Nevertheless, I thought my boy was on the right track. So we did spend more time together.

But around midnight, when the cabin was silent with the exception of the crackling fire, I had the urge to write. I sat down at the table, turned on some jazz thanks to Georgia Public Radio and put a pen to paper.

It's definitely not my preferred way of writing. I hate looking at my own ugly handwriting, a product of having a distractingly pretty third-grade teacher. And ever since that first Commodore 64, I've found that the "delete" key is my friend.

But I found writing the old-fashioned way to be cathartic. To me, words still have more power on paper than on a computer screen or a cell phone. LOL.

I figured if Mark Twain could sit in a gazebo at Quarry Farm and write "Huckleberry Finn" with a pen and paper, then certainly I could sit in a cabin and write a bad short story.

I at least started a halfway decent one, heard some good jazz and got a few crazy ideas out of my head and down on paper. They can't be deleted as so many of my ideas have been. They can be scratched out, thrown away and burned, but, by golly, they won't disappear with one keystroke.

I think "delete" keys have made life too clean. How many great ideas have been typed out, looked at with a "nah" and then vanished forever with a click click click?

I think more people need to get re-acquainted with the pen and paper. People need to feel the weight of words in their hands again. They need to keep journals and write letters. (Letters, by the way, are much safer than e-mail. When was the last time you accidentally mailed a letter to 400 people calling your boss a looney tune?)

There's a permanence with real writing that computers can't replicate. Blogs won't be the Dead Sea Scrolls of 2,000 years from now.

Now, if you'll excuse me, I've got a letter to write. Wait, stamps are how much now?! Oh well, there's always e-mail.

That's one big Mr. Coffee

New technology has always kinda scared me, I must confess. It could be genetic and explain why I grew up as the last kid on the block to get a VCR, a push-button phone, a color TV and chest hair (only one, but I sure was proud of it; still have it framed).

The latest technological innovation I've had to confront is the gargantuan coffee-dispensing machine. OK, maybe these aren't quite so new. Must not be because the one we just had installed downstairs at work accepts nickels, dimes, quarters and talents.

But they're new to me. And the other day, I came face-to-face with this great human (I'm assuming) achievement. It was like meeting someone you know you're supposed to recognize, but don't. Happens to me a lot during the holidays:

"And you are?"

"I'm your sister, moron!"

"Oh, yeah."

Anyway, the machine ain't your ordinary Mr. Coffee that Joltin' Joe used to pitch on TV. This one's almost my height, though somewhat wider and less aerodynamic. I'm also prettier. At least, I feel pretty. Oh, and if you push my buttons, trust me, you won't get extra sweetener.

I'm used to coffee in newsrooms, of course. With all the weird hours we journalists have, you've got to have caffeine. But I'm definitely used to the smell of it and the sounds of it percolating. I've even once had to duck a flying coffee cup thrown by a reporter (at another paper) with anger-management issues.

Yet, I've never been much of a coffee drinker at work because I'm just not willing to put in the extra work to make it. Put me in a diner with a waitress who will call me "darlin" and keep refilling my cup, and I'm all about some coffee. A machine, though, seems like a decent compromise. I don't get served, but I don't have to make it, either. Fair enough.

However, I'd never used a giant coffee machine before. I didn't know whether you were supposed to insert your own cup or what. And with the way my 2009 is going so far, I just knew that if I stuck 60 cents in there that coffee would gush out uncontrollably and flood half of downtown. Those kinds of things just happen to me. I once had a bag of fast food burst into flames in the newsroom when I microwaved it with a ketchup packet inside.

However, I finally mustered up the courage to drop some talents in and see what happened. I figured the worst-case scenario was that I'd be scalded and then drown, but at least the smell would keep folks awake at my memorial service — that and the fun Jimmy Buffett tunes and limbo contest I'm planning for the occasion.

To my surprise, the coffee was good and no helicopters had to fly me to the burn center. They'd have crashed anyway.

Now, if I can just find the button on this machine that makes it call you "darlin," all will be right with the world once again.

Tell me what I want to hear

In the more than 20 years I've been in the newspaper business, I've heard every complaint you can imagine:

How dare you run SPORTS on the front page?! Why is the Georgia football story not on the front page?! You're too liberal! You're too conservative! My toe hurts!

At least on television you've got obviously left-leaning networks like MSNBC and obviously right-leaning networks like FOX News. And thank goodness you no longer have to rely on one of those news channels trying to give BOTH sides and have to use your God-given gift of reasoning. Whew — you can now hear only what you want to hear and not have to worry about, you know, thinking and stuff.

But I'm planning to go into the TV news business and take it a step further with the Things I Want to Hear Network. No more getting bogged down with balance or facts. My network's broadcasts will be tailor-made for each individual viewer. We had a pilot news broadcast last night tailored just to me. Here's a sample …

And, now, from the Things I Want to Hear Network World Headquarters in — uh, where are we again? oh yeah — Possum Holler, (bom! bom! bom!), it's News for Chris. Sitting in tonight for our distinguished-looking gentleman in a suit is a random hot Argentinian broadcast journalist in a bikini. Take it away — um, what's her name? oh — Gabriella.

Thank you. Our top story tonight: All the foods you thought were unhealthy are now healthy. The government is now urging everyone to eat more cheeseburgers, cheesecakes and those little marshmallows in Lucky Charms. Please avoid such food as celery and lettuce at all costs. Now, let's go to our bikini meterologist, Trixie.

Well, as you see, Garbellia, it's gonna be a beautiful day in Possum Holler because all this red stuff here is gonna go thattaway and I'm gonna wipe this green stuff off the radar with some Windex. Our high temperature tomorrow will be like 70 or 80 or something. I know it's a number.

Thank you, Trixie. Now, time for sports with Sally, the bubbly blonde who almost knows the difference between a hockey puck and a basketball. Also in a bikini.

Thanks, Gabnella. The big news today is that tennis star Anna Kournikova, auto racing's Danica Patrick, softball's Jennie Finch and golf's Natalie Gulbis have teamed up to form a new sports league!

Oh really, Sally? Which sport?

I don't know.

Thanks, Sally. And thank you for watching, Chris. Stay tuned for four straight episodes of "The Andy Griffith Show," all with Miss Peggy in them. Norah Jones will now hum our closing theme music.

Bom! Bom! Bom!

Cell phone concert

A couple of weeks ago, my old cell phone went for a swim. And, once again, I was forced to take another step forward in the technology arena.

I got as fancy-shmancy a cell phone as a cheap guy is willing to buy. It has a keyboard for texting and many other buttons that do something or another. I think you might even be able to make calls on it.

Actually, I'm sure you can make calls on it because I took yet another first step in the technology world this week. This new phone is equipped with the handy "butt-dial" feature.

I'd heard of butt-dialing before. I've heard of teenagers whose misdeeds were overheard when they butt-dialed their parents. And I've wondered what kind of idiot could butt-dial.

Now I know.

Blame Jerry Reed, though, not me. Somewhere between Buena Vista and Ellaville, Ga., I stumbled across some wonderfully eclectic radio station. It's not often you're scanning channels and bump into Jerry Reed belting out "Lord, Mr. Ford."

I did what any red-blooded Georgia boy would do in that situation — I sang along and helped Jerry out with a little air guitar. Apparently I was putting on such a good show that my cell phone decided to call someone and let them know. It couldn't find any music industry agents on my contact list, so it called my friend Rhonda instead.

For over five minutes, she and her husband, Felton, enjoyed my concert. I know they enjoyed it because she said she kept screaming my name into the phone — kinda like someone screaming "Bruce!" at a Springsteen concert, I guess.

She should consider herself lucky. Depending on the hour I'm driving and how loopy I am, I could be belting out anything from Abba's "Dancing Queen" to "The Star-Spangled Banner." But "Lord, Mr. Ford," that's classic stuff.

I've been on the receiving end of such calls. I once got one from my wife when she was on a girls trip to Atlanta. It was still on as they ate at a classy restaurant, and I tried to get her attention, but she couldn't hear me over the ambient music — "It's Raining Men" — in the background. Those restaurants can get loud. I didn't even know she had a friend named Hank the Hunky Handyman until that day. I still think that's a strange name for a girl.

Rhonda hung up after being overwhelmed by my mobile musical

talent and called my wife to let her know I just might be waking up all the residents along Highway 26. My wife then called and said, "So, you're singing in the car, huh?"

Lucky guess, I figured. She explained what happened, so I called Rhonda again and she said that it was indeed the highlight of her day.

"Who was that?" she asked of the music I was playing.

"Jerry Reed!" I said proudly.

"Who's that?"

That did it. I love Rhonda, but such a question is blasphemy in Georgia. Just for that, her next cell phone performance will be "Afternoon Delight."

Do not try this at home

I've always been a weather freak. Granted, some would argue the need for the word "weather" in the previous sentence.

Of course, if I had my druthers, it would always be 80 degrees with a light breeze. But I don't have my druthers. Either someone stole them or I lost them in my recent move.

I spent numerous days on our front porch during my youth watching summer thunderstorms roll into Oglethorpe almost on a 5:30 p.m. schedule. I'll watch snowflakes fall for hours, check radars online and watch Jim Cantore and Stephanie Abrams get blown around by hurricanes. I marvel as far-off lightning spider-webs through the sky when I'm driving at night.

So, as we put out a newspaper last Sunday while keeping one eye on the TV and one eye on the computer screen and one eye on the Atlanta Hawks, I grew ever more excited about the approaching "mini-super cell," as the local guys called it. (Is mini-super cell an oxymoron? Like minor tornado?)

We kept waiting for it to die out, but it quite obviously didn't. And when the TV guys bolted for the bathroom, I did what any genius would do: I charged up the stairs to the roof of the Ledger-Enquirer. (I'm sure that's some major violation of company policy, but so is what I wear to work every day.)

That's when lightning flashed and I saw the funnel cloud coming in from the west. Someone asked me how I knew for certain it was really a funnel cloud. That would be (a) because it was shaped like a funnel, and (b) because it was a cloud. I'm no Jim Cantore (I have a little more hair), but I recognized this was either (1) a tornado, or (2) God was changing the oil in the Chattahoochee.

From the roof, I could hear rumbling that sounded like giant 18-wheelers cranking up in Phenix City. I assume that was a bunch of giants hanging out at a truck stop and cranking up their giant 18-wheelers to get the heck away from the tornado. I was listening for a freight train.

But it got quiet and still for a moment as the funnel cloud apparently hopped over the Chattahoochee in the darkness. Then, reflected by the streetlights, its top reappeared over our heads.

Yes, our heads. I'd reveal my co-worker's name, but I can't because Alan's supposed to have more sense than to follow me to the highest, most vulnerable spot during a tornado. He's supposed to do what the TV guys said they did … head for the bathroom. About the time it reappeared over us and some lady flew by on a bicycle, I thought I might need a bathroom myself.

I can't give you the actual transcript of our conversation when we saw it had arrived because this is a family newspaper, but it went something like this:

"Well, by golly, it is a tornado," I said. "That is quite a remarkable feat of nature. I'm somewhat intimidated at the moment."

His response was something to the extent of "goodbye, you small-town hick, I'll be downstairs."

City boys. Geez!

Where are the people?

I've decided that the biggest problem in America isn't the stock market decline or the housing crisis. Nor is it the high gas prices that no one will acknowledge as the pin that burst the housing bubble and blew up the economy. Nor is it out-of-control spending. Nor is it a decline of moral values, politics as usual, drugs or peanuts.

No, the biggest problem in America is that there are no more people.

Of course, I don't mean we now have a population of 0. That's ridiculous because if that were the case, home prices would be even lower than they are now.

What I mean is that instead of people, we have taxpayers. Customers. FTEs. Uninsured. Jobless claims. Homeless. Stockholders. Constituents. Parishioners. Viewers. Households. Dependents. Elderly. Teenagers. Baby Boomers. Users. Subscribers. Recipients. Personnel. Executives. Buyers. Sellers.

What's missing from that list? Bob. Ethel. Gene. Fred. Jennifer. Earl. Samantha. Ed. Louise. Tony. Wanda. Jimmy. Mary Lou. Dave. Laurie Ann.

We now live in a society that — with the exception of celebrities — deals with people as groups, not individuals. It's why such well-meaning concepts as No Child Left Behind, No Pass/No Play or Three Strikes are so flawed. Because actual people are no longer part of the formula.

Everybody on welfare is lazy. Every corporate executive is greedy. Everybody who is foreclosed upon bought a house they couldn't afford. Every Muslim is dangerous. Everybody who works for AIG is a crook. Every journalist is a liberal. And white men can't jump.

But it's not so much the stereotypes that bother me. It's that too many schools, businesses, banks and governmental institutions aren't aware that no two people are alike.

My wife encountered this recently when going to work before daylight and stopping at a convenience store. She accidentally parked in a handicapped spot that was marked only by a small sign on the store. A police officer reprimanded her, and she profusely apologized and promptly moved her vehicle. But her apology was met with "that's what they all say" and "use some common sense" and on and on and on. At least we now know what happened to that annoying hall monitor from junior high school.

But recently while purchasing a home from a real estate service in Utah that behaved like an entire group of former hall monitors, we were able to lean on several people who knew we were good folks trying our best to play by the rules. All we were doing was trying to buy a house. It must be really tough for decent folks facing foreclosure or job loss who don't have people who will see them as individuals.

And at the very end, we sat in a small lawyer's office in Ellaville, Ga., just a few normal folks acting like reasonable people. We all were the kind of folks who could still do business with a handshake — if institutions would let us.

Too bad those days are gone.

Too many shoes

One of the stalkers who occasionally comments on my columns online likes to say I'm gay in lieu of an intelligent, unique insult.

Maybe that would bother me if I were gay. Probably not, though. Anyway, all you've got to do is take one look in my closet and your first reaction upon seeing my out-of-style wardrobe and my dearth of shoes would be: "Oh, no, you are so not gay." And your second reaction would be: "What's that furry thing in the closet growling at me?"

I call him Igor. But back to shoes.

I don't think a lot about shoes. I guess this is a sexist remark, but I think shoes are a far bigger concern for women than men. Really, an attractive woman can be wearing a $1,000 pair of shoes and pass by two guys and we could watch her for a whole block and not even notice whether she has feet, much less shoes.

I thought about shoes a lot more when I was younger and playing tennis 150 days a year. Back then, I regularly needed new pairs, which I'd learn when I could see my big toe through the sole. But, now, the only time I know I need new shoes is when women tell me so. I think women live in perpetual hope that men can someday make such discoveries on their own.

But I did think about shoes last weekend, when I had to attend the funeral of an old friend out of town. I thought I'd packed fairly well until the morning of the funeral when I opened my bag and discovered I had two black dress shoes, all right. But one was a slide-on and the other a lace-up. One had a bigger heel, and the other was narrower. The only saving grace was that there was one for the left and right foot.

I called my wife and told her how stupid I was. She didn't consider that a news flash.

"I'm amazed you took a left one and a right one," she said.

My sister Laurie, whom I adoped at age 37, called a few minutes later and I told her my situation. As much as I hated it, I was gonna have to make a trip to the — cringe — mall.

"Please tell me you're not gonna walk in the mall wearing those two different shoes," she said.

I told her yes and got a "bless your heart," which we all know is Southernese for "moron."

Sure enough, I hobbled into the mall looking like someone from that "Ministry of Funny Walks" sketch on "Monty Python." I consider any mall a foreign land, but even more so those in other cities, so I headed straight for the mall directory. Unfortunately, no shoe stores were listed, so I waddled down the mall like a deranged duck seeking any store that might sell dress shoes.

(By the way, guys, I learned Sbarro is not an Italian shoe.)

Luckily, I found a shoe store, wasted money on yet another pair of Sunday-go-to-meeting shoes (as my Dad used to call them) and proceeded to rectify the problem by finishing getting dressed right there in the middle of the food court.

I now have three pairs of Sunday-go-to-meeting shoes, which would no doubt cost me guy points if I had any idea what style or brand they are.

Let the stars fall

In case you missed it, the Perseids meteor shower peaked in the wee hours of Wednesday morning. And if you're anywhere in this newspaper's coverage area, you probably did miss it because all those falling stars hid behind a blanket of clouds and rain.

The Perseids is one of the best meteor showers of the year, although the Draconids in October, the Leonids in November and the Geminids in December promise to be pretty spectacular this year. I hear the Eyelids in January might not be bad, either.

I love meteor showers because I'm easily entertained. Plus they're free this year in the United States, thanks to a generous corporate gift from Exxon-Mobil. Many other countries have had to trim their showers to just a falling star or two or have had to cut them out altogether because of the global recession.

Problem is, I have a tendency to get wrapped up in the beauty of the heavenly spectacle and forget to use the opportunity to wish on the falling stars. And those wishes come true. That's how Barney and Betty Rubble got Bamm-Bamm. Plus those showers are especially spectacular out here in the country away from the light pollution of Columbus and other cities. And if you're not ready to make your wish upon seeing a falling star, another falling star could appear. And if you don't make your wish before the next falling star appears, said wish is thereby and henceforth and thereto declared null and void.

Don't look at me like that. I don't make the rules.

During a particularly busy shower — such as the 60 per hour the Perseids was expected to produce — I could get flustered trying to wish under pressure. I could stammer out something ridiculous like "I wish I had a blueberry Pop Tart!" instead of something truly important like "I wish I had a double-chili-cheeseburger with no onions!"

I have a bit of trouble with getting organized, kinda like a hippopotamus has a bit of trouble getting airborne. So I took a page out of the playbook of some of my OCD friends and made a list of wishes. I took the paper outside with me about midnight and still got flustered when lightning struck nearby.

Of course, I hadn't bothered to check the radar and had no idea the weather was getting bad, so my first thought was: "Wow! That last falling star dang near hit me!"

And, yes, I know they're not really stars falling. I'm not a complete idiot. Everybody knows they're really UFOs.

Once I realized the stars weren't literally falling, I whipped out my paper and prepared to barrage the heavens with requests. Lottery numbers! Falcons in the Super Bowl! Those last 10 pounds! Norah Jones performing (and swimming) at my next pool party! And, if there are enough falling stars, world peace or something like that.

Alas, the only thing I wound up wishing for was that it weren't so cloudy. So, once again, I'll fail to hang out with Norah Jones or win the lottery this year. That was my last hope of retiring before age 132. Guess if I'm ever gonna get rich, I'll have to do it the old-fashioned way — embezzlement.

Grindin' my teeth

Quick, somebody. I need a good excuse to keep from having to go to the dentist for a cleaning this week. That's a teeth cleaning, by the way. They don't do all-over cleanings. Have to get those at the car wash.

I know the call is coming this week, reminding me of my appointment. I'd rather get a call from that guy in the "Scream" mask telling me he can see me in the kitchen.

It's not that I don't like the feel of freshly cleaned teeth. I do. Even more when they're mine. But I don't like sharp objects or metal touching my teeth. I can't even stand to hear metal touching someone else's teeth. If I hear someone's teeth touch a fork in a restaurant, I'll need therapy. Or a cooperative waitress who will spit in their food for me.

And my dental hygienist, Ginger Vitas, is slightly nicer than Mother Teresa and cuter than every Disney Channel star put together. You'd think I'd be a little bit happy to see her.

But you can't flirt with her because you're lying there with your mouth wide open, wearing a bib and having spit and various organs sucked out of your body by this nuclear-powered mini-Hoover as you make small talk like, "Ho, nife day owfide, huh?"

You also can't flirt with her because your wife goes to the same dentist. And when she says, "Your husband drooled all over me," she'll likely have DNA evidence to prove it.

Fortunately, all my dental hygienists have been female. Call me homophobic or whatever, but I just don't like guys touching me for any longer than a handshake or high-five. I wasn't too keen on those butt-slaps when I was a kid playing football and baseball, either. So, I doggone sure don't want a guy sticking his hands in my mouth. My dentist is a guy, but I usually throw some gummy worms in my mouth right before he comes in, so he just takes a peek and says, "You can go."

My hygienist thinks I'm putting on when she dives in with the sander or whatever they use to clean your teeth and I grip the armrests of the chair as if I'm an airline passenger bracing for a crash. I literally leave finger marks in the chair. I'm in a state of terror from the moment they call me back until they tell me there's no charge.

My son, however, loves going to the dentist. Of course, he doesn't know the horror of an oral surgeon sawing your wisdom teeth in half and breaking them with pliers while you're wide awake. That'll scar you for life. Even moreso when it happens on Sept. 10, 2001.

I don't even think my son appreciates the feel of clean teeth, though there is a strong possibility a cute hygienist interests him. He holds court in the dentist's office and has everyone laughing. Meanwhile, I go in and they all hide and say, "Here comes that neurotic weirdo."

Of course, Saylor gets to go to the treasure chest after his teeth cleanings. Maybe I could be more cooperative if they had a treasure chest for adults who act like big boys. It could be filled with those little airplane liquor bottles, Braves tickets and giant-sized Slinkys.

If so, I promise to act like a big boy. For once.

Give the all-you-can-eat buffet its due

During my slightly chubbier and far more artery-clogged days, I was a big fan — literally — of the all-you-can-eat buffet.

Actually, I'm still a fan, but I hardly ever go to such buffets anymore. My wife is the main reason. She doesn't feel like she gets her money's worth because she doesn't eat enough.

So, you don't get your money's worth at $7.99 for all-you-can-eat, but the $14 pecan-encrusted, cinnamon-buttered, parsley-surrounded, blackened pork loin that is slightly bigger than a Tic Tac is a good deal because it's "presented" better?

I don't go to restaurants for presentation. I go to the theater for presentation. The only presentation I want at a restaurant is for a lady to hand me a plate and say, "The food bar's over yonder, honey."

My wife also doesn't like the "atmosphere" of most buffets. Again, I don't need atmosphere in my restaurant. By "atmosphere," all folks really mean is that the patrons are dressed uncomfortably, the place plays annoying music and it's so dark you can't actually see the food or whom you're with.

I don't need any music playing. All I want to hear every now and then is a worker yelling, "We need more chicken!"

I want the whole place well-lighted, too, especially at the actual buffet where the heat lamps help that vat of macaroni and cheese get that yummy crusty orange coating on top after no one's touched it for a while.

And I don't want to see anyone sitting around me while wearing a tie. Let me see folks comfortable in their buffet-eating, stretchy pants. Ties have no function. After a half-hour at the buffet, stretchy pants are the definition of functionality.

I like buffets because I decide what I want on my plate and how much of it instead of the restaurant. My wife can attest to the fact that I've made a scene at more than one restaurant where a server tells me what sides a dish comes with — even if they're the same dang price.

And at the buffet, not only can I pick all my sides, but if I want to put 12 pounds of meatballs on my plate, by golly, no snotty waiter named Francois will sneer at me. My waitress, Gladys, will simply smile, refill my Diet Coke (yes, I see the irony) and say, "Like meatballs, huh?"

But the main reason I love buffets is that they don't screw up your mashed potatoes. At fancy restaurants, not only do they put weird things in your mashed potatoes, but the food gets smaller the more you pay.

They're potatoes. You mash them. You eat them. Don't complicate it.

One day when I've got the meatballs to stand up to my wife, I'll find me a new, hot pair of stretchy pants and return to conquer the buffet. Until then, save some of that crusty orange stuff for me.

Leave 'em with a smile

There was probably no person in Oglethorpe, Ga., more well known than Grover Hobbs. His constant smile, hearty laugh and storytelling magic were well known back when he was a mere master of the backhoe.

Then came the biscuits.

And Grover, the entrepreneur, made the leap from the ranks of the merely well known to bona fide local legend.

In a land where biscuits and grits power a way of life, Grover was a true power broker through Grover's Grits, a small but bustling operation in downtown Oglethorpe.

Every morning — except Sundays, of course — there was a small gathering outside Grover's Grits, housed in a tiny shack next door to his sister's hair salon. Black and white. Young and old. Men and women. Folks on the go and folks killing time with old stories. Strangers in town and everyday customers from down the street.

It wasn't so much that the biscuits were hearty — I can verify that just one of Grover's biscuits could get you all the way from Oglethorpe to Orlando. Nor was it that you could fill up on just a couple of bucks.

It was that man smiling and laughing under that straw hat in the back, the same man who'd been up since the wee hours of the morning on a mission to get a community's day started on the right foot. It was a labor of love, and you could taste the love in the biscuits.

Few people possess Grover's self-deprecating charm, a charm that may have been born of necessity with 11 brothers and sisters.

Before I'd tried one of Grover's biscuits, I had my doubts that such a funny guy could whip up a serious biscuit. While working the backhoe on a project for my dad, Grover touted his breakfast joint. He told me he did it up right, but there was one little problem:

"Sometimes we get the orders a little wrong," he admitted, still smiling. "But I tell them, 'Just eat whatever's in that bag because whatever I put in that bag is good.'"

I found that funny but not all that reassuring as a potential customer. The sign where you place your order didn't reassure me, either: "Order what you want. Eat what you get." Only Grover could turn such a "problem" into a chuckle.

But one bite and I was hooked, making me one of many. I also found he was stretching the truth a bit (as we Oglethorpe folks are prone to do), for not once did I get a wrong order and have to "eat what you get."

Grover died unexpectedly on June 5 at the age of 64. He was laid to rest on Monday. It was his second burial. The first one, back in the '70s, didn't take. (He was briefly buried in a ditch.)

It was the first time I'd walked into a funeral, saw the deceased and wanted to smile. It's an involuntary reaction upon seeing Grover. And it's a hard instinct to suppress, especially through a service with more laughs than tears.

When people recall Grover, forever more, they will picture him with a smile on his face.

If only we could all leave that impression.

At least I didn't hear banjo music

It'd been a long time since I'd had a can of Beanee Weenies. But I was headed out into the wilderness, and when you're gonna be having lunch alone on some sandbar while kayaking along a lonely stretch of the Flint River, you gotta have some Beanee Weenies. And a can of Pringles in that wonderful "stay crisp" can.

I didn't need much more than that last Sunday. I wanted peace and quiet. I wanted to get away from everybody

My wife and son dropped me and my kayak off at the Highway 127 bridge over the Flint River several miles north of my hometown of Oglethorpe. It was the site of Georgia's last working ferry, near an old Indian encampment called Miona Springs, where we used to collect arrowheads and pottery when I was a kid. The bridge is also known as the place where a mother once hurled her two children to their deaths below.

But this trip wasn't about the past; it was about the future. It's been a stressful year, good and bad. I just wanted an easy day of paddling with no distractions. I just wanted to drift along and wonder what lay around the bend. I didn't even let the spitting noises my wife made as I floated underneath the bridge distract me from my mission.

Though the river was quite swift, I took it easy for the first 3 miles or so. I'd paddle a little, then prop my feet up on the kayak and lean back. I stopped off at a sandbar to powder my nose and took pictures with my cell phone of giant footprints obviously made by Sasquatch (or me) and sent a picture message to my Bigfoot-obsessed 9-year-old.

It was sunny with temperatures in the mid-60s. Yet, the water was cold, so I wouldn't have to bother with gators and snakes. I pushed away from the sandbar and again went to pondering what lay around the bend. I didn't have to wonder long.

WHAM! What lay around the bend was a stump, possibly a giant sequoia stump. One so perfectly positioned as to tilt my kayak just so that the rushing Flint could fill it and spill its contents, including me.

After being bashed against this misplaced tree hiding in the cold, murky water, I managed to grab the kayak with one hand and my paddle with the other. I tried to swim toward either bank, but the swift Flint would have none of it. It pushed me along, banging my legs against stumps and rocks for nearly 30 minutes while I kept swimming in vain with limbs that were growing colder and more numb by the minute. And I was almost to the point where I couldn't hold on any longer.

I should note at this point that I'm not much for doing things in groups. No group exercise classes. No group paddling excursions. I relish my alone time.

Well, let me tell you, when you are hanging onto a kayak with one hand and being dragged along like a waterlogged rag doll 3 miles from the nearest human, you feel plenty alone. I got enough alone time last Sunday to last me all of 2010.

I also should note that I've gotten quite lackadaisical in my two years of kayaking. When I first started, I had a whistle, a life preserver, an air horn, a spray skirt and a waterproof bag for my phone and such. But after breezing encounters with waves, alligators, a cottonmouth who nearly fell into my kayak from a bush and angry mess of wasps, I may have eased up on the precautions.

My life preserver last Sunday looked an awful lot like a mere long-sleeve Addidas shirt. Ironically, under it was a T-shirt with a whale on it and the words "Save the humans." It didn't seem as funny in the river as it did in the store, but I hoped some largemouth bass would see it and get the message and lend a helping hand, or fin.

Fortunately, after being dragged along through the deep waters and turned into an ice cube, I maintained my quick-thinking skills and smartly lunged for a jagged tree limb with my nimble ribs and thigh. For several minutes, I stayed pinned there between the kayak and the tree while I caught my breath.

I tilted the kayak to get some of the water out and rummaged through the cockpit for my belongings. I found my cell phone and put it in the branch of a tree to dry out. Of course, it was dead. My UGA duffel bag that was full of soggy Pringles (stay-crisp can, my backside!), sunscreen, flip-flops, water and, yes, the Beanee Weenies then got away from me and disappeared.

I climbed onto the tree and back into the half-full kayak, then strapped my phone under a bungee cord in hopes of a miraculous cellular resurrection. I paddled over to another sandbar and tried to dry out. That's when I learned one of the symptoms of "mild" hypothermia, violent shaking. I looked like I did that time as a kid when I stuck my finger in a light socket to see if it still has electricity even with no bulb in it. In case you're wondering, it does.

I figured the only way to warm up was to dump the rest of the water out, take off my wet shirts and get back to paddling. Seven miles later, I made it to a boat ramp with not a soul in sight. An hour later, a fisherman arrived let me borrow his phone to call for help.

By the time my wife picked me up, the sun was going down and I was standing there alone, barefoot, shirtless and shivering. I also felt thankful and stupid at the same time. And to this day, my bones feel cold. I'm not afraid of the water, but I now have a great fear of trees. Especially ones who don't know their place.

So, please, learn from my stupidity. If you kayak that stretch of the deserted Flint, wear your life jacket and don't go alone.

And if you get hungry, there's a can of Beanee Weenies waiting on you.